THE HIGH HOLY DAYS

THE HIGH HOLY DAYS

A Commentary on the Prayerbook of Rosh Hashanah and Yom Kippur

by
HERMAN KIEVAL

Book One: Rosh Hashanah

THE BURNING BUSH PRESS
NEW YORK

This volume has been prepared for publication by the National Academy for Adult Jewish Studies of the United Synagogue of America.

Library of Congress Catalogue Card Number: 59-14794
Manufactured in the United States of America

Rabbi Eleazar said:

"One should always set his prayers in order before beginning to pray."

Rosh Hashanah 35a

"The worshipper must direct his heart to each word that he utters. He is like a man who walks through a garden collecting rare and precious flowers, plucking them one by one in order to weave a garland. So we move from word to word and from page to page combining the words into prayers. Each word seizes hold of us and cleaves to us; it entreats us not to abandon it, saying,

" 'Consider my light, notice my grace. Be careful as you take hold of me, take care as you pronounce my name.' "

Rabbi Naḥman of Bratzlav

DEDICATED TO THE MEMORY OF

MY BELOVED FATHER

יצחק בן רפאל

FOREWORD

The High Holy Days are undoubtedly the most widely observed of all Jewish religious occasions. On Rosh Hashanah and Yom Kippur, large numbers of worshippers have the opportunity to hear and participate in the stirring liturgy of the Days of Awe. Its key phrases and melodies are often remembered long after the holidays themselves have passed.

These facts notwithstanding, the High Holy Day Prayerbook is far from being fully appreciated or understood in our own time. The Maḥzor is a microcosm of Jewish thought, reflecting much of Israel's historical experience. Some of the most sublime concepts of Judaism find expression in its language of prayer. In addition, the prayers in their origins span centuries of time and move across the space of continents.

Hence the need to devote time to the careful study of the prayerbook, its meaning and history. As our understanding of it is deepened, we find ourselves enabled to develop a prayerful attitude and become steeped in the spirit of these sacred occasions.

Over the ages, the inspirational treasury that is the Maḥzor has elicited a wealth of commentaries and homilies. Withal, its full riches have not yet seen the light of day, accessible to the general reader.

Our generation is therefore particularly indebted to Rabbi Herman Kieval who has undertaken the task of presenting to the lay reader the Maḥzor, its meaning, structure and historical development. At the same time, the full notes he has provided make possible an even deeper understanding keyed to sources, both ancient and modern.

Rabbi Kieval has brought to bear the results of his studies in the field of liturgy, accompanying the insights of scholarship with the gift of popular presentation. This volume has evolved from his teaching as a rabbi in the congregational ministry as well as from his lectures at the Jewish Theological Seminary of America. Written simply and clearly, it examines the structure of the Maḥzor and comments on each of the major prayers of Rosh Hashanah.

The National Academy wishes to acknowledge its indebtedness to the following for their cooperation in the preparation of this volume: Rabbi Bernard Segal, whose sustained interest encouraged our efforts; Rabbis S. Gershon Levi and Baruch Silverstein, readers of the original manuscript, who offered valuable comments; Mr. Moshe Sheinbaum, representing the Burning Bush Press, for his wise guidance; Rabbi Jules Harlow, who made a number of helpful editorial suggestions; and Rabbi Jack Riemer, who prepared the glossary and bibliography.

In the spirit of advancing *may-ḥa'yil el ḥa'yil,* from one spiritual achievement to another, we anticipate bringing to publication in the near future the companion volume, Book Two: Yom Kippur.

MARVIN S. WIENER, Director
National Academy for Adult Jewish Studies of the United Synagogue of America

Tammuz, 5719
July, 1959

CONTENTS

INTRODUCTION

The Prayerbook of Rosh Hashanah and Yom Kippur, for many Jews in the Western world, has become the most important text in the vast library of Judaism. Even in the classic East European period, the Siddur was more familiar to the man in the street than the Bible or Talmud; indeed much of what he had absorbed from these basic sources of Judaism had come to him through the Prayerbook. Franz Rosenzweig accurately described the relationship of the Prayerbook to the other classic works of Judaism when he wrote:

> The biblical literature of antiquity is the fountainhead of all living Judaism: the talmudic-rabbinical literature of later ages constitutes its encyclopedia; and in the philosophical writings we see its subtlest sublimation; yet the sum and substance of the whole of historical Judaism, its handbook and memorial tablet, will ever be the Prayer book: the Daily and the Festival, the Siddur and the Maḥzor. He to whom these volumes are not a sealed book has more than grasped the "essence of Judaism." He is informed with it as with life itself; he has within him a "Jewish world."[1]

The central role of the Siddur as an instrument of education as well as inspiration has been further accentuated in the Jewries of the West where the chief expression of Jewish consciousness is Synagogue worship. Even those who may still confine their worship experience to the High Holy Day season are nonetheless exposed to the Maḥzor for many hours within a concentrated time span. Our synagogues and temples are increasingly crowded with men and women of all ages who hold in their hands, hour after hour, a classic text they yearn to know and possess; yet, because of its complexity and archaic style, the Maḥzor remains a "closed book" for all but the initiated.

"Seek ye the Lord while He may be found, call ye upon Him while He is near" (Isaiah 55:6). The Talmud cites this Biblical verse as a prophetic allusion to the unique spiritual opportunities afforded by the Days of Awe; even in those ancient times the High Holy Days were very special days. "Like lighthouses on the shores of eternity, Rosh Hashanah and Yom Kippur have flashed their message of holiness and have proved potent agencies for spiritual renewal to a hundred generations in Israel" (Joseph Herman Hertz). Contemporary generations, even more than their predecessors, have come to rely on the religious inspiration and educational experiences of the Days of Awe to provide these "messages of holiness" without which their Jewish existence would be largely barren of meaning.

At the High Holy Day season, more than at any other time of the year, the newly awakened hunger for a return to the sources of Judaism manifests itself. Not infrequently a worshipper will even bring with him to the Synagogue a reference work on Jewish history or literature into which he might delve during the long hours of the service. Yet the Maḥzor for Rosh Hashanah and Yom Kippur, properly understood, is itself the richest single source book for authentic insights into the essence of Judaism. Here we may find the embodiment of its highest values and aspirations — not only what Israel claimed to be but what it actually was. As the late Chief Rabbi Hertz acutely observed, "Whatever Judaism has to say on God, man and duty is enshrined in the prayers and hymns of the 'Days of Awe' . . . These prayers and hymns are the spiritual epitome of the devotion of Israel's prophets and psalmists, rabbinic teachers and medieval hymn-writers."

II

The purpose of this Commentary is to help open the "closed book" which the Maḥzor for Rosh Hashanah and Yom Kippur has become for the majority of our people. It is intended as a knowledgeable (though not pedantic) companion to guide the worshipper through the High Holy Day services page by page, introducing him to the treasures of prayer, poetry and ritual. Its ultimate purpose, however, is not to give information but to induce the worshipper to identify himself with the Maḥzor as the sublime expression of his own spiritual aspirations as a faithful Jew. The author is heedful, in this respect, of the wise caution voiced by Solomon Schechter in his discussion of the *Malkhuyot* benediction of Rosh Hashanah, the sublime prayer for the universal sovereignty of God: "We can easily lecture on the history of this prayer, and even make a guess as to its date and authorship, but we should certainly fail were we to try to make one understand what the Kingdom of God on earth really meant for the saints of Israel, whose whole life was nothing else than a preparation for entering into the Kingdom."[2]

The challenge that faces any aspiring guide or companion for the High Holy Day worshipper is a formidable one, and, to judge by the host of commentaries through the ages, it has never been simple. The Jewish Prayerbook is not a mere manual of devotion. It is (in Theodor H. Gaster's felicitous metaphor) "Israel's personal diary, catching, as in a series of exquisite vignettes, the scenes and moments of her entire life, and recording, in a diversity of moods and styles, her deepest and most intimate emotions."[3]

The approach of this Commentary is therefore multi-dimensional. On one level, it attempts to reveal the underlying *form* of the complex Maḥzor: the origin and development (in main outline) of the several worship services and of the individual prayers they comprise; the authorship (wherever available) and the structural design of the prayers, poems and hymns. On another level, however, the Commentary is concerned with *meaning*: it endeavors to interpret the religious message of the prayers, poems and rituals — in terms both of their original thought and of their evolving meaning as revealed by Jewish teachers through the centuries down to the present. Wherever they shed a special light on our prayers, the insights of "the righteous among all nations" are also utilized.

Conscious at all times of the web of interrelation between faith and folk in Judaism, this Commentary views the Maḥzor against the total historical experience of the *people of Israel.* It is historically as well as theologically oriented. It strives to echo some of the drama that pulsates yet behind the words worn smooth by centuries of repetition. Illustrative material is brought from every major period of Israel's pilgrimage and from diverse branches of its literature — from both Hebrew sources and from the many vernaculars in which Jews have expressed their spiritual aspirations (Yiddish not least among them). Premised as it is on the concept of *Kelal Yisrael,* this Commentary is intended for all Jews. Though it interprets primarily the Ashkenazic rite, it makes frequent reference to that of the Sephardim as well, particularly those of the Occident (as reflected in the prayerbooks for Rosh Hashanah and Yom Kippur edited by Rabbi David de Sola Pool). Eschewing partisanship, it attempts to present a point of view that will be readily recognizable to all who strive earnestly (in Schechter's phrase) to "appreciate and fall in love with everything Jewish."

III

The Commentary proper is prefaced by more detailed accounts of the historical development of, first, the Siddur and the Maḥzor and, second, the body of synagogal poetry known as *Piyyutim.*

The main body of the work consists of Commentary on the most significant prayers, poems and rituals of the Days of Awe. Page references are provided in the Index to several editions of the traditional Maḥzor currently in wide use in the English-speaking countries. The Commentary treats primarily those prayers associated specifically with Rosh Hashanah and Yom Kippur; those which are recited equally on other occasions throughout the year are discussed only insofar as they may possess a special aspect relevant to the High Holy Days. This policy was dictated, on the one hand, by limitations of space, and, on the other, by the fact that a number of excellent commentaries are available in English for the daily and Sabbath prayerbooks.

A special section has been provided for the ritual of Sounding the Shofar. The brief text included in the traditional Maḥzor, moving as it is in its simple dignity, does not adequately state the central role of the Shofar in the High Holy Day tradition and in Jewish lore generally. This Commentary accordingly endeavors to draw together, under a number of themes, some of the vast store of legal material, customs and folklore, homilies and parables, poems and anecdotes that have accumulated through the centuries around the Shofar.

This Commentary is intended primarily for the layman; nevertheless, it is hoped that the more advanced student will also find much that is of interest. The sources of passages quoted and of opinions cited are given in the notes along with more detailed information. The body of the Commentary is, however, self-contained and may be read, if so desired, independently of the notes. A short bibliography of non-technical books and pamphlets is included to guide the reader in further study in the Jewish liturgy. A glossary is provided which gives the meaning of Hebrew terms used in the Commentary. A detailed discussion of the structure of the *Kerovah* form of sacred poetry is contained in a special appendix.

IV

A word is in order concerning the effective use of this Commentary, not only by the individual but by groups of students and worshippers.

The experience of numerous congregations has demonstrated the growing appeal of High Holy Day institutes, seminars and study groups. These may be held on *Seliḥot* night, prior to the worship service, on other occasions preceding Rosh Hashanah or between Rosh Hashanah and Yom Kippur. The present Commentary is intended to provide a continuing curriculum for this type of study.

Many congregations have been skillfully utilizing recess periods during the High Holy Day services themselves — especially on Yom Kippur — for purposes of study. Rabbis and lay leaders have long been aware that frequent opportunities for instruction in the prayerful mood present themselves even in the course of the worship service.

The enthusiasm for Jewish learning generated by the High Holy Day season gives the Maḥzor a unique appeal as a subject of study in the continuing adult institutes and study circles that form an integral part of the congregational or communal program. Furthermore the Maḥzor constitutes a splendid unit for discussion in the increasingly popular week-end laymen's institutes and at the Torah sessions which are coming to characterize conventions and conferences.

It is hoped that this Commentary may prove useful in all these areas.

V

Like the Maḥzor itself, the commentaries it has inspired since the earliest times have inevitably rested upon the work of distinguished predecessors. I am humbly aware of the inestimable debt I owe to those who have pioneered in this field and my dependence is freely acknowledged by reference to their work throughout the Commentary.

My indebtedness extends to many teachers and colleagues who have given me guidance and encouragement during the more than fifteen years I have been preparing the work at hand. I wish to record my gratitude especially to: Dr. Louis Finkelstein, for having introduced me as a Seminary student into the delightful treasure-house of liturgical research; Dr. Saul Lieberman, whose mastery of Jewish sources has elucidated for me many difficult questions; Dr. Moshe Davis, who helped conceive the plan for this Commentary and has encouraged my efforts to consummate it; Dr. Max Arzt, who has generously shared with me his valuable insights and who has extended gracious assistance over a period of many years; my revered teachers, Drs. Robert Gordis, Simon Greenberg, Louis L. Kaplan and Shalom Spiegel and my esteemed colleagues, Rabbis Morris Adler, Solomon B. Freehof, Albert I. Gordon, Philip Kieval, Simon Noveck, Max B. Wall and the late Rabbi Philip Graubart, *zikhrono li-verakhah*, for having read portions of the manuscript and for their many valuable suggestions. Their inestimable assistance does not, of course, in any way relieve me of responsibility for the final result.

Rabbi Marvin S. Wiener, Director of the National Academy for Adult Jewish Studies, has devoted hours without number to the task of helping me prepare the manuscript for the press and has seen it through the publication process. I cannot adequately word my feelings of gratitude.

To my congregation, Temple Israel of Albany, N.Y., I am thankful for the encouragement I have received to pursue my studies and writing in the midst of pressing congregational duties. In a large measure, the eagerness of our people to deepen their appreciation of the classic Jewish sources has stimulated me to prepare this Commentary.

Aḥaron aḥaron ḥaviv. Finally, I wish to record my eternal gratitude to my cherished mother, who prepared my heart for a life of service to God, Torah and Israel, and to my wife, who more than any other mortal has kept my feet from faltering on the path we have chosen to walk together.

Herman Kieval

Burlington, Vermont
Tammuz, 5719
July, 1959

CHAPTER ONE

THE SIDDUR AND THE MAḤZOR

"No beautiful synagogues were built; instead bridges were built leading from the heart to God."[1] In these loving words, Abraham Joshua Heschel paid homage to a millennium of religious creativity by that East European Jewry which was done to death in our time. If prayers were their "bridges," the blueprint by which the spans were constructed was the Siddur, the sacred Prayerbook.[1a] Rooted in the language and spirit of Scripture, enriched by the exquisite insights of the Sages, and adorned with the piety of thirty generations, it has served as the daily guide and constant companion of the Jew. Throughout history, the Siddur has been his literary fare more consistently than even the Bible or Talmud; to the extent that the man in the street knew the latter, it was usually through the medium of the Prayerbook which quotes liberally from them (this is especially true for the Psalms). "One of the greatest products of the Jewish genius," in the words of Hermann Cohen, the Siddur constituted the fountainhead of public and private prayer in the Western world. Like the Synagogue itself, the Siddur is one of the truly original contributions of Judaism to the religion of mankind.

For the major festivals, a special Prayerbook eventually came into being, known to Ashkenazic Jews as the Maḥzor. The full title was *Maḥzor shel Tefillot,* meaning "cycle of prayers." Strangely enough, the use of the word *maḥzor* for a prayerbook is borrowed from the Syrian Christian Church.[2] The term had a variety of applications in the early Middle Ages. It was originally used for the nineteen year cycle of the lunar calendar *(Maḥzor Levanah).* It also designated the cycle of *Haftarot,* the readings from the prophetic books of the Bible prescribed for each Shabbat and Festival.

The name *Maḥzor* was also employed for the cycles of *Piyyutim,* synagogal poems composed for the annual round of Sabbaths and Festivals; the first and most famous work of this type is *Maḥzor Yannai,* an ancient poetical Midrash on the entire Torah.[3]

The Middle Ages saw the flowering of the Maḥzor as an encyclopedic compendium of calendar lore, rules and regulations for worship and Jewish life generally, legal opinions, the text of the prayers, commentary, Scriptural readings and *piyyutim.* The classic example of such a work is the twelfth century *Maḥzor Vitry,* reflecting the usage of French Jewry at the time of Rashi. This work — like the *Maḥzor Italiani* (or *Maḥzor Roma)* and others — covers the daily and Shabbat services as well as those of the Festivals; yet it includes significantly, in addition to the poetical material of the main work, a special appendix with over a hundred *piyyutim.* Such *piyyutim* eventually became the primary content of the Maḥzor and its distinguishing characteristic while the calendar emphasis receded into the background.[4] The terms *siddur and maḥzor* for many centuries were not clearly differentiated among Ashkenazic Jews and, to this day, are used interchangeably among the Sephardim.[5]

Each of the five Biblical holidays (Pesaḥ, Shavuot, Sukkot, Rosh Hashanah and Yom Kippur) has its own Maḥzor, but the most widely used and most elaborate are those for the *Yamim Noraim,* or "Days of Awe,"[6] i.e., the New Year and the Day of Atonement. The text of the Maḥzor like that of the Siddur varies with the *minhag,* the rite of the country or city in which it developed. Leopold Zunz listed some sixty different *minhagim,* but local rites of this type tended to give way as a result of migrations and expulsions.[7] The two chief geographical groups are the Arabian-Spanish, stemming from the old Babylonian tradition, of which Spain was the center, and the German-Roman, whose roots were in Palestine — with Germany as the focus of influence in the West, and Poland in the East of Europe. This division corresponds respectively to the chief historical groupings of Jews in Sephardic (Spanish) and Ashkenazic (German) communities. Even so, the variations are usually found in the auxiliary hymns, poems and supplications rather than in the statutory or obligatory prayers — such as the Benedictions of the Shema and the *Amidah.* These statutory prayers *(tefillah shel ḥovah)* were stabilized during the earlier Talmudic period and have remained relatively uniform and unchanged down to the present. In America and other Western countries most congregations use Maḥzorim based upon the Polish *minhag* of the Ashkenazic tradition, and it is this text which is used as the basis of this Commentary.

How the Siddur and the Maḥzor Were Created

From the standpoint of the worshipper, the Siddur and Maḥzor may aptly be described as "the treasure house of Israel's faith to which every generation has brought its choicest gifts of aspiration and hope" (Robert Gordis). From the vantage point of the scholar, they may be compared to a geologic formation in which one may trace the successive strata of every age. Long before the Synagogue had its origin, public prayer was an element in the sacrificial system of worship at the Temple in Jerusalem. After the latter was destroyed in the year 70 C.E., prayer remained as the sole medium of public worship. Nevertheless the legacy of the Temple ritual enriched the Synagogue with many familiar prayers and blessings, psalms, responses and doxologies.[8]

The basic element of Jewish liturgy is the *Shema Yisrael* ("Hear O Israel") taken from the Book of Deuteronomy 6:4-9, plus companion passages from Deuteronomy 11:13-21 and Numbers 15:37-41. These passages are included in the term *Keri'at Shema*, "Reading of the Shema." This proclamation of faith in the true and universal God, who is linked in a historic covenant-relationship with the People of Israel, has remained the core of Jewish worship down to the present.[9] Early in the Second Commonwealth (sixth century B.C.E. to first century C.E.) various benedictions and petitions, notably the prayers before and after the Shema and at least some of the benedictions of the statutory *Tefillah* ("Prayer") — known also as *Amidah* ("Standing") or *Shemoneh Esray* ("Eighteen") — were formulated by the anonymous "Men of the Great Assembly" and their successors of the Persian period.[10] These pioneering "Interpreters of the Book" *(Soferim)* created the formulas of prayer and laid down the lines along which Jewish worship has moved ever since. By this period too the practice of reading and interpreting appropriate passages from Scripture, a practice which may have originated among the exiled Judeans in Babylonia, had become an integral part of worship. In addition, the Psalms — which previously had been a major element in the Temple ritual — became prominent in the Synagogue service as well, notably in *Hallel,* the festive service of praise and thanksgiving.

All these elements were edited and expanded by the authorities of the Mishnah and Talmud (both Palestinian and Babylonian) during the early centuries of the Common Era. The divisions of the service as we now have them, namely, Shaḥarit, Musaf, Minḥah, Arvit and — on Yom Kippur — Ne'ilah, were consolidated. Simple hymns, litanies and poems, new occasional prayers and more elaborate settings for older prayers, a few private meditations of the Sages and selections from the Oral Law were set into the framework surrounding the more ancient *Shema* and *Tefillah* (i.e., *Amidah*). The texts of certain (though not all) previously elastic prayers were fixed. By the year 550 C.E. the basic structure of the Prayerbook, including some sections perhaps a thousand years old, was virtually complete.

Many individual rabbis are mentioned by name as having been especially active in the composition and editing of prayers. In the liturgy of Rosh Hashanah, the hand of Rabbi Akiba is prominent among the Palestinian sages; the influence of his contemporary, Rabbi Yoḥanan ben Nuri, reporting the Galilean tradition, is also felt. The great creative flowering in the composition of prayers for New Year and Atonement came, however, in third century Babylonia. The chief architects of the High Holy Day liturgy, as it existed prior to the influx of the *Piyyutim*, were Rav and Samuel. Rav appears to have been the supreme innovator. He had studied in Palestine with the Patriarch Judah the Prince and with Rabbi Ḥiyya, the scholar who consistently underscored the extraordinary sanctity of Rosh Hashanah and Yom Kippur by urging special observances.[11] Along with Samuel, Rav pioneered in the establishment of new academies for the study of the Mishnah in Babylonia, at that time a populous Jewish center but poor in Torah learning. The intense revival of interest in Judaism which Rav and Samuel stimulated at Sura and Nehardea, respectively, resulted in an extraordinarily creative output of new prayers and refinement of older ones.[12] There is hardly a service in the Siddur or Maḥzor which does not reflect their activity.

The late Chief Rabbi Joseph H. Hertz aptly called Rav, "a genius in the realm of prayer." His name is associated prominently with such well-known High Holy Days prayers as *Malkhuyot* (including *Alaynu*), *Zikhronot* and *Shofarot* — the three-fold prayer structure known collectively as *Tekiata d-Rav* or *Tekiata d-bay Rav* ("Shofar service according to the School of Rav") ; the formulas, *Ha-Melekh ha-kadosh* and *Ha-Melekh hamishpat; Melokh al kol ha-olam* and *Meḥal la-avonotaynu* (the central benedictions for Rosh Hashanah and Yom Kippur respectively) ; and, together with Samuel, the *Viddui* confessionals which feature the various services of Yom Kippur. (Detailed comment on all these prayers will be made as they occur in the service.)

The Maḥzor as a Mirror of Religious Development

The Maḥzor differs from the Siddur chiefly through the inclusion of hymns and religious poems known collectively as *Piyyutim*. These began to find their way into the service for special occasions in the early centuries of the Common Era in Palestine, yet some of them have retained their freshness and popularity down to the present. Many of the *Payyetanim* or synagogal poets — and certainly the earliest ones — were themselves *Sheliḥay Tzibbur*, "emissaries of the congregation," in the conduct of the worship. During the medieval period there was a rich flowering of synagogal poetry in Spain and Italy, the Moslem lands, France, Germany and Eastern Europe, especially Poland; so prolific were the Spanish singers that almost every city had its own ritual. This treasury of sacred verse furnished the contents of such important services as the *Seliḥot* and the *Avodah* of Yom Kippur. The Rosh Hashanah service of the Sephardim is almost devoid of *piyyutim* but the Ashkenazic service in generously endowed with them. This Commentary will discuss the most important *piyyutim* as they occur in the text. The subject of *Piyyut,* however, is so highly complex and its historical development so obscure that a separate chapter follows for the purpose of examining this characteristic element of the Maḥzor more thoroughly.

Throughout the Middle Ages, the Siddur and Maḥzor reflected the conditions of Jewish life and the influence of changing emphases in Jewish thinking. The far-reaching Kabbalah movement, stemming from Safed in Galilee in 16th century Palestine, exerted an important influence down to the end of the 18th century. It is echoed in many a mystical reference and passage from the Zohar. The meditations during the Shofar sounding (including the names of angels in the older texts) are a legacy from these mystics. Needless to add, the Kabbalists compiled their own prayerbooks and commentaries; the most influential were those of Rabbi Isaac Luria *(Nusaḥ Ha-Ari)*, Rabbi Isaiah Horowitz *(Shenay Luḥot Ha-Brit)* and Rabbi Nathan Hanover *(Sha'aray Zion)*. The Ḥasidic movement followed the Kabbalists in their liturgical practice. The modern era itself added readings and petitions, as in the Yizkor or Memorial service, or adaptations of ancient formulas to new circumstances, as in the prayer for the heads of State. With the translation of the Hebrew text into the many vernaculars (the first into Italian in 1538; the first into English at the close of the 18th century) the practice arose of including readings, meditations and notes in the language of the land to supplement the traditional ritual. The rise of the Reform and later the Conservative (and Reconstructionist) movements in Western Europe and America produced and continues to produce new Prayerbooks, all of which derive in greater or lesser degree from the classical Siddur and Maḥzor. The rebirth of the State of Israel has led to the creation of a number of prayers for special occasions, chiefly military and political. Who can say with certainty which of these modern and contemporary innovations will gain universal acceptance by *Kelal Yisrael,* the totality of Israel?

Mention should also be made of the host of formal commentaries and random notes on the various prayerbooks which have characterized the Jewish liturgy from Geonic times to the present. The earliest prayerbooks, like those of Rav Amram and Saadiah, themselves provide commentaries on the prayers and poetry. Certainly the worship of no other faith is so lovingly annotated with learned discussion, both historical and hortatory, in Hebrew and in the vernacular, and this from the hands of the outstanding scholars of their time, from men of affairs as well as from bookmen. There is no more eloquent tribute to the vital role of worship in Jewish life than the fact that spiritual and intellectual giants like Akiba, Rav and Samuel, Saadiah, Rashi, Maimonides, Isaac Luria and Elijah of Vilna — to name only the most prominent — dedicated so much of their genius to the liturgy. An entire literature of commentaries on Maḥzorim lies in manuscripts still unpublished. In more recent generations, splendid commentaries on the Siddur and Maḥzor have been prepared by eminent scholars and religious personalities like Wolf Heidenheim, Samson Raphael Hirsch, Seligmann Baer, Israel Abrahams, Wolf Jawitz, and the Chief Rabbis, Abraham Isaac Kuk of Palestine and Joseph Herman Hertz of the British Empire. Aside from formal commentaries, the history and meaning of Israel's prayers have engaged the reverent attention of virtually all scholars from the earliest centuries down to the present.[13]

To be sure, all of these statutory prayers were at first handed down orally like the rest of the post-Biblical tradition. The written Siddur was unknown until the ninth century and not widely used at that for several more centuries.[14] It appears that the religious life of Babylonian Jewry was so thoroughly organized and disciplined, "that there was no occasion for the Geonim to occupy themselves with the task of fixing the order of the prayers. With centuries of religious development in Babylonia the conduct of the divine service lay in the hands of men who would do the right thing without the necessity of special instruction" (Louis Ginzberg).[15] Such was not the case, however, with the communities outside Babylonia. These turned to the heads of the academies of Sura and Pumbeditha with requests for guidance. Authoritative rulings were urgently needed, moreover, because the Karaite schismatics were arguing effectively that wide variations in local customs of prayer belied the claim of their Rabbanite opponents to an authentic, binding Tradition (based on Talmudic law). Indeed the Rabbanite liturgy of that period reveals Karaite influence.[16]

In a famous Reponsum *(Teshuvah)* on "The Order of Benedictions," which was known for centuries only through quotations by later authorities until it was rediscovered in the Cairo Genizah, the Gaon Natronai provided "the nucleus of the prayerbook" as we know it. The oldest "Order of Prayers" that has come down to us is the famous *Seder Rav Amram,* Gaon of the Sura Academy, prepared at the request of Spanish Jewry about 870 C.E. This important work has unfortunately been changed so much by copyists over the centuries that it is difficult to reconstruct Rav Amram's original text. Perhaps — as the great Talmudist, Louis Ginzberg, suggested — his manuscript was "used until it was used up."

In the tenth century, Saadiah Gaon compiled the oldest authentic prayerbook which has come down to us. It is a highly individualistic work intended to educate the Jews of his time (probably in the Egyptian communities) in the proper forms of worship. Hai Gaon, head of the academy of Pumbeditha until his death in 1038, also prepared a text for communities outside Babylonia; Louis Ginzberg suggested that it may have been intended for the Jews of the Crimea or of Byzantinum.[17] How successful the efforts of the Geonim to establish a standard liturgy for Diaspora Jewry were is proved by the fact that these medieval prayerbooks are basically the same as those used in traditional synagogues today. As Ginzberg observed, "Upon no other department was the activity of the Geonim so decisive as upon the Liturgy." On the other hand, their chief rivals for spiritual hegemony in the Jewish world, the Palestinian authorities of that period, were equally active in the same area. The Land of Israel, where the Siddur and Maḥzor as we know them were born and structured, retained its influence in the field of liturgy longer than in any other area of religious usage. Even at the zenith of the influence exerted by the flourishing Babylonian academies, and after the disappearance of the academies of Palestine, the latter country remained the center of the next major development in Jewish worship, the *Piyyutim,* to which we shall shortly turn our attention.

From Palestine and Babylonia, the practice of compiling Maḥzorim spread into all the lands of the Diaspora. We have record of such collections edited by luminaries of the Torah like Rabbenu Tam and Naḥmanides; indeed, most of the authorities of that period arranged their own Maḥzorim, which came to be accepted as binding in matters of religious practice. The Maḥzorim grew to be ponderous tomes of an encyclopedic nature — a good example is the famed *Maḥzor Vitry*, composed by R. Simḥah of Vitry, France, a pupil of Rashi, and reflecting the master's views in prayer. In the 12th century we see the beginning of the process of breaking down the outsized Maḥzorim into specialized volumes of worship for daily use, for Shabbat, the Three Festivals (Pesaḥ, Shavuot and Sukkot) and the Days of Awe. In addition, smaller collections for specific occasions begin to appear: *Haggadah, Seliḥot,* etc. The laws and customs relating to liturgical usage are collected in books of *Minhagim.*

With the invention of the printing press, the texts of the various Maḥzorim tended toward increasing stabilization.[18] The first critical edition of the Ashkenazic Maḥzor, the model for all later editions in Western Europe and America, was published by Wolf Heidenheim in Roedelheim, Germany beginning in the year 1800. This pioneering scholar, whom Zunz called "the Mendelssohn of the Maḥzor," was the founder of the scientific study of the *Piyyutim* and the first to purify the Maḥzor of its more extravagant Kabbalistic excesses. In our own day new editions of the High Holy Day Maḥzor continue to appear along with translation into the vernacular, offering eloquent testimony equally to the vitality of Jewish worship and to the growing role of Rosh Hashanah and Yom Kippur in the religious consciousness of the modern Jew.

The Music of the High Holy Day Service

One of the factors which helped stabilize the traditional prayers of the Siddur and Maḥzor and keep them popular and ever-fresh is the musical setting which was developed for each part of the service, and even for individual prayers, by Synagogue authorities through the centuries.

Hebrew prayers chanted in the traditional manner could be repeated at almost every occasion without producing a sense of monotony in the worshipper. In the first instance, the traditional congregant was an active participant in the ritual instead of being a member of a silent audience. The old psychological principle of "no impression without expression" embodied in Jewish prayer made the experience emotionally vibrant and satisfying. Second, the characteristic musical modes and Scriptural cantillations which differ with the varying occasions of the year, served to create a distinct mood appropriate to the day and added variety and interest, even when the text remained the same (Robert Gordis).

Another historic function of the *Nusah*, or traditional melodic structure, has been to maintain the musical integrity of the service. Although our sacred music has always echoed the contemporaneous musical fashion of the world at large, the accepted prayer-motifs served to restrain cantors from the temptation of catering to the current tastes.

The High Holy Day prayers in the Ashkenazic rite are chanted according to a *Nusah* which differs markedly from the musical modes for Shabbat and Festivals. Within this overall mode there are the usual variations for each of the several services of Rosh Hashanah and Yom Kippur — the evening service (Arvit), the morning service (Shaharit), the additional service (Musaf), the afternoon service (Minhah), and the concluding service of Yom Kippur (Ne'ilah). Finally, specific prayers and *piyyutim* at each of these services, for example, *Kol Nidre* or *U-netaneh tokef*, have developed their own hallowed melodies into which Jewish musical genius through the ages has woven its infinite variations. These themes, expressing by turn every mood of the Jewish soul, constitute a veritable symphony. Some of the melodies have inspired classic composers like Beethoven and Max Bruch as well as contemporaries like Arnold Schoenberg and Ernst Bloch. This Commentary will cite brief explanations of the musical settings of key prayers and *piyyutim* for Rosh Hashanah and Yom Kippur as they appear in the services.

With characteristic charm, Israel Zangwill has summarized the significant role of music in the religion of the traditional Jew, as the author observed him in London's East End. "Their religious consciousness was largely a musical box: the thrill of a ram's horn, the cadenza of a Psalmic phrase, the jubilance of a festival 'Amen,' and the sobriety of a workaday 'Amen,' the Passover melodies and the Pentecost, the minor keys of Atonement and the hilarious rhapsodies of Rejoicing, the plain chant of the Law and the more ornate intonation of the Prophets." Here is striking corroboration of the insight of Sir James G. Frazer, the famed student of religion and folklore: "Every faith has its appropriate music, and the difference between the creeds might almost be expressed in musical notation."

The *Nusah* did not exist primarily for its own artistic sake nor even to create an emotional attitude. It was felt to be an organic part of the total experience of group worship. Such an integration of musical form and inwardness of spirit is possible only when the individual worshipper can participate intimately and directly in the service, not when he is merely a spectator at a performance, however polished. The sainted leader of Liberal Judaism, Rabbi Leo S. Baeck, warned, "The Jewish people . . . always were and should remain a singing people, singing in their synagogues, maybe unsolemnly, but singing themselves — not by proxy, by the Choir."

It is of such Synagogal music that the Zohar, classic source of Jewish mysticism, speaks when it declares, "There are halls in the heavens above that open only to the voice of song." It is melody in this traditional sense that the Ḥasidic master, Rabbi Naḥman of Bratzlav, had in mind when he observed, "Tears open the gates but music razes the very walls of Heaven."

The Future of the Jewish Prayerbook

It is clear from the foregoing that, when we read our Prayerbook for the High Holy Days, we make use of an exquisite mosaic of Jewish piety whose pieces have been set in by reverent hands over many centuries in lands too numerous to mention.[19] Not all the pieces are of equal beauty and significance, and recent editions of the Maḥzor have removed some of the less worthy items. Yet our generation must exercise great caution lest a momentary passion for expediency undo beyond repair the hallowed pattern woven by our forbears.

Nor should we confine ourselves to deletions. Though ours may not be an age especially gifted in religious expression, neither is it free of the obligation to strive after fresh and creative forms of devotion. Encouragement in this direction comes from the new State of Israel where inspired verse is being written in the finest traditions of Jewish spirituality.[20] In the work of such contemporary masters as Yaakov Cohen, Yosef Tzvi Rimmon, David Shimonovitz (Shimoni) or Sh. Shalom, as in that of the sainted Hillel Zeitlin and Rabbi Abraham Isaac Kuk and the immortal Bialik, the Jewish people may well find the winged words to express the spiritual yearnings of the present and thus continue to enrich the Siddur and Maḥzor. The mosaic need not yet be complete; the "bridges leading from the heart to God" require constant maintenance.

"When Jews prayed sincerely, one Siddur sufficed for all; now that the urge to pray is weak, new Siddurim are multiplied." Such was the wry observation of Solomon Schechter, and our generation has accelerated the process which caused him concern. Yet the publication of new Siddurim and Maḥzorim need hold no dangers as long as a decent regard for Jewish authenticity is preserved. The history of the Prayerbook is one of growth and development within a framework fixed by tradition yet hospitable to new content, a spiritual dialectic of "form and freedom," to use the expression of Shalom Spiegel. It is this framework, the "mould cast by the Sages," which has insured the unity and integrity of Jewish worship in the face of the vicissitudes of history and geography and the hazardous criteria of prevailing fashion.

Fundamental to the framework is the sacred Hebrew tongue. Contrary to the popular notion, Hebrew was *not* the language of the Jewish "everyman" during the period when the text of the major prayers was established. Yet the Sages ordained that the language of devotion remain classical Hebrew. This insight into the folk-psyche, which proved to be a priceless safeguard against many a future threat to Jewish unity, guaranteed the continuity and unique quality of Jewish worship down to the present. The use of the vernacular was never forbidden; such an important prayer as the Kaddish (written largely in Aramaic) is a case in point. Yet any Jewry which radically displaces the traditional Hebrew prayers loses the historic sense of oneness with all Israel and with Israel's pilgrimage and courts the fate of excision from the mainstream of Jewish tradition. Solomon Schechter's warning to American Jewry, first stated in 1904, takes on urgency with the years: "There is no future in this country for a Judaism that resists either the English or the Hebrew language."[21]

The Siddur and Maḥzor are the finest products of the traditional Synagogue which the poet Bialik justly called *"Bet ha-yotzayr l-nishmat ha-umah* . . . the potter's shop wherein the folk-soul was fashioned." By all means, let our manuals of devotion be pleasing in form and possess content relevant to contemporary needs. But let them also bear the trademark of that same potter's shop, the genuine stamp of those reverent craftsmen who fashioned the Siddur and Maḥzor of which Yaakov Cohen has sung in his modern Hebrew classic:

The old tear-stained prayerbook will I take in my hand
And call upon the God of my fathers in my distress,
To the God of my fathers who was their Rock and Refuge
In ages past, I will pour out my woe
In ancient words, seared with the pain of generations.
May these words that know the heavenly paths
Bring my plaint to the God above,
And tell him that which is hidden in my heart —
These words, faithful and true, will speak for me before God,
They will ask His pity.
And God in Heaven who has heard the prayers of my fathers,
The God who gave them power and strength —
Perhaps He will hear my prayer, too, and my distress,
And will be a Shield unto me as He was unto them.
For, like them, I am left a spoil unto others,
Degraded and despised, a wanderer over the face of the earth.
And there is none who can help and sustain me,
Except God in Heaven.[22]

CHAPTER TWO

THE PIYYUTIM

The High Holy Day services, especially in the Ashkenazic rite, are distinguished by a large number of Hebrew poems composed for Synagogue use since the early centuries of the Common Era by poets, cantors and scholars in practically every land where Jews have dwelled. These poems, though of many different types, are generally subsumed under the collective name *Piyyutim* or simply *Piyyut*. The name comes from the same Greek word which gives us our "Poetry"; the root-word is found in Talmudic literature.[1] The story of *Piyyut* constitutes a colorful and dramatic chapter in the history of our sacred literature. Indeed, a study of its origin and successful struggle for recognition as a legitimate element in public worship will be instructive to those who are searching for a method to modify the traditional liturgy of our own day in a positive, creative fashion. For through *Piyyut* medieval Judaism discovered a formula for preserving both adherence to tradition and self-expression in the worship of God.[2]

The *Piyyutim* are the product of no one man, country nor century. "They represent in a real sense the collective soul of Israel throughout the centuries" (Max Arzt). Originating — like the Siddur itself — in Palestine,[3] *Piyyut* spread to Babylonia, Byzantium, Spain, Italy, France and Northern Europe, the Balkans and the Middle East, introducing new material into the classic Prayerbook for a thousand years (and in some Oriental communities down to the present day). A touching *piyyut* in the style of the classic *Seliḥah*, lamenting the Nazi destruction of six million Jews, has been included in a recent edition of *Seliḥot* for the entire year.[4] Israel Davidson devoted a lifetime to collecting over 35,000 titles of extant *piyyutim* by almost 3,000 poets (in Hebrew called *Payyetanim*).[5] The rituals of our fellow-Jews who worship in the Spanish, French, Italian and Yemenite traditions contain many soul-stirring and beautifully written *piyyutim* not included in our Ashkenazic ritual. Leopold Zunz, pioneer in Jewish liturgical studies, has revealed how *Piyyut* preserved not only historical memories,[6] but even the special intellectual interests of communities of the past — the Spanish with its predilection for philosophy, science and linguistics, the Northern European with its penchant for Talmud and Midrash, law and legend.[7]

How Piyyut Began

The origins of *Piyyut* are veiled in the obscurity of the post-Talmudic period in Palestine;[8] but the sensational discovery of long-lost manuscripts — especially in the Cairo Genizah — has shed new light on the problems and it is now possible to reconstruct some picture of how this important form of literature arose.

By the year 550 C.E. — as we have seen in Chapter One — the basic structure of the Jewish Prayerbook was well established, with some sections a thousand years old,[9] notably the Benedictions of the Shema and the *Amidah*. These statutory prayers were attributed to the "Men of the Great Synagogue (or Assembly)," the anonymous Sages of the Persian-Greek era, roughly 500-150 B.C.E. They had been designated as the standard pattern of worship *(matbay'a shel tefillah)*, legally binding on all Israel. Indeed it might have been expected that the text of the Siddur, as it existed in the sixth century, would become as fixed as the texts of the Bible, Mishnah and Gemara. There was a real danger that the wellsprings of Hebrew prayer would be stopped up, especially in view of the deterioration of the Jewish political and economic position in Palestine. That this did not come to pass may be attributed to the rise of *Piyyut*.

About the fifth century C.E. — or even earlier, according to some scholars[10] — a fresh channel of liturgical expression was opened for a people still richly endowed with creative religious genius. Shortly after the compilation of the Palestinian Talmud (end of the fourth century), the relatively artless prayers of the earlier Talmudic age began to take on more stately poetic embellishment. The leader of the worship — who played a much more decisive and creative role before the spread of printed prayerbooks, especially in the East — while reciting the standard prayers from memory, would interpolate newly-composed sacred poems into the Benedictions of the Shema and the still-fluid *Amidah.* These poems might be of his own composition or the work of other poet-cantors, often chanted to appropriate melodies. To judge by the large collection of *piyyutim* appended to the *Maḥzor Vitry,* the precentor had the freedom, as late as the twelfth century, to select the poetry he deemed suitable for insertion into the worship service.

Saadiah Gaon and others in the Geonic period describe the art of *Piyyut* composition by the term *Ḥazzanut.*[11] This designation was popular in the East until the twelfth century and served as a key to modern scholars in reconstructing the origins of *Piyyut.* The interpolation of these new poems was especially frequent on festival and fast days and on the special Sabbaths of the calendar in order to interpret the particular significance of these occasions to the congregation. The themes were frequently drawn from the Midrashim on the Bible; the effect — if not the purpose — was that the *piyyutim* thus popularized these latest products of Rabbinic genius.[12] Especially common were poetic embellishments of the weekly Torah portion *(Seder).* The *payyetan* Yannai, for example, composed poems (known as *Kerovot*) for each *Seder* of the triennial cycle according to which the Torah was read in Palestine at that time.

The forms employed were novel, strikingly at variance with the sharp images and the balanced strophes of Biblical poetry, on the one hand, and the simple prose of the earlier liturgy, on the other (the statutory prayers employ a modified Biblical vocabulary and rhythm). The new poetry differed in style and appearance even from the relatively unadorned hymns and litanies (e.g., *El adon, Tikanta shabbat, Mi she-ana*) which had been added to the obligatory prayers in earlier Talmudic times. Ever more complex acrostic devices succeeded the simple alphabetical sequences already familiar from the Psalms, Proverbs and Lamentations of the Bible. A word artistry of increasing ornateness replaced the "quiver of arrows" (to use Herder's phrase) that is Biblical Hebrew and the restrained neo-Hebrew of the Mishnah. Rhyme was introduced as a conscious technique, replacing the sporadic or even accidental rhymes of the standard prayers. In the course of time (especially in Spain, under the influence of Arabic literary models) regular meters of varying complexities replaced the simple stress rhythms of older Hebrew verse.

These revolutionary developments in style launched a fertile new era in Hebrew literature as well as liturgy. One may question the superiority of the new over the old but one cannot quarrel with history. The pattern was now set for infinite variety of literary and musical expression in harmony with the evolving needs and changing tastes of the people of Israel in its wide dispersion.

What historical conditions provided the impetus for this fresh burst of liturgical creativity? For one, there was an ancient and authoritative tradition that prayer must not be allowed to congeal into fixed forms but must ever retain an element of spontaneity and surprise. Rabbi Aḥa, a scholar of the fourth century, states in regard to the *Amidah,* "It is necessary to make some innovation in it each day."[13] Thus the leader of the worship service had a certain freedom of improvisation. This tradition of spontaneity was especially strong in Palestine where *Piyyut* originated. Some scholars believe that the earliest *Piyyut* and the form of standard prayer existed side by side for centuries.

Another explanation has gained wide currency: it is the theory that *Piyyut* originated as the result of persecution. Judah ben Barzillai, a rabbi of Barcelona, (end of eleventh — beginning of twelfth centuries) preserved an older tradition that the *Piyyutim* were originally instituted "when the Jews were forbidden by their oppressors to engage in the study of the Law."[13a] This repression is taken by some modern scholars to be the persecution of the Babylonian Jews by the late Persians, 450-589 C.E.[14] Others identify the persecution referred to as the prohibition in 553 C.E. by Justinian, the Christian Emperor of Byzantine Rome, against the teaching of "deuterosis," that is, the Rabbinic interpretations of the Bible, by the Jews in his domain, of which Palestine was a part.[15] In either case, the didactic or instructive *Piyyut* — associated with Yannai and Kallir — would have its origin as a disguised lesson in Jewish law, a sort of secret sermon in which the Ḥazzan — as it were — substituted for the Rabbi.[16] The Talmud records the use of cryptic messages of a legal character as well as prayers, both artfully designed to circumvent decrees against public instruction in Jewish traditions.[17]

Israel Davidson suggested that the first *Payyetanim* were merely adapting an old method when they conveyed the teachings of the Law to the Jews of Palestine through cryptic poems during the suppression by Justinian of sermons and public teaching of Halakhah.[18]

Whether *Piyyut* actually originated in this dramatic fashion, or whether the motivating factor was the need to interpret the Aggadic literature or simply to adorn the standard prayers, there can be no doubt that such heroic employment of sacred poetry could not but endear the new form to the Jewish worshipper, both in Palestine, the land of its birth, and in Babylonia, where it was quickly adopted. Another strong appeal of *Piyyut* to the populace may have been its musical possibilities; the voice of song was being heard again in the Synagogue, thanks to the *piyyutim,* which were sung by the worshippers as well as by the Ḥazzan.

The Payyetanim

The writers of *Piyyut,* called *Payyetanim,* during the earliest period were not known by name,[19] except for Yose ben Yose. Nothing is known about his life but it is assumed that, since he bears his father's name, the latter died before Yose's birth. For this reason he is sometimes referred to as *Ha-Yatom* ("the orphan"). The name Yose (= Yosef) is common in Palestine in the third and fourth centuries; an Amora bearing the very name Yose ben Yose, who flourished about 300 C.E., is mentioned in the Palestinian Talmud.[20] The *payyetan* Yose lived possibly in the early fifth century in Palestine.[21] He authored several *Avodah* compositions for Yom Kippur. Unfortunately, only a few fragments of his verse remain in the German, French and Italian rituals for the High Holy Days. Much of his work probably lies buried in manuscripts.

Yose is represented in our Ashkenazic Maḥzor only by a few simple unrhymed fragments written in a simple Biblical style. These are *Darkekha Elohaynu* and *L-ma'ankha Elohaynu* (part of a *Viddui,* or Confession, for Yom Kippur that begins, *Omnam ashamaynu*). Our Ashkenazic service includes these two fragments in the *Seliḥot* for Yom Kippur night. In the Rosh Hashanah service we have only the single verse in the *Yotzayr* section of Shaḥarit, *Or olam* [*b*] *otzar ḥayyim, orot may-ofel amar va-yehi.*[22]

The first great Palestinian *payyetan* whose extant work presents a true picture of his genius is Yannai. Many of his long-lost creations have been recovered only in the past generation from the Cairo Genizah. The most dramatic find was the *Maḥzor Yannai*, a "cycle" of *piyyutim* based on the old triennial Torah reading, published in 1919 by Israel Davidson. His use of the term *Maḥzor* is the oldest on record. Menaḥem Zulay published no less than eight hundred poems which he identified as Yannai's. Thus has scholarship rescued from oblivion a great Hebrew poet of the Synagogue, forgotten for almost a thousand years, whose very name was unknown a century ago. Yannai was probably the creator of the *Piyyut* form known as *Kerovah* (a chain of poetic interpolations into the *Amidah* for Shabbat and Festivals).[23] He was also one of the first to use rhyme and the name-acrostic as a stylistic device. Shalom Spiegel dates Yannai about 550 C.E.[24] Saul Lieberman has shown that Yannai may have flourished in a much earlier period; his poems are a rich source for the Palestinian Halakhah, according to the school of Rabbi Ishmael.[25] It is also recorded[26] that Yannai influenced Anan, the founder of the Karaite sect which in the eighth century revolted against the prevailing Talmudic law.

In spite of Yannai's vast output and his great fame among early authorities, only a single poem of his found its way into the Ashkenazic rite; a section of this *piyyut* is preserved in our Passover Haggadah, beginning *Az rov nissim.* There is, however, evidence for also ascribing to Yannai the authorship of one of the best-known *piyyutim* in our High Holy Day Maḥzor, *V-khol ma'aminim.*[27] Tradition has it that Yannai was the teacher of the illustrious *payyetan,* Eleazar Kallir; a fanciful medieval legend tells that Yannai grew envious of his disciple and caused his death. Yannai's poetic style is simple compared to that of Kallir and others who followed. Yet many of his images continue to baffle us, probably because we are ignorant of the many shades of meaning conveyed by certain Hebrew words and expressions then current. Further reasons for the neglect of Yannai's poems which led to their virtual disappearance were, first, the fact that they were tied to the triennial cycle of Torah readings which later became obsolete and, second, the fact that their content was heavily legalistic, whereas his successors utilized material from the Aggadah, legends and homilies much better suited to devotional purposes.

The most famous of all the *payyetanim* is Eleazar ben Jacob Kallir (or Killir) known familiarly as (the) Kallir. This prolific poet of the Synagogue lived in Palestine in the sixth or seventh century[28] and created a style of *Piyyut* which prevailed for centuries. Many critics, ancient as well as modern (notably Abraham Ibn Ezra), have deprecated his poetic style and obscure allusions and charged him with reckless abuse of the Hebrew language.[29] Nevertheless, his *piyyutim* have won an enduring place in Jewish hearts. To this day they remain like uncut jewels embedded in our festival prayers; our Ashkenazic High Holy Day Maḥzor is studded lavishly with them. Some scholars even credit Kallir's "daring innovations" in Hebrew grammar and vocabulary with paving the way for that linguistic resiliency which has made a living, spoken Hebrew possible after a lapse of twenty centuries. Shalom Spiegel holds that the allegedly exotic Hebrew of Yannai, Kallir and their contemporaries is not at all an artificial personal idiom, but actually mirrors the Hebrew which continued to be spoken in rural Judea long after Aramaic became the vernacular of the rest of Palestine. Indeed, the editor of Yannai's poems, Menaḥem Zulay, continually urged the linguistic authorities of contemporary Israel to reclaim some of the vocabulary and usages of Yannai, Kallir and other Palestinian *payyetanim* for the evolving Hebrew language of our time.[30]

Kallir and his muse became legendary among medieval Jews. Along with his teacher Yannai, he was considered to have been a Tanna of the Mishnah[31] — a tradition which bestowed a sort of ecclesiastical legitimacy upon his embellishment of the statutory prayers. His inspiration is traced to the celestial chorus; he is reputed to have seen angelic visions as a babe in the cradle while bees filled his gifted mouth with honey. Thus did Jews venerate their *payyetanim!*

Until recently, only a few other early *payyetanim* were known by name (e.g., Joshua and Phineas, who are mentioned by Saadiah Gaon). The new material from the Genizah of Cairo, however, has brought to light a host of hitherto unknown poets. Scholars have identified hundreds of Palestinian *payyetanim* who flourished between the sixth and eleventh centuries, thus establishing the existence of a period of high intellectual and spiritual creativity in that heretofore obscure period. These *piyyutim* constitute a rich new source for the recovery of the lost *midrashim,* legends, traditions and synagogue practices of Palestinian Jewry during the Byzantine and early Arab periods. We cite one fascinating example: a *piyyut* of the Yannai-Kallir period reveals a previously unknown tradition that Hillel and Shammai were brothers, like Moses and Aaron.[32]

The art of the Palestinian poets was carried on in Babylonia, even though some authorities, notably the Geonim of Pumbeditha (the Geonim of Sura were closer to the Palestinian usage) opposed the practice for fear that the text of the statutory benedictions might be altered.[33] No less distinguished an authority than Saadiah Gaon (882-942) was an admirer of the "ancient poets" of Palestine, whom he names as Yose ben Yose, Yannai, Eleazar (Kallir), Joshua and Phineas. Saadiah wrote *piyyutim,* notably the two petitions *(Bakashot)* which earned the lavish praise of Maimonides and Abraham Ibn Ezra, among others, and were translated into Arabic by the poet and by his admirers.[34] Hai Gaon (died 1038) wrote *piyyutim,* especially a number of moving *seliḥot.* Indeed, some leading modern scholars (S. D. Luzzatto, Wolf Jawitz) considered Babylonia, rather than Palestine, to be the birthplace of *Piyyut.* Paradoxically, however, the new prayer-form struggled unsuccessfully to strike roots in Synagogue worship there.

The personal history of Saadiah Gaon reveals the different attitudes toward *Piyyut* in Palestine and in Babylonia. In his native Egypt, the congregations, especially those which were deeply influenced by Palestinian practice, undoubtedly used many *piyyutim* in their ritual. When Saadiah came to Babylonia, however, he found the situation to be quite different: though the populace, as everywhere, favored the practice of inserting new poetry into the time honored statutory prayers, the academic authorities vigorously resisted the pressure to change the character of traditional worship. That is why Saadiah, who was brought up in a country where *Piyyut* was firmly established and who personally composed a considerable amount of liturgical poetry, nevertheless practiced abstinence in his historic *Siddur* (which was to serve as an authoritative text for Jewry). He apologized every time he quoted a *piyyut,* found fault with the extravagances of some *payyetanim,* and excused his inclusion of *piyyutim* by referring to the popular trend.[35] His ambivalent approach notwithstanding, Saadiah remains one of the central figures in the history of *Piyyut.* He may have been the living link between the pioneering Palestinian school and the Spanish "Golden Age" which created the most perfect gems of medieval Hebrew poetry.

From Palestine and Babylonia, the art of *Piyyut* spread eastward and southward into Moslem lands; it also spread west and north to Byzantium and southern Italy and thence to Germany and France. In the Rhineland of the tenth and eleventh centuries, the Kalonymus family, Simon ben Isaac ben Abun of Mayence and a host of others enriched the Prayerbook with *piyyutim,* many of which grace our own High Holy Day services to this day. Such luminaries of the Law as Gershom ben Judah and Meir of Rothenburg are also represented by *piyyutim* in our Maḥzor. Many *piyyutim* are attributed to Rashi. Ephraim of Regensburg (died 1175) is among the foremost of the German *payyetanim.* A familiar *piyyut* recited on Kol Nidre night *(Omnam kayn)* has been ascribed by some to another rabbi of the twelfth century, Yom Tov of Joigny, who was martyred at York, England in 1190.[36]

The Kallir-mode in sacred verse did not give way until the eleventh and twelfth centuries when the masters of the Spanish "Golden Age" developed a new metrical style based on classical Arabic models. The recognized giants of secular poetry (with the exception of Samuel Ha-Nagid) also excelled in *Piyyut.* Solomon Ibn Gabirol, Judah Halevi and Moses Ibn Ezra — to mention only the chief masters — skillfully adapted Arabic meter, rhyme and rhetoric to the Hebrew liturgy. Even Abraham Ibn Ezra, who opposed in principle the interruption of the obligatory prayers by optional *piyyutim,* wrote scores of sacred poems which fall within the *Piyyut* category. For the first time now, men who were distiguished as secular poets, men of science and philosophy, lent their ample talents to sacred song. Nor was there any contradiction in this versatility. Careful students of Hebrew poetry — ancient, medieval or modern — know that the line which separates sacred from secular (the very concepts are basically foreign to normative Judaism!) is frequently an arbitrary one. There is only one essential tradition in Hebrew poetry from the Bible down to the present day, and *Piyyut* is perhaps the strongest bridge between the old and the new.

In eastern Europe, the poets of the Synagogue veered away from the elegant arabesque verse of the Sephardim in favor of *Seliḥot.* These were penitential prayers and elegies commemorating tragic experiences; their theme is God's quality of forgiveness *(Seliḥah).* The style of *Seliḥot* is generally simpler than that of the other *Piyyut* types. "On the lips of the Ashkenazic Jews Hebrew was freed from the golden chains of a complex rhetoric, and it came to be as easy and natural as the Hebrew of the authors of the Midrash in the early centuries of the Common Era" (Abraham J. Heschel).[36a]

The Main Types of Piyyut

The generic term *Piyyut* includes several major categories of liturgical poetry, each of which may be further sub-divided. The *piyyutim* are of four main types; the names of the categories indicate either their location in the service or the nature of the contents. *Ma'aravot* (also called *Ma'arivot* or *Ma'aravim*) are poems intended to adorn the Benedictions of the Shema in the Arvit or evening service. *Yotzrot* (singular, *Yotzayr*) are poems inserted in the Benedictions of the Shema in the Shaḥarit, morning service. *Kerovot* (singular, *Kerovah*) are poetic insertions in the *Amidah* of both the Shaḥarit and Musaf services. The *Kerovah* is the characteristic type of Rosh Hashanah *piyyut,* and the most elaborate. On Yom Kippur, the *Seliḥah* (singular of *Seliḥot)* is the ubiquitous form of *piyyut.* It is found in all services of the Day of Atonement and tends to absorb all other types. So voluminous is the *Seliḥot* literature — the hymns of penitence, the pleas for God's forgiveness, the elegies over Jewish disasters through the centuries — that it has often been considered a category of its own, parallel to the more positive *Piyyutim,* whose mood is one of praise and thankful acknowledgment of God. A full discussion of the *Seliḥot* will be provided in the Yom Kippur volume of this Commentary.

Ma'aravot are not recited in the Rosh Hashanah evening service, even among Ashkenazim; we may therefore dispense with further discussion at this point. In Chapter Three, however, the commentary on the Arvit service mentions several little-known rites which included *Ma'aravot.*

Yotzrot are regularly found in the Shaḥarit of the Ashkenazic rite for the High Holy Days, and it will be helpful, therefore, to present a brief outline of the chief sub-types. The first sub-type is called a *Yotzayr* (this is the limited use of the term). It is so designated because it follows the opening sentence of the first benediction preceding the Shema, "Who formest *(yotzayr)* light." After the "Thrice-Holy" *(Kadosh, kadosh, kadosh)* and before the phrase, *"V-ha-ḥayyot yeshorayru* . . . the heavenly beings sing," there is a second sub-type of *Yotzrot* called *Ofan* ("Wheel," alluding to one of the heavenly beings envisioned by the prophet Ezekiel). This completes the sub-types of *Yotzrot* actually used in our services for the High Holy Days. On other occasions, additional sub-types of *Yotzrot* are employed, such as *Me'orah*, so-called because it precedes the finale of the first benediction, *yotzayr ha-me'orot; Ahavah,* a *piyyut* inserted near the end of the second of the two benedictions preceding the Shema, whose key word is *Ahavah* ("love"); and *Zulat* and *Ge'ulah,* poems inserted in the single benediction following the Shema. To the extent that the Sephardim use *piyyutim* on Rosh Hashanah, they are generally inserted among the preliminary hymns *(Zemirot)* or after the Bible lessons — in short, they appear outside the body of statutory prayers.

The *Kerovah* in its classical form is actually a chain or cycle of *piyyutim* inserted at prescribed intervals during the Cantor's repetition of the *Amidah;* the number of links in this chain depends on the particular *Amidah.* In Shaḥarit, *Kerovot* appear only in the opening three benedictions: *Avot, Gevurot* and *Kedushah;* in Musaf, they may appear in the middle benedictions as well.[37] The Sephardic rituals use some *Kerovot* on Yom Kippur[38] but not on Rosh Hashanah. The *Kerovah* originated at a time when the Reader of the service still had considerable freedom in presenting his own individualized insertions in the *Amidah,* especially in the *Kedushah* section (which in ancient Palestine was recited only on Shabbat and Festivals).[39] The *Kedushah* is heavily weighted with allusions to the Midrash; in fact, as Shalom Spiegel observes, it was actually "a rhymed homily on the portion of the Writ read that week in the Synagogue."[40]

The greatest master — and probably the creator — of this *piyyut* form was, as we have already noted, the Palestinian Yannai. He wrote *Kerovot* based on each *Seder* (weekly portion of the

Torah) of the three-year cycle then employed in Palestine, as well as for festivals and fasts. His *Kerovot* contain considerable Halakhic (legalistic) and Aggadic (homiletical) material.

For the first day of Rosh Hashanah in our Ashkenazic rite, there are two *Kerovah*-cycles, both from the pen of the prolific Eleazar Kallir. The first, for the Shaḥarit service, is called — after the opening verse — *At ḥil yom pekudah;* the second, for the Musaf service, begins with the phrase, *Upad may-az.* For the second day of Rosh Hashanah, there is only one *Kerovah*-cycle, namely in the Shaḥarit service. Composed by Rabbi Simeon ben Isaac ben Abun of Mayence, it is entitled — after its initial phrase — *Atiti l-ḥanenakh.* Some recent editions of the Maḥzor include only selections from the original cycles, which, in their entirety, consisted of ten distinct poems (in Kallir's *Kerovot*) and eleven poems (in the *Kerovah* of Simeon ben Isaac). The *Kerovot* were provided, by the medieval Ashkenazic authorities, with melodies which became traditional and were considered binding on later generations.

The original meaning of the term *Kerovah* is still disputed.[41] It has long been connected with the familiar Hebrew verb *karav,* "approach," because the Reader would approach the Ark in order to recite the *Amidah.*[42] The name is likewise used in Syrian Christian liturgy. More likely the term is connected with *karova,* a synonym for cantor-poet found in the Midrashic literature.[43] In medieval France and Germany, *Kerovot* were called *Kerovatz* or *Kerovetz.*[44] So prominent is the *Kerovah* type of poetry on the High Holy Days in the Ashkenazic rite that the prayerbook is sometime designated *Sefer Kerovot* instead of *Maḥzor* (e.g., the Heidenheim prayerbooks for Rosh Hashanah and Yom Kippur).

Any description of the highly complex structure of the *Kerovah*-chain would necessitate a lengthy and technical discussion. For those who might wish to examine the *Kerovah* apparatus in all its details, a special Appendix has been provided at the end of this volume. In Chapter Four, THE SHAḤARIT SERVICE and Chapter Seven, THE MUSAF SERVICE, the reader will find commentary on the individual *piyyutim* which have retained a wide appeal in the contemporary synagogue. As they appear in the text, more will be said about their content and religious message, as well as their structure.

The Age-Old Controversy over Piyyut

As we have indicated, *Piyyut* was not welcomed into the service of the Synagogue unchallenged. Paradoxically, despite its learned character, *Piyyut* was popular among the masses in every land; yet, among scholars, there raged a heated controversy for centuries over the interpolation of *piyyutim* into the well-established statutory prayers.[45] Authorities as far removed in time and clime as Hai Gaon, Judah ben Barzillai, Maimonides, Joseph Caro and the Vilna Gaon[46] opposed the indiscriminate insertion of *piyyutim* into the obligatory prayers. *Piyyutim* were attacked as unwarranted interruptions of the classic Rabbinic rite, as repositories of obscure ideas out of harmony with normative Judaism (e.g., anthropomorphism), and as barbaric examples of Hebrew composition.[47] Even in medieval times we find complaints that they prolong the services unduly; indeed, from the fifteenth century on abridgements are common. Nevertheless, the ferocity of the attacks has been matched by the passion of the defense. Equally distinguished authorities — Rashi, Rabbenu Tam and Rabbenu Gershom, the "Light of the Exile," among them — praised the art of *Piyyut* and claimed for it and its authors heavenly inspiration or, at the very least, Talmudic sanction. Even the Karaite schismatics borrowed *piyyutim* from the Synagogue.[48] In general, the Oriental Jews and other Sephardim have followed the Babylonian tradition; the *piyyutim* which they have introduced into the prayers have been largely relegated to positions *outside* the main body of the statutory prayers. The Ashkenazim, loyal to the ancient Palestinian practice, have inserted *piyyutim* in profusion directly into the benedictions of both the Shema and the *Amidah*.

What is the abiding value of *Piyyut*? The answer would seem to lie between the extremes of partisanship, as Zunz, Berliner, Idelsohn, Davidson and other modern critics of medieval Hebrew poetry have argued with great cogency. Ismar Elbogen, one of the most distinguished scholars of Jewish liturgy, summarized this position: "The modern era has, on the one hand, set aside the great mass of unintelligible and worthless *piyyutim* unsparingly; on the other hand, it has correctly evaluated the historic significance of these poems and has had no hesitation about retaining *piyyutim* of poetic value in the Maḥzor."[49] There can be no shadow of doubt concerning their historic significance. The *piyyutim* preserved the Jewish liturgy from stagnation and from irrelevance to changing conditions of Israel's existence. They served as an outlet through which Jews told of their suffering at the hands of the nations and their touching hopes for redemption from the bondage of exile and restoration to ancient glory. *Piyyutim,* moreover, served as a pathetic form of mutual aid and comfort between Jews in different lands and regimes. Many Sephardic elegies were taken into the Ashkenazic liturgy; Italian Jews tearfully recited *Seliḥot* over the persecution of their German and Polish brothers. Above all, it was the passionate love of the rank and file for the *piyyutim* that won the day over the learned objections of the scholars.[50] The great Zunz lovingly summarized it: "In the course of time, *Piyyut* entwined the entire religious life and entered into every area of the service of God. Nor did it remain only in the Synagogue. It entered the (Jewish) household; it visited with the family at the Shabbat table and at the departure of the Shabbat; it accompanied all domestic occasions, both joyous and sad, on birthdays and anniversaries of death."[51]

It is undeniable that many *piyyutim* offend the modern canons of aesthetics; but even deficiencies in form are not necessarily crucial from a religious viewpoint, as Solomon Schechter, the discoverer of many lost *Piyyut* treasures in the Genizah, caustically observed:

> One likes to think of the old days when devotion was not yet procurable ready-made from hymn-books run by the theological syndicates . . . You can see by their abruptness and their unfinished state that they were not the product of elaborate literary art, but were penned down in the excitement of the moment in a "fit of love," so to speak, to express the religious aspirations of the writer. Their metre may be faulty, their diction crude, and their grammar questionable, but love letters are not, as a rule, distinguished by perfection of style. They are sublime stammering at best though they are intelligible enough to two souls absorbed in each other.[52]

Can Piyyut Still Play a Role?

The *payyetanim* did more than create a new form of Hebrew

literature. They also established a precedent for worthy additions to the ritual by every Jewish community which has felt the need. Their example might also arouse our own generation to the continuing need for creative liturgical expression as a reflection of recent Jewish experience and thought. *Piyyutim* like *Adon olam*, *Yigdal* and *U-netaneh tokef* were once optional but they have become so hallowed by usage that even radical theologians hesitated to excise them.[53] Yet synagogues today resist the addition to the ritual of modern Hebrew verse of a high spiritual order. The question suggests itself: why should our generation not encourage its gifted poets to voice in public worship our own anguished quest for God and for the spiritual significance of Israel's continuing history? It is intriguing to speculate what lasting contribution to our liturgy a poetic genius like Bialik might have made had the modern Synagogue enlisted his inspired muse as the medieval Synagogue did that of Halevi and Gabirol.

Fortunately, the Hebrew singers of our time have by no means abandoned the old *Payyetanic* tradition of articulating religious emotions in newer forms of expression. An able student of Hebrew poetry, A. M. Haberman, has edited a collection of liturgical poems wherein he reveals the direct and intimate relationship between religious poetry to be found in modern Hebrew literature and the earlier periods of sacred poetry.[54] He links some of the religious — even synagogal — moods in modern Hebrew poets to similar moods in the work of time-honored liturgists. One finds the verse of Bialik following (in alphabetical arrangement) that of Baḥya ben Joseph (1040-1090); that of Braudes, the Israeli poet, followed by poetry of Barukh ben Samuel of Mayence (died 1221); the work of American-born Reuben Grossman beside that of Rabbenu Gershom (died 1028). Each of the modern poems included is written in a form and spirit which renders it suitable for incorporation into a Synagogue service. A contemporary poet like Mordecai Temkin has issued a whole volume of "Poems and Prayers," many of them closely resembling the classic *Seliḥot*. Joseph Tzvi Rimmon wrote occasionally in almost pure *Piyyut* style. It is hardly necessary to mention in this connection Chief Rabbi Kuk, who was a masterful religious poet.

The well-nigh universal impression has been that modern

Hebrew poetry is secular, even irreligious, in spirit. Qualified and unprejudiced students of Hebrew verse including the poet-critics, Simon Halkin and Hillel Bavli, have demonstrated, however, the frequent religious moods in the work of Yaakov Cohen, Shlonsky, Lamdan, Uri Tzvi Greenberg, Sh. Shalom and other leading Israeli poets.[55] In the Diaspora, too, such poets as the sainted thinker and mystic, Hillel Zeitlin, have written verse eminently suited for liturgical purposes. One is encouraged by the inclusion of an occasional gem from this untapped treasure in recent editions of Siddur and Maḥzor,[56] but only a beginning has been made in claiming for Synagogue worship the sacred themes in Hebrew verse of recent generations.

The *payyetanim* of ancient Palestine interpreted in sacred music the intricacies of Halakhah and Aggadah to their congregations. The sweet singers of the medieval Spanish synagogues added new philosophic dimensions to the popular God-faith of their time. The Ashkenazic saints and sages intoned God's praises and lamented Israel's tragedy through the dark centuries. And, in our own day, perhaps the poets of Israel's supreme martyrdom and miraculous rebirth shall voice in sacred accents to their contemporaries, gathered in far-flung sanctuaries, fresh insights into the fate and destiny of the Jew and of every man.

CHAPTER THREE

THE ARVIT SERVICE

- THE ORDER OF SERVICES FOR ROSH HASHANAH
- MIZMOR SHIR L-YOM HA-SHABBAT • BAREKHU
- HA-MA'ARIV ARAVIM • THE SHEMA • EMET VE-EMUNAH
- V-SHAMRU • TIK'U VA-ḤODESH • THE HALF KADDISH
- THE AMIDAH • VA-TODI'AYNU • KADDISH TITKABAL
- KIDDUSH • SHE-HEḤEYANU • ALAYNU
- AL KAYN NEKAVEH • MOURNER'S KADDISH
- (L-DAVID) ADONAI ORI • YIGDAL
- ROSH HASHANAH GREETINGS

THE ARVIT SERVICE

The Order of Services for Rosh Hashanah

Rosh Hashanah does not differ essentially from Shabbat or the Three Pilgrimage Festivals in the overall design of the worship. The order of services is basically the same. The holiday is inaugurated with the brief evening service of Arvit (or Ma'ariv). The morning worship begins with Shaḥarit, followed by *Keri'at Ha-Torah* (the reading of the Biblical portions). The climax of the New Year festival worship comes — as always — in the "additional" service of Musaf. The twenty-four hour cycle is concluded with the afternoon prayer, Minḥah. This order is duplicated on the second day of the holiday.

The only unique variation on Rosh Hashanah is the insertion of the Shofar sounding ritual. This ritual is performed twice: first, after the conclusion of the Torah reading and the *Haftarah* and, second, during the Repetition of the *Amidah* of Musaf. The sounding of the Shofar too is omitted when Rosh Hashanah coincides with Shabbat. Unlike the Three Pilgrimage Festivals *(Shalosh Regalim)*, Rosh Hashanah lacks *Hallel*, the service of praise and thanksgiving; the reasons for this omission will be given below, at the close of Shaḥarit where *Hallel* ordinarily is recited.

The uniqueness of the Rosh Hashanah worship lies not in the basic format of the worship but in the special New Year prayers and poetry included in the familiar services, as well as in the heightened significance attached even to the year-round prayers by the High Holy Day motifs. It is to these prayers, poems and motifs that we now turn our attention.

Mizmor Shir L-yom Ha-Shabbat מזמור שיר

The 92nd Psalm, entitled "A song for the Sabbath day," was recited on Shabbat by the Levites at the offering of the *Tamid,* the morning sacrifice in the Temple of Jerusalem. In the Midrash[1] this Psalm is ascribed to Adam, who recited it after he learned the efficacy of repentance as demonstrated by Cain. The Midrash elsewhere[2] states that Adam was created, sinned, was judged and absolved — all on Rosh Hashanah; therefore, this day was ordained for all generations as the Day of Judgment. Rashi explains the appropriateness of this Psalm for the Sabbath on the grounds that its portrayal of the world's perfection corresponds to what life will be in Messianic times. In the Rabbinic tradition, the "life of the world to come" is described as "a day that is completely Shabbat." Rosh Hashanah commemorates the Creation of the universe.

Barekhu ברכו

The Arvit (or Ma'ariv) service for Rosh Hashanah closely parallels that for the Sabbath and the Three Pilgrimage Festivals with the exception of the *Amidah* which contains distinctive High Holy Day prayers. However, unlike the Arvit of the Three Festivals, the Rosh Hashanah Arvit, in almost all rites, contains no *Piyyutim* (which, in the evening service, are called *Ma'aravot*[3]).

In view of the similarity of the Rosh Hashanah Arvit to that of the other Festivals, great importance is attached to its distinctive musical setting *(nusaḥ).* The musical signature for the entire Arvit is set by the chant for *Barekhu,* which constitutes the call to prayer. Its exultant yet melodious theme is carried through the entire service, with slight variations. This festive *nusaḥ* is also used for the Arvit of Yom Kippur. Because of the majestic motif it sets, this invocation is sometimes called *Barekhu Ha-Gadol* (the "Great *Barekhu*").

The Sephardim introduced the practice of reciting, prior to Arvit on the first night of Rosh Hashanah, the tender lyric *Aḥot Ketanah* ("Little Sister") by Abraham Ḥazzan Gerondi; a number of Ashkenazic prayerbooks incorporated it also.[4] This poem has as its refrain, "Let the old year and its curses come to an end; let the new year with its blessings begin." Another Sephardic usage is to preface the Arvit service with Psalm 81 which contains the verse "*Tik'u va-ḥodesh shofar* . . . Sound the shofar on the new moon."[5]

Ha-ma'ariv Aravim המעריב ערבים

The first prayer of Arvit speaks of the power of God as it is revealed in the orderliness and dependability of the natural order. The recognition on man's part that the Creator has established a harmony of the heavenly bodies which insures a beneficent recurrence of night and day, of darkness and light, helps to establish the foundation of trustfulness upon which genuine faith is built. "The realm of Nature is to the Jew nothing distant, strange, cold or uncanny; it is the workshop of the Almighty, and is ruled by His beneficent Will (Bousset).[5a]

Nature, like man, is God's creation and is therefore thought of as endowed with personality and moral responsibility. Rabbi Judah bar Ilai, a sage of the Mishnah, says: "Everything in nature is judged on Rosh Hashanah and its fate is sealed on various other days — grain on Passover, fruit on Shavuot, water on Sukkot. But the fate of man is sealed on Yom Kippur."[6]

A lovely Ḥasidic legend tells that on Rosh Hashanah life ceases on all the stars. They sink into a deep sleep in which they are strengthened to awake with a new power of shining — "The falling is for the sake of the rising."

The Shema שמע

The centrality of *Keri'at Shema* ("Reading of the Shema") in Judaism has been summarized admirably by Robert Gordis, in his "Note on the Shema" in the Sabbath and Festival Prayer Book of the Rabbinical Assembly and United Synagogue of America:

> The Shema is the most important prayer in the Jewish liturgy. With the Shema upon their lips, martyrs in every age, including our own, have died for the sanctification of God's name and the

glory of Israel. Its words were the very last spoken by pious men in every age, and its sacred syllables the first taught to little children. It is a central feature of the morning and evening service and is recited before retiring at night.
The importance the Shema holds in Jewish law and sentiment is not accidental. It played a central part in the service of the Second Temple and is probably the oldest part of the liturgy. Its three paragraphs, drawn from the pages of the Bible (Deuteronomy 6:4-9, 11:13-21 and Numbers 15:37-41) express the fundamental beliefs of Judaism, which, modified and enriched through the ages, remain essentially the same. The Shema opens with the clarion call, "Hear, O Israel: the Lord our God, the Lord is One," an avowal of Israel's uncompromising belief in the absolute Unity of God, the basis of the faith in the universal brotherhood of man. Then comes a verse based upon the Bible, proclaiming our allegiance to God's kingdom.

On Rosh Hashanah the Shema takes on an extra dimension of significance. In the Rabbinic tradition, Rosh Hashanah's essential message is the re-affirmation of the Kingship of God, and the Sages interpreted the Shema as the Jew's daily proclamation of allegiance to His Sovereignty. The Shema has three distinct themes: *Talmud Torah* (which constitutes a token of daily study in the Torah), *Yiḥud Ha-Shem* (the teaching of God's unity), and finally *Kabbalat Ol Malkhut Shama'yim* (accepting the yoke of Divine Kingship). The *Malkhut* ("Kingship") theme received major emphasis as the Jewish people felt more and more sharply the yoke of foreign political suzerainty. Our ancestors had good cause for making a great issue of the Sovereignty of God and publishing their protest in this manner against mortal rulers, like the Roman emperors, who arrogated divine honors to themselves. The supreme authority of God, already implicit in the Shema, was made crystal clear when, sometime during the later days of the Second Temple, two additional phrases were added to the Shema. They were *El Melekh ne'eman*, "God, the faithful *King*," for individual recitation,[7] and *Barukh shem kevod malkhuto l-olam va-ed*, "Blessed be the Name of His glorious *Kingship* forever and ever," for public recitation.

The liturgy of both Rosh Hashanah and Yom Kippur accentuate the Shema and its response, *Barukh shem kevod malkhuto l-olam va-ed.* The most prominent single prayer of the Rosh Hashanah worship is *Malkhuyot,* the "Kingship" (or "Kingdom") verses with their framework of accompanying prayers. (*Malkhuyot* is ascribed in its present form to the School of Rav, the third century Babylonian sage, though Louis Finkelstein has traced its origins to the time of Rabbi Akiba, the Palestinian sage of the second century who was martyred during the Hadrianic persecutions.) *Malkhuyot* originally consisted of ten verses from the three sections of the Bible to illustrate the concept of *Malkhut,* God's universal Sovereignty. The first three verses are from the Pentateuch, the second three from the Hagiographa (Writings) and the third triad from the Prophets. Finally, there is a tenth verse, from the Pentateuch again, namely, the *Shema Yisrael.* But the word *melekh* (king), which occurs in some form in each of the nine verses, is completely absent from *Shema Yisrael.* The explanation is that, by this stage of its development, the *Shema Yisrael* had become synonymous with *Malkhut Ha-Shem* (The Kingship of God). "The Shema not only contains a metaphysical statement (about the unity of God) but expresses a hope and belief — for everything connected with this verse has a certain dogmatic value — in the ultimate universal kingdom of God" (Solomon Schechter).[8]

The Yom Kippur prayers, in turn, emphasize *Barukh shem kevod malkhuto l-olam va-ed.* Whereas this non-Biblical response to *Shema Yisrael* is recited only *in silence* during the entire year, on Yom Kippur it is proclaimed *aloud.* The reasons for this striking change will be discussed at the point of its occurrence.[9] Both *Shema Yisrael* and *Barukh shem kevod malkhuto l-olam va-ed* are also proclaimed together prior to the sounding of the Shofar that marks the end of Yom Kippur.

Emet Ve-emunah אמת ואמונה

The Sages prescribe that following the Shema one must mention the crossing of the Red Sea.[10] The benediction following the Shema, in both the morning and the evening services, accordingly describes the wondrous deliverance of the Israelites from Egyptian bondage. The prayer is therefore known as *Ge'ulah,* "Redemption."

Like Shabbat and the Three Festivals, Rosh Hashanah is also observed as "*zaykher li-yetzi'at mitzra'yim* . . . in commemoration of the Exodus from Egypt." As if to document this historical association, the sage, Rabbi Eliezer, explains that on Rosh Hashanah Joseph was liberated from his Egyptian dungeon, and again on Rosh Hashanah the Hebrew bondsmen in Egypt began to desist from their slave labor. According to this same authority, the final redemption of the Messianic era will also come in Tishre, the month of Rosh Hashanah.[11]

V-SHAMRU ושמרו

When Rosh Hashanah occurs on Shabbat, it is necessary to include appropriate prayers and readings for the latter. The coincidence of Shabbat and Rosh Hashanah has elicited brilliant and profound homiletical comment from gifted preachers in Israel. Prominent among these was R. Levi Yitzḥak of Berditchev, a renowned Ḥasidic sage of the early nineteenth century, and one of the most unconventional saints in Israel's large gallery. No one ever had a more passionate and unqualified love for his people. Once, when Rosh Hashanah fell on Shabbat, he began in his familiar way to talk to God: "Master of the Universe! On this day You must decide our fate and write down Your verdict. But it is Shabbat and writing is forbidden — even for You. There is but one solution: 'Inscribe us in the Book of Life!' Then it is permitted for You to write; for the saving of life *(pikuaḥ nefesh)* takes precedence even over Shabbat."

TIK'U VA-ḤODESH תקעו בחדש

On Rosh Hashanah night, when the sky is clear, we may behold a thin pencil-line of the new moon. The Hebrew months are based upon the phases of the moon. *Rosh Ḥodesh*, the day of the new moon and thus the "head of the month," was in ancient times a major holiday on a par with Shabbat. Rosh Hashanah, falling as it does on the first day of the month Tishre, is the only festival which coincides with *Rosh Ḥodesh.* These verses from the Psalms (81:4,5) are recited at this point in the Ashkenazic rite because they were construed as alluding both to the new moon and the sounding of the Shofar. On ordinary new moons, silver trumpets were blown; but this obscure verse was taken by Rabbinic interpretation[12] to refer to the special new moon of the seventh month, Tishre, which was to be heralded by a Shofar. Sephardic and Yemenite Jews recite here a different verse entirely: "Also in the day of your gladness and in your appointed seasons and in your new moons, you shall blow with the trumpets, etc." (Numbers 10:10). The Italian ritual cites Leviticus 23:4 (the verse Ashkenazim use for the Three Pilgrimage Festivals only); the Romanian rite cites Numbers 29:1.[13]

A favorite homily of the Sages derives from a play on the word for new moon, *ḥodesh*, and on the word *shofar.*[14] The former is related to the verb "renew" and the latter to the verb "improve." Thus Rosh Hashanah is the auspicious psychological moment for the erring Jew to "renew his deeds" and to "improve his conduct." The Midrash thus emphasizes the familiar Jewish belief that it is never too late to make a new start. The new moon is a constant reminder of the infinite possibilities of renewal and rebirth in the human personality. Elijah, the Gaon of Vilna, took the word *ḥodesh* to refer to the first day of Rosh Hashanah, which was ordained by God, and *keseh* to the second day, which is *yom ḥagaynu* ("our festival") i.e., an extra day for repentance which Jews have voluntarily added to the Biblical commandment.[15] *Keseh*, however, is now usually taken to refer to the "full moon" and would thus indicate Sukkot, which begins on the full moon of Tishre. In ancient times, Sukkot was part of the new year season (see Exodus 23:16, 34:22).[16]

A Kabbalistic commentary on *Tik'u va-ḥodesh* is based upon the word *keseh*, which is related to the Hebrew verb for "conceal." The moon "conceals" herself on the Day of Judgment and thus escapes a summons to testify for the prosecution against Israel. The sun, on the other hand, readily bears witness that the Jews have neglected God and Torah. Homilists have gone on to explain the parable: the sun represents the bright days of our history when Jews enjoyed freedom and prosperity and consequently tended to neglect the idealism of their fathers. The moon symbolizes the dark nights of persecution and suffering when Jews scaled great heights of heroism and sacrifice for their beliefs. The moon does not testify against Israel for she knows full well the tragic conditions under which Jews have had to exist throughout the ages.

"It is a statute for Israel, an ordinance of the God of Jacob." The Sages found a contradiction in these words: either Rosh Hashanah is a "statute for Israel" or "an ordinance of the God of Jacob" but how can it be both? Their answer, in typical Midrashic form, shows the strong democratic flavor of Rabbinic thought. "If there is no 'statute' already established in Israel, there can be no 'ordinance' on the part of the Holy One, blessed be He."[17] In a similar vein, the Rabbis observed that it is Israel who determines the Day of Judgment (by determining the calendar months and festivals) rather than the Heavenly Court. It is from Psalms 81:4,5, indeed, that the Rabbis derived the tradition that Rosh Hashanah is *Yom Ha-Din,* the Day of Judgment.

The phrase *Tik'u va-ḥodesh shofar* is also interpreted by the medieval authorities as Biblical precedent for the custom of sounding *(tik'u)* preliminary blasts on the Shofar during the entire month *(ḥodesh)* of Elul, which immediately precedes Rosh Hashanah.[18]

The Half Kaddish חצי קדיש

The Kaddish appears throughout the service in several forms, marking the end of a complete service or some significant segment thereof. This one is called the "Half" *(Ḥatzi)* Kaddish because it lacks three passages found in the "Complete Kaddish" *(Kaddish Shalaym* or *Kaddish Titkabal)*. The latter will be found at the conclusion of the *Amidah*. Sephardim call the briefer form *Kaddish L-ayla.* The Half Kaddish here marks the conclusion of the first section of Arvit, namely, the Shema and its escort of benedictions; the second section is the *Amidah*. In the Talmudic period, the recital of only this first section was obligatory; this Kaddish then originally marked the end of Arvit.

There is a slight change in the text of our Kaddish for the High Holy Day season: the word *l-ayla* is repeated — *L-ayla* [*u*] *l-ayla.*[19] *L-ayla* is the Aramaic for "higher," "above" — referring here to the greatness of God, whose name is exalted beyond the power of mortal praises and blessings. From Rosh Hashanah to Yom Kippur, and Mercy and is exalted even higher than usual.[20] Therefore, the homilists of old explain, God ascends the thrones of Justice (they say) we add the second *l-ayla* — "(exalted) above, yea, above and beyond all the blessings and hymns, praises and songs, which are uttered in the world, is our God."[21]

In point of fact, however, no such fanciful explanation is necessary. In rituals other than the Ashkenazic the double form of *l-ayla* is used throughout the year. Our usage for the High Holy Days is clearly a recourse — for reasons of sentiment — to a variant reading. Other examples of this phenomenon are well-known (for example, *Oseh ha-shalom* is used as the closing benediction of the *Amidah* during the High Holy Day season only). Many Maḥzorim join the second *l-ayla* to the first by the conjunction *u,* "and." This is not necessary and is probably incorrect. *L-ayla l-ayla* is the Aramaic translation of the Biblical phrase *ma'alah ma'alah,* "higher and higher" (Deuteronomy 28:43).[22]

THE AMIDAH עמידה

The *Tefillah* or *Amidah* (also called *Shemoneh Esray*) of Rosh Hashanah is constructed on the classic framework laid down by the Talmudic sages for all Sabbaths and Festivals. This consists of seven statutory benedictions: the three fixed initial blessings *(shalosh rishonot)* and the three fixed final blessings *(shalosh aḥaronot)* plus a central benediction that varies with the special occasion, Shabbat or Festival. This central prayer establishes the specific religious character of the day and is therefore designated *Kedushat Ha-Yom,* "the Sanctification of the Day." On Rosh Hashanah this unique benediction ends with the words, *"melekh al kol ha-aretz, mekadesh Yisrael v-yom ha-zikaron* . . . Sovereign of all the earth, who sanctifies Israel and the Day of Memorial."

To the framework of these seven statutory benedictions, whose authorship is attributed to the pre-Maccabean "Men of the Great Assembly," several supplementary prayer-groups for Rosh Hashanah were added during the centuries that followed the destruction of the Temple. First came the *Malkhuyot-Zikhronot-Shofarot* group, which convey the concepts of God's Kingship, Remembrance, and Revelation, respectively. They were developed during the first two centuries of the Common Era and put in their final form by the third century Babylonian School of Rav. This three-fold section was attached to the fourth benediction of the *Amidah* (i.e., the central benediction, *Kedushat Ha-Yom*). Originally intended, it seems, for the Shaḥarit service, the *Malkhuyot-Zikhronot-Shofarot* prayers were eventually confined to the Musaf service, to the accompaniment of the sounding of the Shofar whose several meanings they were intended to suggest.[23] They are not recited on Yom Kippur, since the Shofar is not blown until the Atonement service is concluded.

Another prayer-group, similar to *Malkhuyot-Zikhronot-Shofarot*, is the three-fold *U-v'khayn* prayers, probably composed in the same period. These are included in *every* service of Rosh Hashanah and of Yom Kippur. The *U-v'khayn* group (variously interpreted as parallel to *Malkhuyot*[24] alone or to the entire *Malkhuyot-Zikhronot-Shofarot* group) was attached to the third benediction of the *Amidah,* designated *Kedushat Ha-Shem,* "the Sanctification of the Divine Name."

The third of the supplementary prayer-groups did not come into the Rosh Hashanah and Yom Kippur worship until the early Middle Ages, in the period of the Geonim, and then only after long-standing opposition. This group — sometimes called *Zikhronot* or, more accurately, *May-ayn Zikhronot* (i.e., "miniatures" or "facsimiles" of the older *Zikhronot* or "Remembrance" prayers) — consists of four brief petitions, one of which is inserted in each of the first two and last two fixed benedictions of the *Amidah.* They begin, respectively, with the words: *Zokhraynu l-hayyim, Mi khamokha av ha-raḥamim, U-khetov l-ḥayyim*, and *B-sayfer ḥayyim.* They are also recited during the Days of Penitence between Rosh Hashanah and Yom Kippur.

The second and third of these supplementary prayer-groups appear in the *Amidah* for the evening service, Arvit; only the Musaf contains the first as well. More detailed explanations will be given as these prayers appear in the various services for Rosh Hashanah and Yom Kippur.

Va-todi'aynu ותודיענו

When Rosh Hashanah coincides with the conclusion of Shabbat, this brief prayer is inserted into the *Amidah*. It is attributed to the Babylonian scholars of the third century, Rav and Samuel,[25] though the text has changed considerably over the centuries. We pray "that, through our observance of the Sabbath, a new realization of the infinite difference between holy and profane, between light and darkness, between Israel and the heathen, abide with us throughout the coming week; and that such realization lead to peace of soul, freedom from sin, and fervent attachment to the God-fearing life" (J. H. Hertz).

The key word of the prayer is *havdalah,* meaning "separation." The frequency of its use attests to the refined ethical sense which Judaism requires of its adherents to distinguish not only the sacred from the profane but even the more holy from the less holy. The distinction between Shabbat and Festivals in the matter of sanctity is reflected in observance: on the Sabbath, all work is prohibited, whereas on a Festival (such as Rosh Hashanah) only "servile work" is forbidden while the preparation of food is permitted.[26] The distinction "between Israel and the heathen" lies in the heightened sense of responsibility which a Jew should feel because God has brought him closer to the Torah. There is no idea of inherent racial superiority here or elsewhere.

Kaddish Titkabal קדיש תתקבל

Kaddish is an Aramaic word meaning "holy," equivalent to the Hebrew *kadosh*. The origins of the Kaddish are still obscure, but it is now generally agreed that it first came into use in Palestine during Mishnaic times as a prayer (following a period of Torah study) for the establishment of God's Kingship.[27] (Analogous is our use of the *Rabbanan* or "Scholars" Kaddish today.) The teacher or preacher, having completed his discourse, would dismiss the assembly (hence the use of the pronoun "your") with an allusion to Messianic hope, which is the main theme of the Kaddish. Those present would respond "Amen" and "May His great name be blessed for ever and ever." The language of the Kaddish, except for the final Hebrew clause, is Aramaic,[28] the vernacular of Palestinian Jewry of the period and thus of the Torah discourses. This epilogue to Torah study passed gradually from the school into the Synagogue and the Kaddish became a favorite doxology (a lofty hymn of praise to God) marking the end of the service.

Today we are accustomed to think of the *Alaynu* as our closing prayer, but for many centuries it was actually the Kaddish which fulfilled that function while *Alaynu* was recited only on Rosh Hashanah and Yom Kippur. In point of fact, however, the two prayers have the same theme, viz., the universal sovereignty of God and man's fervent hope for the establishment of His kingdom "in the world which He has created according to His will."

The Kaddish appears in several forms in the course of the service, generally marking terminal points of major sections of the worship. This Kaddish, which marked the end of Arvit before *Alaynu* was appended, is designated *Titkabal* (or *Titkabayl*) because it includes the passage beginning "*Titkabal tzelotehon* . . . May the prayers, etc." It is also known as the "complete Kaddish" *(shalaym)* because it contains passages omitted in the Half Kaddish and Mourner's Kaddish.

KIDDUSH קדוש

The ceremony of publicly consecrating Shabbat and Festivals over a cup of wine is known as *Kiddush Ha-Yom,* "Sanctification of the Day," abbreviated to simply Kiddush. As is true in most cases of translation, the English term for Kiddush cannot convey the warm associations of the ceremony as it is practiced in the traditional Jewish home. Essentially it belongs to the home rather than to the Synagogue.[29] Kiddush signifies joyous fellowship, the delights of a festive family table, and songs of thanksgiving to a gracious God who has "chosen us from all peoples . . . and has sanctified us through His commandments."[30]

Samson Raphael Hirsch sagely observed, "The catechism of the Jew is his calendar," and Kiddush is the epitome of Shabbat and *Yom-tov,* those "firebrands of vision and torches of dream hurled into the blackness of workaday reality" (A. Steinman). The poet Bialik, who was also a gifted interpreter of Jewish tradition, keenly analyzed the role of the holidays in the consciousness of the Jew: "They rise out of the flatness of the week-days like mountains rising out of the plains. The loftier the peak, the more it bears testimony to successive upheavals and revolutions which have taken place beneath that mountain on many ancient occasions, all of which combined in turn to push a level of earth up through the surface and to raise it on high. So, too, every festival is witness to deep, sometimes volcanic, upheavals which tossed about beneath the soil of the nation — not once but many times in rapid succession." In the Kiddush, then, we recall the hallowed hills of Jewish history — none of them richer in layers of meaning than Rosh Hashanah, here called by its most ancient names, *Yom Teruah* and *Zikhron Teruah,* as well as by its more familiar liturgical designation, *Yom Ha-Zikaron.*[31]

SHE-HEḤEYANU שהחינו

This benediction, of Talmudic origin, is recited at the initial performance of a commandment prescribed for special occasions. *She-heḥeyanu* is attached to the Kiddush prayer because the latter is the public proclamation of the beginning of the Festival.[32] On Yom Kippur it is said after *Kol Nidre;* Kiddush is, of course, not recited on a fast day.

Some question, however, arose concerning the recital of *She-heḥeyanu* on the *second* evening of Rosh Hashanah. Since the two days of Rosh Hashanah are considered by the Talmud as "one long day," why should this inaugural prayer be repeated? To resolve the difficulty and to provide, in any case, a fresh occasion to offer praise to a bountiful Creator, the custom was instituted in medieval times of eating on the *second* night some previously untasted sweet fruit such as grapes, melons, pomegranates or olives.[33]

ALAYNU עלינו

Since the thirteenth century, every public worship service —

for Festivals, Shabbat or week-day, morning or evening — has closed with the ancient prayer, *Alaynu*.[34] This magnificent crown of the service has been borrowed from another place in the liturgy, namely, the Rosh Hashanah Musaf service. It is a noble example of the transfer to daily use of a ritual originally designed for a special occasion. A fanciful medieval legend traces the composition of *Alaynu* to Joshua at the walls of Jericho.[35] The prayer was probably edited by the School of Rav, the distinguished legal authority of third century Babylonia, who is responsible for so much in our High Holy Day prayerbook.

The prayer consists of two paragraphs, each built up of Biblical phrases, which proclaim God as King over Israel and over the entire universe. The first paragraph, beginning with the word *Alaynu,* calls upon all Jews to laud the God who has chosen them for a life of consecrated service while pagan nations reject the true way. The second paragraph, beginning *Al kayn nekaveh,* expresses our hope that the entire human race might speedily recognize the benevolent sovereignty of God and submit themselves to His will. Ashkenazic Jews recite both paragraphs at the end of each service; some Sephardic communities, only the first.

Alaynu has had a dramatic existence through the centuries. It was a victim of censorship on the part of church authorities in medieval and even modern Europe. It served as a martyr's song among Jews. A fuller discussion of the roles *Alaynu* has played in Jewish history will be found in the commentary on *Alaynu* in the Musaf service of Rosh Hashanah.

Al Kayn Nekaveh — על כן נקוה

While the opening portion of *Alaynu* stresses the uniqueness of Israel among the heathen nations, this concluding part emphasizes the universal mission of Judaism, "to establish the world under the Kingdom of the Almighty." Solomon Schechter pointed out that, in Rabbinic literature, the two ideas, "Kingdom of the Almighty" and "Kingdom of Heaven" are synonymous. He goes on to draw the significant conclusion, "We learn first that the Kingdom of God is in *this world.*" A Ḥasidic master, Rabbi Ḥanokh said: "The other nations also believe that there are two worlds. They speak of 'the other world.' The difference is that they think of the two as separate and severed, while Israel professes that the two worlds are essentially one and shall, indeed, become one."[35a] When the prophets of Israel spoke of "a new heaven and a new earth" they meant that "this, our world, will be purified to the state of the Kingdom, that creation will be made perfect, but not that our world will be annulled for the sake of another world. Moreover, they refer not to a more righteous order, but to 'righteousness,' not to mankind grown more peaceful, but to 'peace' " (Martin Buber).

Judaism teaches that injustice and evil can be banished from the universe if men desire wholeheartedly to do God's will. True, there have been periods when Jews too were driven by a sense of weakness and frustration to despair of ever improving this world. Then, as in so many other religions, they tended to relegate the Kingdom of God to another life. But the dominant ideal in Judaism is the establishing of God's sovereignty in *our* world. "While it denies that history by itself redeems or that men will ever achieve perfection, it still envisages him as achieving something, and that of consequence" (Milton Steinberg).

Mourner's Kaddish קדיש יתום

The Kaddish originated, we have seen, as a scholar's prayer and was adopted by the Synagogue as a fitting doxology with which to close the worship service. The final step in the evolution of the Kaddish as we now know and revere it was its use as a prayer for mourners. This usage did not take root until the twelfth or thirteenth centuries in northern Europe[36] but at that time there was already an ancient legend concerning Rabbi Akiba that associated the saying of Kaddish and *Barekhu* with reverence for a deceased father. The practice was certainly not unknown in the post-Talmudic period.

The significance of Kaddish for mourners appears to stem from two ideas contained in the prayer. First, the bereaved is strengthened by reflecting on the Kingship of God, which is the main theme of the Kaddish. In his hour of grief, the mourner stands before the congregation — frequently in the company of fellow mourners —

and proclaims aloud his faith in the supreme authority of God and his confidence that all men shall yet acknowledge the Kingdom of Heaven on earth. Secondly, the mourner is reminded by the Kaddish that creatures of flesh and blood are incapable of expressing in words the magnitude of God, much less comprehend His justice and wisdom.

Much of the importance of the Kaddish derives from the responses in which all the congregation must join, especially the words, "*Yehay shemay rabba*, etc. . . . May His great name be blessed forever and ever."[37] The Talmud declares that since the destruction of the Temple, the world has been sustained by this sacred verse and by the *Kedushah* of the liturgy.[38] Joining loudly and in unison in this congregational response has the power, the Rabbis state, of moving God to forgiveness.[39] Considered in this light, the mourner is actually leading a miniature service of his own in which he summons forth the sacred responses from his fellow-worshippers.

(L-David) Adonai Ori לדוד יי אורי

The 27th Psalm is recited daily from the first of Elul, the month preceding Rosh Hashanah, until Yom Kippur, or, in some communities, till the end of Sukkot. Several reasons for this practice are advanced by the Midrash and later homiletical works. "The Lord is my light" is taken to refer to Rosh Hashanah; "and my salvation," to Yom Kippur; "whom shall I fear," to Hoshana Rabbah.[40] The phrase, "for He will hide me in His tabernacle" (verse 5) alludes to the festival of Sukkot (Tabernacles). The "enemies" referred to in the Psalm are explained homiletically as man's own evil inclinations and temptations.[41] The letters of the word *lulay,* "if not," toward the end of the poem, when arranged backwards, spell *Elul;* in the Masoretic text of the Bible, these letters are marked with the special points that traditionally indicate a homiletical interpretation of this kind.

More cogent than all the homiletics is the simple fact that the sentiments of the Psalm are most appropriate for the penitential season. "With wonderful delicacy of touch the Psalmist fuses together the material Temple and the spiritual communion which it inspired . . . We are reminded on the one hand of the value of the institutions of Judaism when rightly observed and on the other of that yearning for illumination which is the mark of true penitence" (Israel Abrahams).

Some communities — Sephardic as well as Ashkenazic — recite the 24th Psalm after the *Amidah*.[42] This psalm, beginning, "The earth is the Lord's and the fullness thereof," is especially appropriate for Rosh Hashanah since the New Year festival also commemorates the Creation of the world described in the opening verses of the psalm.

YIGDAL יגדל

The Shabbat and Festival services customarily close with a hymn. In most of our congregations it is *Adon olam* for the morning and *Yigdal* for the evening service. Both are philosophic definitions of God in poetic form and thus illustrate the influencc of medieval theology upon the Prayerbook through the poetry of the Synagogue; *Yigdal* is the best known among approximately forty poetic renditions of the classic "Thirteen Principles of Faith," enunciated by Maimonides in the twelfth century. It was probably composed by Daniel ben Judah the *Dayyan* (i.e., Judge) of fourteenth century Rome. Like much of medieval Hebrew poetry it is written in a simple rhyme and meter. Its popularity is attested to by the fact that it has had many musical settings.

The charm of this hymn, as Israel Abrahams points out, consists in the subtle manner in which Jewish theological doctrines are associated with the simplest religious thoughts. They delight the child as well as the theologian, depending upon the level of religious development with which one approaches this *piyyut*.

ROSH HASHANAH GREETINGS לשנה טובה

The worshippers traditionally greet one another at the close of the evening service with the blessing, "*L-shanah tovah tikataytu* . . . May you be inscribed for a good year." This practice originated among medieval German Jews.[43] Another form of greeting was "*Tikatayvu l-shanah tovah* . . . May you be inscribed for a good year." Sephardim greet one another, "*L-shanah tovah tikatayv, tizkeh l-shanim rabbot* . . . May you be inscribed for a good year; may you be deemed worthy of abundant years." The response is, "*Tizkeh v-tiḥyeh v-ta'arikh yamim* . . . May you be deemed worthy of life and length of days."

A quaint distinction is drawn concerning the use of our Ashkenazic greeting. One may use the greeting after the first evening service but not on the following morning. Why? Because the Talmud[44] states that there are three types of Jews: the righteous, the sinner and the average person. The righteous gain prompt acquittal on Rosh Hashanah morning and thus need no further good wishes. The sinners are condemned with equal dispatch, hence any blessings to them would be a "mockery of the unfortunate." The average person has his judgment postponed until Yom Kippur. To give one's neighbor a *L-shanah tovah* greeting *after* the Rosh Hashanah morning service is to imply that he is in need of special intercession.

Upon reaching home, we observe the custom of eating at the beginning of our holiday meal some sweet, traditionally apples or *ḥallah* dipped in honey. The food is accompanied by the prayer, "May the New Year be a good and sweet one." This charming custom has its precedent in the book of Nehemiah (8:10). There Ezra the Scribe and Nehemiah, the governor of Palestine, bid their sorrowing people to rejoice on "the first day of the seventh month" (which became our Rosh Hashanah) in these words: "Go eat rich foods and drink sweet drinks . . . for this day is sacred unto our Lord." Though, in the course of time, Rosh Hashanah acquired more of a solemn character, this emphasis on its essential joyousness was never entirely lost.

CHAPTER FOUR

THE SHAḤARIT SERVICE

• HA-MELEKH • B-FI YESHARIM
• SHIR ḤA-MA'ALOT, MI-MA'AMAKIM • THE HALF KADDISH
• YOTZROT: OR OLAM • MELEKH AZUR • MELEKH AMON
• KADOSH, KADOSH, KADOSH • KEVODO IHAYL
• V-HA-ḤAYYOT YESHORAYRU • V-SHINANTAM L-VANEKHA
• ELOHAI NETZOR • REPETITION OF THE AMIDAH
• THE RESHUYOT: MI-SOD ḤAKHAMIM • ZOKHRAYNU L-ḤAYYIM
• MEKHALKAYL ḤAYYIM • YIMLOKH ADONAI—V-ATAH KADOSH
• ATAH HU ELOHAYNU • ADERET MAMLAKHAH
• MELEKH ELYON, AMITZ HA-MENUSA • ADONAI MELEKH
• L-EL ORAYKH DIN • KEDUSHAH OF THE AMIDAH
• THE U-V'KHAYN PRAYERS • KADOSH ATAH • VA-TITEN LANU
• YA'ALEH V-YAVO • MELOKH AL KOL HA-OLAM • RETZAY
• B-SAYFER ḤAYYIM • AVINU MALKAYNU
• WHY WE DO NOT SAY HALLEL ON ROSH HASHANAH

THE SHAḤARIT SERVICE

HA-MELEKH המלך

Up to this point, the preliminary morning service has consisted of introductory benedictions *(Berakhot)* and hymns and psalms *(Pesukay d-Zimrah,* among Ashkenazim; among Sephardim, *Zemirot).* With *Ha-Melekh* the Shaḥarit proper begins, even though the formal call to prayer does not come until *Barekhu.* The Cantor for the morning service, the *Ba'al Shaḥarit,* takes over from the introductory Reader. (It is permissible, of course, for the same man to lead both parts of the service.)

On Shabbat, the *Ba'al Shaḥarit* does not begin chanting until the verse, "*Shokhayn ad marom* . . . Thou abidest to eternity." On the Three Festivals, he begins with the preceding verse, "*Ha-El* . . . Thou art God." But on the Days of Awe, when we reassert our belief in God as Sovereign of the Universe, it is eminently fitting for the first word of the morning service proper to be *Ha-Melekh,* "the King."[1] *Ha-Melekh* is the favored name for God in the Rosh Hashanah and Yom Kippur services; at several places in the text it replaces the word *Ha-El* which is used during the remainder of the year. Another slight change is the omission from our printed texts of the definite article before the word, *yoshayv.*[2]

For many centuries it has been the custom in Ashkenazic congregations for the Cantor to chant the opening *Ha-Melekh* in a special mode: beginning in a hushed minor he raises his voice by degrees to a majestic but reverential major. This practice was instituted by the great Ashkenazic authority of the 13th century, Rabbi Meir of Rothenburg, and was popularized in the next century by Maharil (Rabbi Jacob Moelin of Mayence) who himself served regularly as Cantor for the Shaḥarit service of Rosh Hashanah. In some congregations (e.g., Worms) it was customary to sing *Ha-Melekh* in this fashion each time it occured in the service. In many congregations even today, the Cantor will chant the initial *Ha-Melekh* while on the floor level and lift his voice as prescribed while he ascends the steps to the *bimah.*

B-FI YESHARIM בפי ישרים

The initial letters of *Yesharim* ("the upright"), *TZadikim* ("the righteous"), *Ḥasidim* ("the faithful") and *Kedoshim* ("the holy") form the name *Yitzḥak,* Isaac. (The name Rebecca, Isaac's wife, appears in a similar acrostic in this passage.) An old *midrash* interprets this prayer as a tribute to the faith of Isaac, who, though bound upon the altar of sacrifice, nevertheless uttered words of praise to God.[3] The *Akaydah,* the Binding of Isaac, was so prominent in the Jewish consciousness that it found its way even into this simple passage. Subtleties of this type in worship may strike us as bizarre; lovingly understood, however, they cannot fail to impress us as illustrations of the Talmudic ideal, to strive to become "skillful in piety" *(arum b-yir'ah).*

SHIR HA-MA'ALOT, MI-MA'AMAKIM ממעמקים

It is an ancient Ashkenazic custom (followed, however, in few recent editions of the Maḥzor) to recite the 130th Psalm before *Barekhu* in the morning service of Rosh Hashanah and during the entire Ten Days of Penitence. In the old Palestinian order of prayer, Psalm 130 — and not *Kol Nidre* — opened the evening service of the Day of Atonement.[4] Thus, most appropriately, the Psalm which preceded *Barekhu* in the Arvit service of Yom Kippur was transferred to precede *Barekhu* of the morning service during the entire Ten Days of Penitence which culminate in the Day of Atonement.

The Half Kaddish

חצי קדיש

The short or half Kaddish *(Ḥatzi Kaddish)* marks the division between the two main sections of the Shaḥarit service. We recite it here to indicate that the introductory psalms and hymns are now concluded and that we have reached the formal invocation to congregational worship, namely, *Barekhu.*

On no occasion during the Jewish year does the Kaddish receive such prominence as it does on the *Yamim Noraim,* the Days of Awe. For this credit is due those great cantors throughout the centuries who interpreted the Kaddish of the various services of the High Holy Day worship in magnificent melodies that bear the imprint of Israel's soul.[5] The motif for this particular Kaddish is "energetic and lively, full of strength, a joyous sound, mingled with a note of concern but sung in an exalted and sublime spirit" (M. S. Geshuri).[5a]

Concerning this Kaddish, there is recorded a dramatic incident from the career of the Ḥasidic master, the God-intoxicated R. Levi Yitzḥak, of Berditchev. One Rosh Hashanah morning, the Hazzan was about to intone the Kaddish. Before he could do so, Levi Yitzḥak was moved to communicate an urgent message to his dear Friend, the Holy One Blessed be He, whom he never hesitated to approach just as a son might approach his father. Halting the service in his unpredictable manner, he began to chant a personal prayer that has come down to us as the *Rebbe's Kaddish,* and which has been arranged as a classic of the concert stage the world over. It is a splendid interpretation of what the inaugural declaration, *Ha-Melekh,* meant to the Jews of Eastern Europe:

> Good morning, Master of the Universe, I, Levi Yitzḥak,
> the son of Sarah, from Berditchev, approach You
> with a grievance on behalf of Your people, Israel.
>
> What do You have against Israel?
> Why have You imposed Yourself on Israel?
> In every matter it is, "Command the children of Israel."
> In every matter it is, "Speak to the children of Israel."
>
> Merciful Father, there are so many nations in the world —

Persians, Babylonians, Romans.
What do the Russians say? Their ruler is the Czar.
What do the Germans say? Their ruler is the Kaiser.
What do the English say? Their kingdom is a kingdom.

But, I, Levi Yitzḥak, the son of Sarah, from Berditchev,
Say, *Ha-Melekh yoshayv al kissay ram v-nissa*
("Thou art the King enthroned on high in majesty")
And I will not leave this place
Until there is an end to the Exile.
Yisgadal v-yiskadash shemay rabba
("Magnified and sanctified be His great Name").[5b]

YOTZROT: OR OLAM אור עולם

The opening statutory benediction of the Shaḥarit service praises God as the Creator of light *(Yotzayr or)*. At this point appear the first *piyyutim*[6] of the service. Since these poems are inserted in the *Yotzayr* prayer, each is called a *Yotzayr*. The name *Yotzrot* is also applied generally to all the *piyyutim* of Shaḥarit in the Shema section, i.e., those which precede the *Amidah*.

The first verse of the *Yotzrot* on the High Holy Days, *Or olam,* appropriately is a fragment from the first known synagogue poet, Yose ben Yose. It is lamentable that the remainder of this hymn has been lost. This verse may reflect the familiar Rabbinic legend that the original light of Creation is preserved in God's treasury for the use of the righteous in the world to come.[7] Another interpretation is "God, the Light of the Universe, is the treasury of life" (Max Arzt).[8] In the Palestinian and Italian rites, *Or olam* was recited every Shabbat morning since Shabbat is a commemoration of the Creation, the subject of Yose's *piyyut*. In the German rite, it is recited only on Festivals.

Yehudah Halevi, peer among Sephardic poets, composed an exquisite poem which would be most appropriate for this point in our service.

To You the stars of morning sing
From You the sources of their radiance spring

And steadfast in their vigils day and night
The sons of God, flooded with fervor, ring
Your praise; they taught the holy ones to bring
Into Your house the breath of early light.

Concerning these lines, Franz Rosenzweig, the sensitive philosopher-poet of German Jewry, remarked:

> This is one of those little poems which — in the service of the congregation — may serve the reader as a preface for the usual morning prayer in somewhat the same way as Bach's preludes provide the organist with an introduction to the hymn. The small congregation praying at early dawn — pervading quiet — but around them, at an immeasurable distance, two vast spheres: the circle of stars and circle of angels all sound the same song of praise — Israel, the lonely heart of the world whose voice is echoed by heaven.[9]

Melekh Azur מלך אזור

This *piyyut* (technically, a *Yotzayr*) is by Eleazar Kallir, the most famous of all the synagogal poets.[10] It is the first of many from his prolific pen that fill the pages of our Maḥzor for Rosh Hashanah. Like most *piyyutim*, it is based on a *midrash* (a legendary or homiletical interpretation of a Biblical text) of the Talmudic sages. The legend here states that God robes Himself in ten different garments *(asarah levushin)* each of which represents a specific work of His in the world.[11] The Sages emphasized that God manifests His reality to each person "according to the capacity" of that person, i.e., in an aspect that will be meaningful in terms of his experience. God is pictured here as *Melekh* (King), undisputed sovereign and righteous judge who will brook no injustice. The pious may take heart for "He will bring our judgment into light" and overcome the powers of darkness.

The poem is composed in the familiar *alef-bet* acrostic. Following the key word *Melekh,* each of the stanzas begins with a succeeding letter of the Hebrew alphabet. (As often happens the letter *tav* is used three times in order to round out the total of twenty-four stanzas.) In characteristic *piyyut* style, the poet weaves many Scriptural phrases into a finished tapestry all his own.

Melekh Amon מלך אמון

On the second day of Rosh Hashanah, new *piyyutim* are frequently substituted for those recited on the first day. Such a poem is *Melekh amon.* Like most of the *piyyutim* for the morning service of the second day in our Maḥzor, it is the work of Rabbi Simeon the Great, of 11th century Mayence. The name of the poet is spelled out, in the fashion of the *payyetanim,* by means of the initial letters of the stanzas.

The name Elḥanan, the son of Rabbi Simeon, is also prominently featured in the poem. This unusual emphasis may well be connected with one of the most fascinating and popular tales of medieval Jewish folklore, the story of the Jewish Pope![12] According to this legend, Elḥanan, the son of R. Simeon, had been kidnapped as a child, reared as a Christian and finally elevated to the office of cardinal and Pope under the name Anacletus II. Though aware of his origin, Anacletus issued a cruel edict ordering the Jews of Mayence to adopt Christianity. The Jews, ignorant of the story of the Pope's life, sent R. Simeon as their representative to plead their cause. During a game of chess, the Pope revealed himself to his father. After reversing the decree, Anacletus (or Elḥanan) escaped to Mayence with his father and returned to the family of Israel. In commemoration of the remarkable event, R. Simeon is said to have composed the hymn, *Melekh amon*, containing the acrostic "May my son, Elḥanan, enjoy length of days and be inscribed for eternal life."

Though appearing in the Shaḥarit service, this *piyyut* is based upon the three-fold prayer which features the Musaf service, *Malkhuyot-Zikhronot-Shofarot.* For this reason the stanza groups begin with *Melekh, Zekhor,* and *Shofar* respectively.

Kadosh, Kadosh, Kadosh קדוש, קדוש, קדוש

The recital of the "Thrice-Holy" (Latin, Ter Sanctus; Greek,

Trisagion) occupies a prominent place in our liturgy. In Christianity, the "Thrice-Holy" is interpreted as an allusion to the Trinity. However, in the main stream of Jewish tradition, the "Thrice-Holy" became the seed-bed for a luxurious flowering of poetry and myth.[13] The book of Isaiah (6:3) is the original source of the "Thrice-Holy." There the prophet describes his vision of heavenly beings chanting in chorus the simple but majestic refrain. The Midrash explains that around God's throne myriads of celestial beings daily rehearse His praises in song.

The three-fold *Kadosh* passage from Isaiah is one of the two verses in the Bible that report the language of the heavenly hosts. The other is Ezekiel 3:12, in which the prophet quotes the celestial chorus, "*Barukh kevod Adonai mi-mekomo* . . . Blessed be the glory of the Lord from His abode."[14] Together these two passages form the basic ingredients of the important prayer known as *Kedushah* or "Holiness," recited at three different points in the daily synagogue service, as well as on Shabbat and Festivals. The present *Kedushah* is designated *Yotzayr,* coming as it does within the benediction of that name which deals with God as Creator. It is of Palestinian origin and the oldest form in which this prayer appears. On the High Holy Days, this *Kedushah* (in the Ashkenazic rite)is given additional prominence by the addition of *piyyutim,* an example of which is the following poem, *Kevodo ihayl.*

Kevodo Ihayl — כבודו אהל

This *piyyut* by Eleazar Kallir, arranged in alphabetical order, begins by alluding to the Talmudic tradition that the world was created on Rosh Hashanah. The poet goes on to beg God's pardon for man's wrongdoings by recalling an ancient *midrash.*[15] When God created the world, He saw that it could not hope to survive on the basis of strict justice *(din).* On the other hand, the alternative of pure mercy *(raḥamim)* was equally untenable. He therefore joined justice and mercy and established the world under their joint rule. Like Kallir's poetry generally, this *piyyut* is intensely rich in Biblical and Midrashic allusions whose full explanation would require an elaborate commentary. The stanza beginning *Na netzor* compresses salient events in the lives of the three Patriarchs into three brief verses.

The category to which this *piyyut* belongs is a subdivision of the *Yotzrot* type designated *Ofan*. The name *Ofan* derives from the fact that this type of poem precedes the prayer beginning *V-ha-ḥayyot yeshorayru*, which speaks of the *Ofanim*, wheeled and winged creatures described by Ezekiel in his celestial vision.[16] In this type of *piyyut*, the poet delves into "the labyrinth of heaven or the music of the spheres, or the mysteries of the Divine Name, or the very secret of prayer. Sometimes stress is laid on the daily experience of God's ubiquity, which is more wonderful than even the celestial chariot" (Shalom Spiegel).[17]

Some of the noblest lines of Hebrew religious poetry may be found in another *Ofan* composition by Yehudah Halevi,[18] the opening of which reads:

Lord, where shall I find Thee?
High and hidden is Thy place;
And where shall I not find Thee?
The world is full of Thy glory.

Found in the innermost being,
He set up the ends of the earth:
The refuge for the near,
The trust for those far off.

V-HA-ḤAYYOT YESHORAYRU והחיות ישוררו

This *Ofan* (probably of ancient Palestinian origin) replaces, in the Ashkenazic rite, the usual prayer *V-ha-ofanim* whenever *piyyutim* are inserted.[19] Both of these passages are striking in that they provide rare instances in which the Prayerbook treats of various types of celestial beings. Angelic and demonic creatures play an important role in many religions, ancient and modern, and Judaism is no exception. Since the High Holy Day Maḥzor makes reference not only to heavenly beings but frequently to Satan as well, a word concerning their role in Jewish thinking is in order.[20]

The word *mal'akh* (like the Greek word *angelos* which is used to translate it) means simply "messenger." God's "angels" are the deputies who carry out His purposes. In the world of nature, "He maketh the winds His messengers *(mal'akhav)*, His ministers flaming fire."[21] The ancient Hebrews understood in this way what moderns would call the "laws of Nature." Similarly, when God wishes to carry out some specific mission in the world of men, He sends messengers in human form who are also called *mal'akhim*. Thus the term corresponding to "angel" is used to include "all the instruments of divine purpose, human and superhuman beings, as well as the forces of nature" (Israel Abrahams). In a like fashion, the word *satan* is used at first to mean simply "adversary," and only in the later books of the Bible (notably Job) is the idea personified in Satan. Even then he remains under Divine jurisdiction; he never becomes, as in Christianity, a "fallen angel" or an opponent of the Deity.[22]

Gradually these messengers, symbols of God in action in His world, acquired the nature of superhuman beings. Particularly under the influence of the Persian religion,[23] so rich in angels and demons, Jewish folklore developed a host of celestial — and even some infernal — beings who were divided into classes, such as those mentioned in our prayer: *ḥayyot* (living creatures), *keruvim* or cherubs (some type of winged creature, mentioned in the Torah as covering the Holy Ark),[24] *serafim* (fiery creatures or winged serpents), *arelim* (the meaning is unknown), *ofanim* (literally "wheels" who bear the Heavenly Throne). The only angels mentioned by name in our prayerbook are the four archangels: Michael, Gabriel, Uriel and Raphael. The first two are found in the book of Daniel. All of them play an active role in mystical Jewish literature, beginning with the Bible, Apocrypha and Pseudepigrapha, continuing in Talmud and Midrash, and culminating in the books of Kabbalah and Ḥasidism. Satan, under several aliases, is also a familiar figure in the Midrash and in mystical lore, chiefly as the *Kataygor*, or accusing angel.[25] There are a number of such references in the *piyyutim* for Rosh Hashanah; and Satan also plays an important role in the legends and mystical lore surrounding the sounding of the Shofar.[26] Since the time of Maimonides (12th century), the dominant trend in Jewish thought has been to treat all references to angelic or demonic beings as metaphorical.[27]

This whole conception is of little more than historical interest in Jewish thinking today — except, of course, for the extreme mystical groups. Yet its presence in the Siddur and Maḥzor serves to color our ritual with poetic tints without which our liturgy would be infinitely less charming. Such passages as the one at hand strive to give expression to certain varieties of religious experience which, though strange to the modern temper, lie as close to the core of our tradition as the more familiar rationalist formulations.

V-SHINANTAM L-VANEKHA ושננתם לבניך

Judaism did not allow this precept to remain merely a pious phrase, but characteristically translated it into a positive commandment. According to the Talmud, every Jewish father is personally responsible for teaching his son Torah and *umanut,* that is, religious culture plus some useful occupation; otherwise he is held liable for exposing his child to a possible life of crime. The Talmud also tells how the authorities established professional teachers for those children who did not receive instruction from their fathers.

The Sages did not fail to relate the commandment of instruction *(Talmud Torah)* to the proper observance of Rosh Hashanah. "In the period from Rosh Hashanah to Yom Kippur, the sustenance of every man (for the ensuing year) is determined with the exception of monies to be expended for Shabbat, the Festivals, and instruction for his children. In these latter cases, he who spends less, will receive less; he who spends more, will receive more."[28]

The proper education of the young has always been the weightiest concern of responsible Jewish communities. The Midrash makes bold to declare that as long as the voices of Jewish children can be heard studying in the schoolrooms, no enemy can prevail against Israel; the universe itself rests on the breath of school-children! Mordecai M. Kaplan reaffirms an ancient Jewish conviction when he states, "The primary prerogative of a civilization is that of molding the minds of the young and endowing them with the fundamental traits of human personality." Ḥayyim Naḥman Bialik in his poem, *Ha-Matmid,* has given us the classic picture of the Jewish student, secret of Israel's eternal youth:

In the Yeshivah reigns a sacred silence
Which he, the sacred youth, is first to break;
For there, in the dark corner, wait for him . . .
Faithful companions since the day he came . . .
Three friends: his stand, his candle, and his Talmud . . . [28a]

Elohai Netzor אלהי, נצר

This beautiful meditation is cited in the Talmud as a private prayer of Mar, the son of Rabina.[29] It is one of the rare examples of a prayer couched in the singular (exclusive of the Psalms) which was accepted into the public liturgy. "Through its beauty it found a place in all Rites, and became a pendant to the *Amidah* when spoken silently" (J. H. Hertz).

A scholar of medieval Provence, Don Vidal Solomon (Menaḥem ben Solomon Meiri), reports[30] an otherwise unknown custom of reciting here on Rosh Hashanah a second personal meditation of this type, *Elohai ad she-lo notzarti.* Here we see the influence of the Yom Kippur liturgy, for there the two meditations are recited together at the conclusion of each *Amidah.* An English rendering of *Elohai ad she-lo notzarti* follows:

> My God, before I was formed I had no worth, and now that I have been formed, I am as though I had not been formed. Dust am I in my life; all the more so in my death. Behold I am before Thee like an object filled with shame and confusion. May it be Thy will, O Lord my God and God of my fathers, that I sin no more. As for the sins I have committed before Thee, cleanse them away in Thine abundant mercy; but not through affliction and suffering.

Repetition of the Amidah חזרת הש״ץ

The service of reviewing aloud the *Amidah* for Shaḥarit is neither as prominent nor as elaborate as that for Musaf; yet its exalted text and unique musical setting alike are worthy of close and reverent attention. In the period of the Mishnah, indeed, the Shaḥarit *Amidah* for Rosh Hashanah may have been even more distinguished than that for Musaf since it probably included the *Malkhuyot-Zikhronot-Shofarot* prayers and the accompanying Shofar sounds, as well, before they were transferred into Musaf.[31]

The basic structure is similar to that of the *Amidah* for Arvit, which has already been discussed in Chapter Three. Added to the seven statutory benedictions, which remain fixed, are a number of *piyyutim,* some of which became especially dear to the Jewish heart. They will be discussed below, as they appear in the service.[32] It may be noted here that, in accordance with medieval custom,[33] the worshippers rise for the recitation of certain important *piyyutim.* For some of the especially distinguished poems, the Holy Ark is opened in addition; the opening of the Ark is called *petiḥat ha-aron* or simply *petiḥah.* The tendency in many congregations today is to reserve these marks of honor for a selected few *piyyutim* (e.g., *L-El oraykh din,* in Shaḥarit; *U-netaneh tokef,* in Musaf).

The Reshuyot: Mi-sod Ḥakhamim   מסוד חכמים

At this point of the service the Cantor prepares to chant the many beautiful *piyyutim* known as *Kerovot*[34] which the Ashkenazim insert into the Repetition of the *Amidah.* As a prelude to his solemn task, he intones the ancient formula, *Mi-sod ḥakhamim,* which recurs at this point also in the repetition of the other *Amidot* of Rosh Hashanah and Yom Kippur.

The Cantor continues directly with another, more elaborate prelude, in which he pleads for God's aid and indulgence in his awesome responsibility of representing the congregration. On the first day of Rosh Hashanah, he recites the poem beginning, *"Yarayti bi-ftzoti . . .* With humility and apprehension." The name of the author, Yekuthiel ben Moses of 11th century Speyer, is spelled out in acrostic style in this poem through the initial letters of each four word phrase. His poem was intended as an introduction to the *Kerovah* of Kallir for the first day. On the second day, this prelude is replaced by a composition of Simeon ben Isaac ben Abun, of 10th century Mayence, which begins, *"Atiti l-ḥanenakh . . .* I come to supplicate Thee." This latter poem is the introduction to the *Kerovah* composed by Simeon ben Isaac for the second day of Rosh Hashanah.

Each of these three *piyyutim* is designated by the term, *Reshut*, meaning "Permission" or "Indulgence"; the more exact designation is *Netilat Reshut* which might be rendered as "by your leave".[35] It has its own musical mode, a plaintive plea. One of the most beloved *Reshuyot* among Ashkenazim is *Hineni*, the Cantor's petition before the silent *Amidah* of Musaf. Two other ancient *Reshuyot* appear in the services of Rosh Hashanah and Yom Kippur. Perhaps the oldest example of this form is *Oḥilah la-El*, used by Sephardim as a prelude to the Repetition of the Musaf *Amidah* and by Ashkenazim as a prelude to the *Malkhuyot-Zikhronot-Shofarot* on Rosh Hashanah and to the *Avodah* service on Yom Kippur afternoon. The Ashkenazic rite also prefaces *Oḥilah la-El* with another somewhat longer *Reshut*, known as *He'yay im pifiyot*. All of these *Reshuyot* will be more fully discussed as they appear in the service.

The nature of these *Reshuyot* clearly indicates that the Ḥazzan and *Payyetan* were frequently one and the same man.[36] *Mi-sod ḥakhamim* is one of the oldest examples of a *Reshut*; as with *piyyutim* generally, its simplicity attests to its antiquity. It may be an appeal by the cantor-poet to the "wise" and the "discerning" present in the synagogue to bear with him in his embellishment of the service.

All *Reshuyot* are personal petitions of the Cantor; they are not intended to be recited by the Congregation. They are eloquent testimony to the deep religious fervor and simple piety of the medieval cantor, who in many cases was a distinguished rabbinical scholar as well. The books of Jewish usage list careful regulations for selecting a cantor; for he is not primarily a performer or artist, but rather *Sheliaḥ Tzibbur,* the Emissary of the Congregation.[37] He should be a mature person of recognized learning, piety, training and skill — though artistry is of lesser importance — and of dignified bearing. The history of the sacred calling of *Ḥazzanut* is filled with the lives of consecrated men who have fulfilled every requirement of this tradition.

ZOKHRAYNU L-ḤAYYIM זכרנו לחיים

Following the close of the Talmudic period,[38] the first interpolation into the Rosh Hashanah service was a series of four brief petitions which utilize the poetic figure of God *remembering* "His creatures unto life" or *inscribing* them "in the book of life." The first two, which begin *Zokhraynu l-ḥayyim* and *Mi khamokha av ha-raḥamim,* are inserted into the first and second statutory benedictions respectively of the *Amidah;* the second two, beginning *U-khetov l-ḥayyim tovim*[39] and *B-ayfer ḥayyim*, are incorporated into the last two benedictions respectively. In each case, the language of the petition offers a connecting link to that of the benediction into which it was inserted.

These four petitions are sometimes referred to collectively as *Zikhronot* (Remembrance passages) or *May-ayn* (i.e., "miniature" or "facsimile") *Zikhronot,* as distinguished from the more elaborate
Zikhronot (Remembrance passages) or *May-ayn* (i.e., "miniature"
tion for their inclusion here is that they parallel the latter.[40] Indeed, there is good reason to believe that the full *Zikhronot* of Musaf originally formed part of the Shaḥarit *Amidah* (along with *Malkhuyot* and *Shofarot*) and were later postponed to the Musaf service along with the sounding of the Shofar.[41] The "miniature" *Zikhronot* are included in each *Amidah* of Rosh Hashanah and Yom Kippur and even during the intervening Days of Penitence.

In the early Middle Ages a controversy raged over the inclusion of *Zokhraynu l-ḥayyim,* et al., in the text of the *Amidah* which had been fixed by the earlier Talmudic authorities. Some authorities objected to them as unwarranted intrusions, especially inappropriate in the opening and closing blessings of the *Amidah* because they constitute petitions for *personal* needs rather than words of praise and acknowledgment as required by tradition.[42] The majority, however, permitted them on the understanding that they are, after all, petitions for *collective* welfare *(tzorkhay rabbim)* and that they are prayers for life itself rather than for material goods.

The bone of contention was thus the petitionary character of these prayers; yet their popularity may well have derived from this very fact. One may speculate on the rank-and-file worshippers' growing dissatisfaction with the noble idealism which constituted the

Talmudic conception of Rosh Hashanah. Such abstract themes as *Malkhut*, the re-affirmation of the Kingship of God, did not forever satisfy the deep yearnings for more concrete and immediate fulfillments which must have motivated the heart of the average Jew in those early centuries (as they do indeed to this day). As in so many instances, the popular will prevailed and the simple petitions, "Remember us unto life . . . inscribe us in the book of life, etc.," took root among the loftier concepts of the older statutory prayers.[43] The fact that Jews today recite them throughout the Ten Days of Penitence is the most eloquent testimony to their timeless appeal.

Mekhalkayl Ḥayyim מכלכל חיים

In the traditional synagogue this prayer is usually sung to a very pleasant and lively tune, wherein lies an amusing tale. Rabbi Ezekiel Landau of 18th century Prague was fond of singing his own melodies during the service and his favorite was that of *Mekhalkayl ḥayyim.*

A certain jester, who eked out a livelihood as a *badḥan,* a kind of master of ceremonies at marriage feasts, decided to capitalize on the popularity of the Rabbi's tune. As part of his entertainment at a wedding party, he would mimic Rabbi Landau's singing of *Mekhalkayl ḥayyim* on Rosh Hashanah. When the officials of the Jewish community heard of these irreverent performances they summoned the *badḥan* to rebuke and to fine him. Finally they threatened to revoke his license to act as a jester unless he sought the Rabbi's forgiveness and promised not to use the melody again. When the great scholar and leader of Prague heard the jester's plea, he was highly pleased to learn of the success of his favorite melody. To appease the over-solicitous officials, Rabbi Landau wrote out an official permit licensing the *badḥan* to exploit his *Mekhalkayl ḥayyim* melody "for purposes of making a living."

The most striking aspect of this amusing anecdote is that the Hebrew words, *Mekhalkayl ḥayyim,* mean literally just what the Rabbi wrote, namely, "provides a livelihood." In our prayer we thank the Divine Provider in joyous melody for sustaining our lives in His bountiful mercy and lovingkindness, for raising up those who have fallen, for healing the sick, liberating the enslaved and for imparting immortality to the souls of those who kept faith with their Maker.

YIMLOKH ADONAI — V-ATAH KADOSH ימלך יי — ואתה קדוש

Whenever *Kerovot* are inserted in the repetition of the *Amidah,* these two Biblical verses are included. *Yimlokh Adonai* is from Psalms 146:10 and *V-Atah kadosh* from Psalms 22:4. They are chanted to an exultant traditional melody. Nevertheless, the reason for their inclusion, in the first place, and their relationship to what precedes and follows in the present text are by no means clear. To compound the difficulty, the words *El na* are appended to the latter verse, *V-Atah kadosh*, even though they neither appear in the Biblical source nor fit into the context of the verse as it now stands in all printed editions of the Maḥzor (to the discomfiture of every translator and commentator!).

The solution to the problem lies in a knowledge of the technical structure of the *Kerovah* form of liturgical poetry. The explanation — too involved to be included here — may be found in the appendix to this volume, entitled THE STRUCTURE OF THE KEROVAH.

ATAH HU ELOHAYNU אתה הוא אלהינו

This beloved *piyyut* is often attributed to Eleazar Kallir though his authorship has never been proved conclusively.[44] In any case it has all the earmarks of one of the most ancient Palestinian *piyyutim.* It is composed in the form of an unrhymed alphabetical acrostic. Each of the brief phrases begins with a succeeding letter of the Hebrew alphabet — *alef, bet, gimmel, dalet,* etc. In an age when prayerbooks were extremely rare (if they existed at all) the acrostic was a valuable aid to the memory.[45]

Such devices are characteristic of the art of the *payyetan.* The simple alphabetical acrostic is the springboard for an endless variety of more complex forms. For instance, there is the triple *alef-bet* device, illustrated in Kallir's hymn beginning, *Adiray Ayumah ya'Adiru*. There is also the alphabet in reverse, called *TaSHRaK* (from the last four letters of the Hebrew alphabet: *tav, shin, resh, kof*). A favorite technique is one in which the poet spells out his name by means of the initial letters of each stanza. This practice — as we have seen — has made possible the identification of many poets. Perhaps the best known example of this device is the *Lekha Dodi* of the Sabbath eve service, composed by Solomon Halevi Alkabetz. Translators of the *piyyutim* have frequently attempted to imitate the alphabetical acrostics in their renditions, but their efforts often result in grotesque effects.

It must not be thought that these ingenious techniques reveal a sense of frivolity or a penchant for literary gymnastics on the part of the poets of the Synagogue. Nothing could be further from the truth. They were motivated by the most reverent and devout purposes, eager to extol God with all their powers of articulation. In utilizing what may appear to the western critic an over-ornate style, they were merely following an ancient Oriental literary device already found in the Bible itself (for example, Psalms 119 and 145; Proverbs, Chapter 31, Lamentations, Chapters 1-4). The Midrash also mentions the singing of "alphabetaries" (Heb., *alfabetarin*) at the circumcision feast of Elisha ben Abuyah, about the year 100 C.E. These songs obviously represented a new form of poetry utilizing alphabetical devices and may have been one of the precursors of the *piyyutim*.[46]

ADERET MAMLAKHAH אדרת ממלכה

In this *piyyut* (part of Kallir's *Kerovah, At ḥil yom pekudah*) the author's name, *Eleazar bay Rabbi Kallir*, is skillfully woven into the text of the poem through the initial letter of each stanza (three phrases per stanza): the *alef* (first letter of the Hebrew, *Eleazar*) begins the word *Aderet,* and so on. "With a wealth of Biblical and Midrashic allusions which cannot be reproduced in translation, the author describes the downfall of Israel's kingdom, deplores the ascendancy of might in the world, and expresses his faith that God's sovereignty will yet be acclaimed" (Morris Silverman).

The brief poem beginning, *Ta'ir v-taria,* as found in the printed Maḥzor, is often erroneously taken as part of *Aderet mamlakhah* but this is not the case. Though both are links in the same *Kerovah* chain composed by Kallir, *Ta'ir v-taria* is technically a conclusion (Hebrew, *ḥatimah)* to the preceding *piyyut, Atah hu Elohaynu.* It concludes with the word *kadosh* ("holy"), an appropriate ending to that section of the *Kerovah* which is designated in the ancient manuscripts *Atah Kadosh.* The postlude to *Aderet mamlakhah* is the brief poem beginning, *U-v'khayn v-Adonai pakad et Sarah*; this likewise ends with the word *kadosh.* The frequency of this word derives from the fact that all the poems mentioned here are insertions in the third benediction of the *Amidah,* which in the old Palestinian rite began, "*Kadosh Atah* . . . Thou art holy, etc." A complete outline of the *Kerovah* form of synagogal poetry is found in the appendix to this volume, entitled THE STRUCTURE OF THE KEROVAH.

MELEKH ELYON, AMITZ HA-MENUSA אמיץ המנשא

Just as the *piyyutim* for the first day of Rosh Hashanah in the Ashkenazic rite are chiefly the work of Eleazar Kallir, so those on the second day are almost exclusively by Rabbi Simeon ben Isaac ben Abun of 11th century Mayence. He is sometimes referred to as R. Simeon the Great. An uncle of Rashi and a brilliant scholar in his own right, he was famed as a wonder worker and helped to save many Jews from their persecutors. As we have already seen, another *piyyut* by R. Simeon, beginning *Melekh amon,* may contain an allusion to his son Elḥanan, the legendary "Jewish Pope," with whom R. Simeon is supposed to have intervened to avert a severe anti-Jewish decree. His greatest fame, however, is as a gifted and prolific *payyetan* whose poems were widely adopted in Germany and France. Writing much in the style of Kallir, he set out to fill in whatever gaps existed in the compositions of his Palestinian model. Thus he composed a complete cycle of *Yotzrot* and *Kerovot* for the second day of Rosh Hashanah. The initials of his first name *(SHiM'ON)* are found in the closing stanza of this *piyyut.*

"This poem contrasts the power, majesty and eternity of the divine King of the universe with the evanescent and inevitably vanishing power of earthly tyrants designated as *melekh evyon* (mortal king) in rhythmic contrast with *Melekh elyon* (Most High King). Thus the poet reaffirms his faith in the sovereignty of God and fears not the power of mortal tyrants" (Morris Silverman).

There is another *Melekh elyon* hymn in the Musaf service, written on the same model, beginning *El dar ba-marom* (see Chapter Seven). Both poems are abridged by half: each *Melekh elyon verse* (referring to God's eternal majesty and power) originally was con trasted with a *melekh evyon* parallel (alluding to mortal man's powerlessness). Our printed editions preserve only two of the eleven *melekh evyon* stanzas: the first (beginning with the letter *bet)* and the last (beginning with the letter *tav)*.[47] The usual explanation for this abridgement is the desire to shorten the services; other examples of this practice in medieval times are available.[48] On the other hand, there is some suspicion of censorship on the part of, or in fear of, the Christian authorities who may have taken offense at the theological implication of the *melekh evyon* verses. Such censorship is well known in the history of Jewish liturgy.[49]

Adonai Melekh — יי מלך

This *piyyut* is part of the *Kerovah* chain of poems composed by R. Simeon b. Isaac for the second morning of Rosh Hashanah. Its intricate structure is based on the three-fold liturgical verse, "The Lord is King, the Lord was King, the Lord forever shall be King." Each stanza consists of three lines which constitute a sort of "divine dialectic": the first refers to the hosts of heaven offering sweet praise to God; the second describes the parallel tributes from His earthly subjects; the closing line links the previous two in the classic synthesis of the *Kedushah,* namely, the union of heaven and earth, of celestial and terrestial beings, in singing the praises of the Holy One.

The name of the poet Simeon ben Isaac (ben Abun, of 11th century Mayence) may be traced through the initial letters of the second Hebrew word in each successive stanza. Close examination will reveal a quadruple *shin, mem, a'yin, vav, nun* — spelling out *SHiM'ON* (Hebrew for Simeon) and so with the rest of his name.

An additional *alef-bet* acrostic can be traced through the second strophe of each line in both noun and verb. Although the complex apparatus may seem to lend artificiality to the poem, "it is a brilliant technical achievement and has also a fine sense of movement" (Solomon B. Freehof).[49a]

L-El Oraykh Din לאל עורך דין

This moving hymn by Eleazar Kallir,[50] is one of the best known and most beloved of all the *piyyutim* in the Ashkenazic Maḥzor. The Cantor chants it in a pleading melody, standard in most Ashkenazic synagogues.

The theme of the *piyyut* is stated again and again through the twin refrains: *Din*, "judgment," and *Yom Din*, "Day of Judgment." The poet enumerates the qualities of judgment associated with the Supreme Arbiter, including His attributes of mercy, compassion and forgiveness. The portrayal of God as judge is as old as the Hebrew people itself. Abraham challenged "the judge of all the earth" to "do justice" (Genesis 18:25). The Book of Proverbs (16:11) speaks of God as holding in His hand the scales of judgment, and in the Talmud this figure is used repeatedly. Medieval moralists (such as Baḥya ben Asher, Menaḥem Meiri) were fond of pointing out that nature herself has designated the first of Tishre as the universal Day of Judgment, since the zodiacal symbol for that month is Libra, the Scales (of judgment).

Kedushah of the Amidah קדשה

The congregation rises for a series of three ancient responses from the Bible (Isaiah 6:3, Ezekiel 3:12, Psalms 146:10). These verses are linked by poetic passages into the prayer known as the *Kedushah* ("Sanctification") of the *Amidah*. This is a parallel to that *Kedushah* which has already been recited at the outset of Shaḥarit, as part of the Creation prayer *(Yotzayr)*.[51] The basic element here too is the three-fold *Kadosh*, the "Thrice-Holy." The heavens are envisioned as ringing with the praises sung to the Holy

One by angelic hosts, while on earth the faithful echo their melodious tributes.

The *Kedushah* is a very solemn, though by no means somber, prayer and the worshippers display the utmost reverence during its recitation, standing at attention, as in the *Amidah.* On the High Holy Days, so many poetic selections, especially in the prayers leading up to the *Kedushah,*[52] are rendered that the latter loses much of its customary prominence. There is, for example, no traditional melody for this prayer in Shaḥarit other than that used generally for Sabbaths and Festivals. The *Kedushah* of Musaf is somewhat more prominent, musically speaking, and contains the *Shema Yisrael* plus other additions.

The U-v'khayn Prayers ובכן

Following the *Kedushah* in the morning service there are no further additions to the statutory benedictions of the *Amidah* in the form of *piyyutim.* The next benediction is entitled *Kedushat Ha-Shem,* the "Sanctification of God's Name." Ordinarily it contains just twelve Hebrew words in our rite but on the High Holy Days it is considerably expanded and the closing benediction is changed to *"Ha-Melekh ha-kadosh* . . . the Holy King."[53] Prominent among the interpolations is a triad of prayers, brief but majestic, each of which begins with the words, "*U-v'khayn* . . . And, therefore."[54] The authorship and date of this prayer-group are still obscure. They are not mentioned in the Mishnah or Talmud, yet by the time of the Geonim they are well known.[55]

In any event their meaning is clear; they "reaffirm loyalty to a universal outlook and world brotherhood, the wellbeing of Israel, and the triumph of moral law. The three forces of internationalism, nationalism and religion, each retaining its own sphere of influence, but reacting upon one another, will hasten the advent of the kingdom of God and bring salvation to mankind" (Morris Silverman). The illustrious poet and philosopher, Yehudah Halevi, explains that these three passages parallel the three levels of the human race: the first is a prayer for the nations of the world; the second, a prayer for the peer of nations, Israel; and the third, for the elite in Israel, namely the prophets, the righteous and the saintly.[56]

Kadosh Atah קדוש אתה

This prayer constitutes the conclusion of the expanded third benediction of the *Amidah (Kedushat Ha-Shem)*. Throughout the year, the third benediction closes with the words, "*ha-El ha-kadosh* . . . the holy God." On Rosh Hashanah — and, consequently, on Yom Kippur and the entire Ten Days of Penitence — the word *El* (God) is replaced by *Melekh* (King). The Talmud[57] attributes this innovation to Rav, in third century Babylonia. The change of wording is taken traditionally as another instance of the emphasis on *Malkhut,* God's Kingship, in the liturgy of the New Year; but it may be simply a variant text in the Babylonian rite.[58]

It is noteworthy that this prayer, recited only on the Days of Awe, is strongly reminiscent of the ancient Palestinian form of the third benediction. Indeed, the only difference is that the Biblical verse (Isaiah 5:16) "The Lord of hosts is exalted through justice, the holy God is sanctified through righteousness," replaces the original verse (Isaiah 6:3), the "Thrice-Holy."[59] The change reflects the significance of Rosh Hashanah as the Day of Judgment. "This declaration of the Prophet Isaiah is among the sublimest utterances ever spoken by human lips . . . Isaiah proclaims justice, i.e., respect for elementary human rights, to be a sanctification of the Holy God!" (J. H. Hertz).

Va-titen Lanu ותתן לנו

On the other Festivals, this prayer includes the words "*mo'adim l-simḥah ḥagim u-zemanim l-sason* . . . appointed times for gladness, festivals and seasons for joy." These words were once recited also on Rosh Hashanah in Palestine. The reason for their deletion (by the Babylonian Geonim) was the evolution of Rosh Hashanah from its purely festive origins into the solemn mood of the Days of Awe, under the influence of Yom Kippur.[60]

The Talmud records an opinion that the forced labor of the

Israelites in Egypt ceased on the Rosh Hashanah which preceded the Exodus;[61] but this has no direct connection with the phrase of our prayer, *zaykher li-yetzi'at Mitzra'yim*, "in remembrance of the Exodus from Egypt." The latter is a formula common to all the Festivals as well as Shabbat. The liberation from Egyptian bondage left an indelible mark upon Israel's memory; there is hardly a ritual that does not in some way allude to it.[62]

Ya'aleh V-yavo יעלה ויבא

This prayer is inserted in the *Amidah*[63] on all festival days and on *Rosh Ḥodesh* but it appears to have a special relevance for Rosh Hashanah in its concentration on the theme of Remembrance *(Zikhronot)*. It should be recalled that the first recorded name for what we call Rosh Hashanah is *zikhron teruah,* (i.e. "memorial of the sounding of the horn"); it is found in the book of Leviticus 23:24. The connection between "remembering" and the sounding of a trumpet is clearly established by the Book of Numbers (10:9 and 10):

> And when ye go to war in your land against the adversary that oppresseth you, then ye shall sound an alarm with the trumpets; and ye shall be remembered before the Lord your God, and ye shall be saved from your enemies. Also in the day of your gladness and in your appointed seasons, and in your new moons, ye shall blow with the trumpets over your burnt-offerings, and over the sacrifices of your peace-offerings; and they shall be to you for a memorial before your God: I am the Lord your God.

The original significance of Rosh Hashanah then was probably *zikaron,* a "remembrance," implying that God should hearken to our prayers and Shofar-sounding and be mindful of Israel's needs. The prayer *Ya'aleh v-yavo* may even have been composed originally for Rosh Hashanah and later extended to other "new moons" and festivals.[63a]

Melokh Al Kol Ha-olam מלוך

This is the unique Rosh Hashanah prayer in each of the *Amidah* services, the central benediction called *Kedushat Ha-Yom,* "the Sanctification of the Day." The closing words also serve as the conclusion of the Kiddush and the *Haftarah* blessings.

The text of this prayer offers a parallel in miniature to the historical evolution of the New Year liturgy. It is actually a combination of two separate prayers: the first half presents Rosh Hashanah as the celebration of God's Kingship *(Malkhut)* reminiscent of *U-v'khayn tayn paḥdekha* or *Alaynu*; the second half reflects the earlier character of Rosh Hashanah as a Festival *(mo'ed)* similar to Pesaḥ, Shavuot or Sukkot.[64] The benediction proper, concluding the prayer, is an amalgam of both themes.

Behind this compromise arrangement lies a long history of liturgical struggle. Traces of the old Palestinian worship (preserved in the Palestinian Talmud, in the post-Talmudical tractate Soferim, in the Palestinian *piyyutim* and in manuscript fragments from the Genizah) include references here to *Rosh Ḥodesh*, for Rosh Hashanah is also the New Moon of Tishre, the seventh month. The Palestinian text includes also the Biblical designations of *Mikra kodesh* ("proclamation of holiness") as well as the "day of sounding" the Shofar of Remembrance. The festive quality of Rosh Hashanah as one of the *mo'adim l-simḥah*, "appointed seasons for gladness," is everywhere apparent in the Palestinian rite. The Babylonian schools, however, suppressed the joyous, festive aspects of Rosh Hashanah in favor of its solemnity as a day of universal judgment.[65]

Strictly speaking, the phrase in the concluding benediction, *Melekh al kol ha-aretz,* "Thou, King over all the earth," applies only in the Musaf service where the *Malkhuyot* or Kingship prayer was eventually inserted. Nevertheless, it is coalesced with the phrase, *Mekadesh Yisrael v-ha-zemanim*, "who sanctifiest Israel and the Day of Remembrance" in *all* the services of Rosh Hashanah.[66]

RETZAY רצה

This prayer, known in Talmudic literature as the benediction of *Avodah* (the Divine Service), is the only statutory benediction of the *Amidah* which is never embellished on the High Holy Days by *piyyutim* or other interpolations. One explanation is that "it is a prayer for the Messianic era and no prayer of contemporary relevance may be attached to it."[67]

B-sayfer Ḥayyim בספר חיים

The metaphor of the "Book of Life" is as old as Moses, who implores God to "blot me from Thy book" (Exodus 32:32). It is further elaborated in other sections of the Bible. The actual expression "book of life" is found in Psalms 69:29.

This figure of speech was never taken literally by Jewish authorities. Even the *Sefer Ḥasidim,* a popular pietistic work of medieval Germany, makes a special point of emphasizing this. The symbolic meaning of the metaphor is explained by the distinguished interpreter of Jewish liturgy, Israel Abrahams: "The *Book of Life* was a spiritual fancy corresponding to a material fact. In ancient Judea, to be enrolled in the Book of Life would imply membership in the Holy Commonwealth; to be blotted out, would be to suffer disenfranchisement. This idea was carried over into the spiritual world."[68]

Avinu Malkaynu אבינו מלכנו

The series of verses beginning with the words *Avinu Malkaynu* is recited not only on Rosh Hashanah and Yom Kippur and the intervening Days of Penitence, but on all the fast days in the Jewish calendar. This penitential litany is the oldest in the Prayerbook. Traditionally it is chanted in a tearful melody,[69] similar to that for the *piyyut, L-El oraykh din.* Likewise, the Ark is opened for *Avinu Malkaynu,* as a sign of its importance.

According to the Talmud, *Avinu Malkaynu* originated in the second century after a severe drought had ravaged Palestine. No rains had fallen for a month and prayers and fasts had not availed. Rabbi Akiba appeared before the congregation and prayed, "Our Father, Our King, we have no King except Thee. Our Father, our King, for Thy sake have mercy upon us." His petition was then answered.[70] The Talmud ascribes the efficacy of Akiba's prayer to his merciful traits of character. The prayer is a simple, almost child-like petition, vividly illustrating the teaching of the Sages that a filial relationship exists which "suffers no interference, whether for good or evil, of a third person between Israel and God . . . Israel may claim their filial privileges even if they have sinned" (Solomon Schechter).[71] The term "Father" or "Our (my) Father, Who is in heaven" is one of the most frequent in Jewish liturgy.[72]

Our text contains forty-four *Avinu Malkaynu* verses. It is not possible to determine just how many verses there were in the original prayer. Some signs point to an *alef-bet* order.[73] Even today there are several different versions. The closing lines are unknown prior to the First Crusade (1096); others date from the Black Death massacres of the fourteenth century. "Among the verses are some which point to periods of persecution, martyrdom, and political danger; others refer to more normal tribulations and human necessities; others again . . . are specially adapted to the penitential season when prayers for forgiveness are particularly appropriate" (Israel Abrahams). The requests for material blessings may date from the early Middle Ages.

Avinu Malkaynu is placed immediately after the *Amidah* as was customary in Talmudic times with prayers of petition for God's grace *(taḥanunim)*. The closing verse was possibly added to make this resemblance clearer (" . . . be *gracious* unto us and answer us . . ."). Just as the familiar daily *Taḥanun* prayer is recited by the individual silently, so is the closing verse of *Avinu Malkaynu,* according to this interpretation.

This prayer is omitted on a Rosh Hashanah which falls on Shabbat, although there have been contrary opinions concerning this ever since Geonic times. A variety of reasons are given: 1) it contains requests for personal needs and desires, whereas the day of rest is to be devoted exclusively to spiritual wants; 2) the original *Avinu Malkaynu* was a prayer for fast days, whereas fasting is forbidden on Shabbat; 3) the *Avinu Malkaynu* is an echo of the *Taḥanun* prayer which is omitted on Shabbat; 4) it contains reminiscences of the weekday *Amidah* and therefore may not be used on Shabbat.[74]

It has also been observed that *Avinu Malkaynu* and the *Amidah* are similar in that both are recited while standing and in the special concentration of intent *(kavanah)* which is enjoined during their recitation. Other commentators compare *Avinu Malkaynu* to the *Hallel* prayer which is recited at this point on the Three Pilgrim Festivals.

Why We Do Not Say Hallel on Rosh Hashanah

The *Hallel* prayer, which is usually recited after the morning *Amidah* on Festivals, is omitted on Rosh Hashanah. Many commentators have sought the reason for this. *Hallel*, the Hebrew word for Praise, is a collection of Psalms (113-118) whose refrain is *Halleluyah*, "Praise ye the Lord."[75] These Psalms are recited on joyous occasions in the Jewish calendar including the New Moon, and would seem to be indicated for Rosh Hashanah as well.

The Talmud gives this reason: "Is it conceivable that, while the King of the Universe sits in solemn judgment, with the Books of Life and of Death spread open before Him, Israel should be singing joyous songs before Him?"[76] This remarkably sensitive explanation is directly in the tradition of the classic *midrash* concerning the angels who chanted praises to God while the Egyptians were drowning in the Red Sea. When God perceived this, He scolded them bitterly: "The creatures of My hand are drowning in the sea, yet you dare to sing songs!"[77] Maharil explains the omission on the grounds that certain verses in the *Hallel* are inappropriate to the penitential character of Rosh Hashanah. Others see in the *Avinu Malkaynu* a substitute for *Hallel*. Another explanation is based on the Talmudic principle, "The prophets enacted the recitation of *Hallel* for those occasions when Israel was redeemed from tragic circumstances."[78] Since Rosh Hashanah does not fall into this category, *Hallel* is omitted.

CHAPTER FIVE

THE READING OF THE TORAH

THE READING OF THE TORAH

The Reading of The Torah קריאת התורה

The Reading of the Torah has always been the center and the crown of the Synagogue worship. Some scholars maintain that the practice of gathering on Shabbat, Festivals and special occasions to read portions of Scripture was actually the genesis of the Synagogue itself.[1]

The Scriptural lesson is of special historical significance on Rosh Hashanah. According to the book of Nehemiah (8:1-14) it was on "the first day of the seventh month" that the Torah was restored to the people of Israel by Ezra and Nehemiah. These leaders of the return to Zion after the Babylonian Exile (6th century B.C.E.) gathered together the handful of Judeans in an historic open air assembly, "And they read in the book, in the Law (Torah) of God, distinctly; and they gave the sense, and caused them to understand the reading."

There may well be a direct historical connection between the restoration of the Torah as the constitution of the Jewish people and the development of Rosh Hashanah as a festival of exceptional significance in Judaism.

Va-yehi Bi-neso'a Ha-aron ויהי בנסע הארן

The curtain *(Parokhet)* is drawn and the doors of the Ark are opened as this Biblical passage (Numbers 10:35) is chanted.[2] The classical commentators point out that the opening of the Ark on

Rosh Hashanah is symbolic of the opening of the gates of heaven in answer to the petition previously made in the *Avinu Malkaynu* prayer: "Our Father, our King, open Thou the gates of heaven to our prayer."

The *Parokhet,* the Torah vestments and other coverings used on the Days of Awe are white in color.[3] So is the *Kittel*, the robe traditionally worn by male worshippers on Rosh Hashanah and Yom Kippur and by the head of the household at the Passover *Seder.* Women also traditionally wear white garments on the Days of Awe. The white robes recall the ancient Jewish festival attire, and not — as popularly believed — the death shroud![4] White is symbolic of purity and atonement (as in Isaiah 1:18, a verse quoted frequently in Yom Kippur prayers). But it is equally the symbol of confident joy, as the Talmud[5] clearly explains: "As a rule, a man who knows he must stand trial dresses in black and lets his hair grow, for he knows not what the verdict will be; but Israel does not act in this way. Instead, Jews attire themselves in *white* garments, shave their hair, eat, drink and rejoice because they know that the Holy One, blessed be He, will do wondrous things for them" (i.e., on Rosh Hashanah, the Day of Judgment, once they have repented).

Adonai, Adonai — ײ, ײ

This passage from the Book of Exodus (34:6,7) is recited before the open Ark, not only on the Days of Awe but on the Three Pilgrimage Festivals as well. The High Holy Day setting and the solemn character of the words combine to make this a very moving ritual. The words of this prayer first occur as part of the narrative of the Golden Calf incident, where they form the burden of Moses' plea to the Lord to forgive the transgression of Israel. The Rabbis spoke of the "Thirteen Attributes" of God's nature as derived from this verse,[6] the salient quality being that of mercy. The choice of the designation *Adonai* is in itself significant; for, according to the Talmudic tradition, it is used to denote *middat ha-raḥamim,* God's attribute of Mercy, while the name *Elohim* is used to call attention to *middat ha-din*, His attribute of Judgment.

The verse also forms part of the Torah reading on the minor

fast days of the Jewish calendar. The Thirteen Attributes are very prominent in the worship for Yom Kippur — especially in those sections known as *Seliḥot* (penitential poems). The prayer is not recited, however, on Shabbat because such requests for God's mercy are deemed inappropriate for the Sabbath day. The recitation of the Thirteen Attributes *(Shelosh Esray Middot)* at the taking out of the Torah is comparatively modern; it was introduced by the mystical school of R. Isaac Luria, the *Ari*, along with the prayer, *Ribbon ha-olam,* which follows. *Adonai, Adonai* is recited three times, a characteristic practice for prayers of Kabbalistic origin.

Ribbon Ha-olam רבון העולם

This meditation, too, is a late addition to our Prayerbook.[7] Like *Adonai, Adonai* (the Thirteen Attributes of God) to which it is attached, *Ribbon ha-olam* came into the synagogue service (neither prayer is for private use) under the influence of Lurianic Kabbalah, a mystical movement which arose in Safed of 16th century Palestine. These embellishments were originally intended for the month of Elul, as a preparation for the Days of Awe. Later they were extended to Rosh Hashanah and Yom Kippur and finally to the festivals of Pesaḥ, Shavuot and Sukkot, as well.[8] The three-fold repetition of the concluding verse, *Va-ani tefillati* (like that of *Adonai, Adonai*) is typical of the mystics.

Rationalists like the Gaon Elijah of Vilna opposed the introduction of both this meditation and the Thirteen Attributes, but (as Israel Abrahams, in his splendid commentary on the Siddur, reminds us) "Some of the best of the most recent additions to the Prayer Book are the work of Jewish mystics." In this connection, it may be noted that some prayerbooks include here the noble passage from the Zohar, the classic text of Kabbalah, beginning, *Berikh Shemay,* "Blessed be the Name." Of this prayer the Zohar states, "When the Scroll is taken out in the congregation to read therein, the heavenly gates of mercy open and the celestial love awakes." In his commentary, Abrahams explains the appropriateness of this recitation, which has been widely adopted for the ceremony of the removal of the scrolls from the Ark:

This combination of the ideas of direct intuition of God and of receptiveness to the Law is a striking feature in Jewish mysticism. The mystic is essentially a law to himself; the Jewish mystic, however, often contrives to reconcile his own free, individual emotions with obedience to the law. He is not in a state of revolt against authority, as the mystic so frequently is, but he finds in authority the goal of his ecstatic devotion.

The mystical dimension in Jewish thought is currently reasserting itself after a long silence brought on by the rational and scientific mood of the modern era. One of the most interesting and influential cultural currents of contemporary Judaism is neo-Ḥasidism. Thinkers like Martin Buber in Germany and Israel, Franz Rosenzweig in Germany, Hillel Zeitlin in Poland, and Abraham Joshua Heschel in America have helped to re-evaluate this important dimension of religious experience, especially for introspection and prayer. A gifted composer of religious poetry in the mystic tradition during our time was the late Chief Rabbi of Palestine, Abraham Isaac Kuk. The first modern Hebrew poet, Moses Ḥayyim Luzzatto, was a Kabbalist. Mystical concepts have widely influenced contemporary Hebrew verse.[9]

EḤAD ELOHAYNU אחד אלהינו

On the High Holy Days, the text of this prayer varies slightly from that used on other Festivals and on Shabbat. In recognition of the solemnity of the *Yamim Noraim,* we append the adjective *nora,* "awesome," "revered," to the customary *kadosh*, "holy," when the scrolls are removed from the Ark. This practice probably originated in late Talmudic times.[10] The prayer, *Eḥad Elohaynu,* is recited only in the Ashkenazic and Romanian rites.

The word *kadosh* has likewise strong associations with the High Holy Days. The "first day of the seventh month" is described by Ezra and Nehemiah as *kadosh (hu) l-Adonai,* "holy unto the Lord" (Nehemiah 8:9). It is further designated, in the following verse, as *kadosh ha-yom l-Adonaynu*, "holy is this day unto our Lord," and this Biblical phrase has been incorporated verbatim into the Musaf service for Rosh Hashanah. A traditional name for

Yom Kippur, still popular in some Jewish communities (e.g., the Hungarian) is *Yom Ha-Kadosh*, "The Sacred Day."

GADELU L-ADONAI ITTI גדלו ליי אתי

This Biblical verse (Psalms 34:4) is chanted in all the rites when the Torah scrolls are removed from the Ark. The *Shulḥan Arukh,* the sixteenth century code of Jewish law and practice, interprets the words "with me" and "together" as a warning to the congregation: they may chant along with the Cantor but they must not sing louder than he. All too often we associate the traditional synagogue with lack of decorum. Wherever such was the case, it was the result of ignorance or poor taste. The codes of traditional practice place a much higher value, as a rule, on restraint in prayer than on exuberance.

To be sure, what is often taken as lack of decorum is nothing more than religious fervor and the desire for self-expression. This is particularly the case of the High Holy Days.[11] Thus the codes are more lenient in permitting the individual to pray as the spirit moves him on these Days of Awe, provided that he does not interfere with his neighbor's devotions. It is said that the Ḥasidic master, Rabbi Shmelke of Nikolsburg, would prepare all sorts of musical scores for the service. However, when the spirit of religious ecstasy came over him, he promptly forgot them and sang whatever came to his lips.

PENTATEUCH READING FOR THE FIRST DAY קריאה

The Pentateuchal readings for the High Holy Days are chanted in a melody reserved for those occasions and intended to convey the dignity and solemnity of the Days of Awe.[12] Five persons are "called up" to the Reading of the Torah on Rosh Hashanah, as on other Festivals (seven if it coincides with Shabbat). It is considered especially meritorious to be honored with an *Aliyah* on the Days of Awe.

The readings for Rosh Hashanah from the Pentateuch and

the Prophets were selected many centuries ago with the purpose of conveying important ideas associated with the festival. Thus, the Rabbinic tradition connects the sounding of the ram's horn with the story of *Akaydat Yitzḥak,* "The Binding of Isaac," in whose place a sacrificial ram was substituted.[13] The Talmud states also that Isaac was conceived on Rosh Hashanah.[14] Similarly, it was on Rosh Hashanah that God "remembered" the childless Hannah and Rachel, both of whom figure prominently in the selections for the New Year. The theme of "Remembrance" *(Zikhronot)* is especially prominent in the Scriptural readings. Samson Raphael Hirsch, striving to find a connecting thread in the several narratives prescribed for the Bible readings, suggested that one may gain insight into the twin aspects of man's religious development through the female and male personalities of the texts. The feminine dimension — i.e., being close to God through pure feeling and spirit, typified by prayer — is illustrated by Hannah, Sarah, Rachel and Hagar; the male dimension — obedience, the loyal strength and pure courage needed to act for God, sacrificing our own will to His — is illustrated by Abraham and Isaac.[14a]

The portion from the Torah for the first day, Chapter 21 of Genesis, tells of the birth of Isaac to Abraham and Sarah in their advanced age. Alarmed over the child Ishmael's harmful influence upon Isaac, Sarah insists that her husband banish his concubine Hagar and her son. Abraham is grieved over this "test" of his fatherly love.[15] Though a champion of justice in other situations, Abraham submits to Sarah's demand when he receives Divine assurance that all is for the best: "Through Isaac shall thy name be carried on."[16] Hagar and Ishmael are sent forth into the wilderness but God's care is extended equally to them: "Fear not . . . for I will make of him a great nation." Ishmael eventually becomes a man of war and the progenitor of the desert tribes. The present day Bedouin of Palestine and Moslems generally look upon him and his father, Abraham, as their ancestors.[17]

Most commentators, ancient as well as modern, see only a formal relation between Chapter 21 of Genesis, the reading for the first day of Rosh Hashanah, and Chapter 22, the reading for the second day. David Polish, however, has suggested that the story of the expulsion of Ishmael is the clue to the meaning of the

Binding of Isaac. The two narratives are connected by a significant verse which intrigued the Sages: "And it came to pass *after these things*" (Genesis 22:1).[18] When God calls upon Abraham to take, "your son, your only son, whom you love, Isaac," Abraham seems to comprehend the unspoken overtones of the summons. He interprets it to mean, "Take him — as you once took Ishmael whom you still love." Rashi's comment on the verse supports this interpretation. Rabbi Polish concludes:

> Abraham's acquiescence, even to God, in the expulsion of Ishmael is his undoing and must be atoned for. He has forfeited his right to the life of one son because of the life of the other whom he has cast away . . . Only by reliving with Isaac what he experienced with Ishmael will expiation come . . . By his act, Abraham articulated man's capacity to deal actively with evil . . . Man, bearing the burden of his guilt, can find the way to grapple with it with instruments placed in his hands by God.[19]

The Kohen Reading כהן

Israel H. Levinthal, one of America's outstanding preachers, has pointed out that the verb *tzaḥak,* which may mean both "laugh" and "make sport," is used by the Torah concerning both sons of Abraham. Isaac was called Yitzḥak in the positive sense of the word,[20] but, in the case of Ishmael, the verb *metzaḥayk* is utilized in its negative aspect of irreverent, cynical behavior. He goes on to draw the implication that it is the sacred responsibility of Jewish parents to rear their children that they become — like Isaac — laughing, joyous, positive Jews rather than mocking, immature youth, unhappy in their heritage and — like Ishmael — destructive of ancestral traditions.

The Levi Reading לוי

"And Sarah said . . . 'who would have said unto Abraham, that Sarah should be suckling a child?' " The Midrash explains why the

Hebrew here reads "children" though Isaac alone is referred to. Legend states that the aged Sarah's neighbors cast suspicion upon her capacity for motherhood. Therefore when Abraham made a feast for all his neighbors to celebrate the weaning of Isaac (as described in this portion), Sarah also nursed the babes of the guests to prove her own motherhood.[21] Tzvi Hirsch Masliansky pointed out that this legend is instructive for the modern Jew as well. He noted that Sarah nursed the strangers only after she had satisfied her own child. Unlike this, many Jews today, while giving freely of their talents and substance to other peoples in every field of endeavor, ignore their own heritage and — in the words of Scripture — "hide themselves from their own flesh."

THE SHELISHI READING שלישי

The universal aspect of Judaism — so much emphasized on Rosh Hashanah — shines through even this episode of ancient rivalry. Divine providence is extended to Hagar and Ishmael as well as to Sarah and Isaac, for God is the God of all peoples. In her anxiety, Hagar is reassured by the angel of the Lord concerning her child: "Fear not . . . for I will make of him a great nation."

"Judged by present day moral standards, the banishment of Hagar and Ishmael seems an unusually severe act. It must be understood in the light of primitive social standards, according to which the child of a concubine enjoyed a lower social status and had no claim to the same rights and privileges as the son of the wife. Our sages find a moral basis for the conflict between Sarah and Hagar. They explain the phrase 'Ishmael making sport' as follows: Ishmael would shoot arrows at passers-by and laugh when he saw them wounded. Another interpretation is that 'immorality, murder and idolatry' characterized the life of Ishmael, while justice, truth and peace were the principles which Isaac was to promulgate. These attitudes cannot long exist side by side. Hence Sarah felt justified in sending Ishmael away in order to maintain the ideals of Isaac" (Morris Silverman).

The severity of the treatment of Hagar and Ishmael is mitigated by the compassion which God extends to them in their extremity.

This note is emphasized by the Talmudic commentators on the verse, "God has heard the voice of the lad, where he is." "Though Ishmael had sinned grievously, God listened to his voice; for no matter how far one has fallen, God hears his prayers and accepts his penitence." The Sages interpreted the last phrase of this verse, " . . . where he is (now)", to mean that God judges the sinner, not as he *was*, but as he *is at the moment of his repentance*.[22]

The Revi'i and Ḥamishi Readings רביעי וחמישי

What significance can be derived for Rosh Hashanah from the story of Abraham's dealings with Abimelekh and the Philistines? The answer is to be sought in the prayers of Rosh Hashanah which express the age-old Jewish yearning for peace, good-will and cooperation among men and nations. The account of Abraham's efforts to make peace even with those who had wronged him is most appropriate, seen in this light. Abraham was not an "appeaser" by nature. When the occasion demanded, he fought manfully for the right. But when, as in this case, an honorable peace was possible, he did not hesitate to seek it out. His example has served as an inspiration to later Jewish generations.

A beautiful *midrash* on Abraham's dealings with Abimelekh sheds further light on the moral stature of our first patriarch. The Torah narrates that Abimelekh, who had evil intentions upon the lovely Sarah, was stricken by God with severe illness. Abraham then prayed for Abimelekh's recovery. Shortly afterwards, Sarah's fervent prayers for a child were answered. The Talmud comments: "Whoever implores God's compassion in behalf of his fellow-man, will have his own need filled when he requires it."[23]

The Maftir מפטיר

The reading in the second scroll is from the book of Numbers, Chapter 29, verses 1-6. There (and in the previous chapter) we find a catalogue of all the festivals observed in Biblical times with particular emphasis on the sacrificial ritual for each occasion.[24] For "the first day of the seventh month" (later called Rosh Hashanah) there is a total of ten offerings for which the Midrash finds mystical parallels in the Ten Days of Penitence, the Ten Sayings by means of which the world was created, the Ten Commandments, etc. This reading is repeated on the second day.

There are many who see no point in continuing readings such as this in view of the fact that the sacrificial system has been obsolete in Judaism for 1900 years. There is an element of embarrassment for the primitive tone of such verses. (Even Maimonides interpreted the cult of animal sacrifice as a concession by Moses to the tastes of his own period.) Instructive, then, is the wise observation of Isaac Arama, eminent Jewish thinker of medieval Spain and author of the influential Torah commentary, *Akaydat Yitzḥak*: "If we have a true understanding of the Jewish religion, then not one iota of religious practice has ever been abandoned. The sacrifices have ceased but the *idea* of sacrifices has never ceased."

From Talmudic times down to the last century, the majority of Jewish children received their first impressions of Jewish literature through the opening chapters of the book of Leviticus that deal exclusively with the sacrificial system. This practice has been ridiculed by modern pedagogues, a situation which elicited this delightful rebuttal from Solomon Schechter:

> The Jew of ancient times was not given to analysis. Seizing upon its bold features, he saw in the Book of Leviticus only the good message of God's reconciliation with man, by means of sacrifice and of purity in soul and body. Perceiving, on the other hand, in every babe the budding minister "without taint of sin and falsehood," the Rabbi could certainly render no higher homage to childhood than when he said, "Let the pure come and busy themselves with purity." Every school thus assumed in his eyes the aspect of a holy Temple, in which the child by his reading performed the service of an officiating priest.[25]

Another beautiful interpretation of the spiritual significance of the sacrificial worship is given by the Midrash. It reminds us that the animals offered up are tame, from among the persecuted and not the persecutors, just as Israel is among the persecuted rather than the persecuting peoples. Scripture states, "God seeks that which is pursued" (Ecclesiastes 3:15). The Midrash comments: "God always avenges the innocent blood of the pursued from the pursuers

. . . therefore offer not unto Me the persecutors but the persecuted."[26]

The Rolling of the Scrolls גלילה

Ordinarily, after we have read from the scrolls of the Torah they are rolled, their vestments are replaced and we return them to the Ark. On Rosh Hashanah, however, in all rites, the Torah scrolls are kept on the pulpit until after the Shofar is sounded. One reason for this exception was given by a Jewish preacher (the Vilna Ḥarif) who compared the Torah to a devoted mother of Israel. Just as a mother wishes to stand by her children in time of danger, so the Torah desires to be present at the Shofar sounding when Israel is judged and the "satanic prosecutor" demands the extreme penalty for us. By its presence, the Torah offers testimony in our defense (see THE SHOFAR IN JEWISH FOLKLORE AND SUPERSTITION, in Chapter Six.)

The Haftarah for the First Day הפטרה

The Reading from the Prophets *(Haftarah)* for the first day of Rosh Hashanah is taken from the book of I Samuel, Chapters 1 and 2. Like the Pentateuch reading, it deals with the birth of a child. Hannah, wife of Elkanah, had suffered the sorrow of barrenness for many years before her prayers for a son were granted. Talmudic legend has it that Hannah like Sarah was "remembered" and that she conceived on Rosh Hashanah.[27] She then fulfills her vow to "lend" her child, Samuel, to God that he might consecrate himself to the service of religion. Like Sarah, Hannah manifests grave concern for the spiritual welfare of her child, and her concern was ultimately rewarded. The boy Samuel later became one of the great leaders and religious teachers of Israel, numbered among the Prophets. A contemporary scholar has drawn an interesting parallel between the Torah reading and the *Haftarah*: in the story of Abraham, man performs and God promises; in the story of Hannah, it is man — actually a woman — who promises and God who performs (Theodor H. Gaster).[27a]

The second half of the *Haftarah* consists of a moving prayer of thanksgiving which Hannah offered to God for the blessing of motherhood. It is a passionate avowal of God's providential care and a conviction that brute power and vast wealth are powerless against God's righteousness and justice. Some commentators consider this latter half of the *Haftarah* more significant for Rosh Hashanah than the former.[28] The Talmud connects the nine-fold praise of God's name uttered by Hannah with the nine benedictions of the Musaf *Amidah*.[29]

The *Haftarah* suggests the vital thought that the future of Judaism in the modern world is largely in the hands of the Jewish mother. It is she who determines in the main whether or not the home shall be permeated with a wholesome Jewish atmosphere. She can inculcate in the child a love for the Synagogue and Jewish learning, or — by her indifference and neglect — render a nascent love stillborn. And the mother can never begin too early: "Hannah brought her child to the house of the Lord while he was young" (adapted from Morris Silverman).

A contemporary preacher, David Aronson, has observed that the Scriptural readings for Rosh Hashanah mention three women who wept over their fate: Hagar, Hannah and Rachel (the latter in the *Haftarah* for the second day). When Hagar saw her son Ishmael gasping for water, she said, "Let me not look upon the death of the child," and she wept. When Rachel (in Jeremiah's vision) saw her descendants being led off into exile, she wept bitterly "because they were no longer." Hannah, too, wept over her childlessness; but she neither closed her eyes to the tragedy, as Hagar did, nor did she content herself with tearful reminiscences of the "good old days" when her children were round about her, as Rachel did. Instead of lamenting, Hannah acted. Not only did she obtain a child for herself, but she was instrumental in providing her people with a great leader. Rabbi Aronson sees reflected in this homily various types of Jewish parents today and urges that the example of Hannah be emulated.[30]

Pentateuch Reading for the Second Day קריאה

Few chapters of the Bible have had a more lasting influence upon both Judaism and its daughter religions than this twenty-second chapter of Genesis — the *Akaydah* or Binding of Isaac. Its inner meaning is basic to the religious development of both the Judaic and Christian faiths and it also plays a significant role in Islam (some Moslem theologians even substitute Ishmael, the progenitor of Mohammed, for Isaac in the story). The *Akaydah* is prominent in the classical liturgy of the Church and is found in Moslem worship, as well; but in the Jewish liturgy it attained its greatest prominence, especially during the Middle Ages, when the career of Israel provided such a graphic commentary to the Biblical narrative. The Mishnah does not associate the Binding of Isaac with Rosh Hashanah; but, by the third century, this association is clearly made. From that time on, the theme of the *Akaydah* permeates the liturgy of Rosh Hashanah.[31]

Many important religious ideas grow out of this chapter. The most familiar — and popular — for the modern Jew is the fact that God did *not* allow Abraham to harm his son. God chooses the most forceful method of demonstrating to Abraham and his posterity that He abhors the human sacrifices which were a regular feature of the pagan religions of the time. The Talmud makes this point very forcefully,[32] although it is not the primary lesson of the *Akaydah* in Jewish tradition. Hermann Cohen pointed out that the incident is never called by the Hebrew word for "sacrifice" *(korban* or *hakravah)* but *akaydah,* "binding" (of Isaac upon the altar). This chapter then marks a milestone in the evolution of religion from primitive barbarism to a lofty spiritual relationship between man and God.

This rationalist level of interpretation, however, by-passes the tragic dimensions of the *Akaydah* narrative, reducing its grandeur and epic proportions. The Talmudic sages, no less than more recent generations, were troubled by the moral and theological dilemma raised by the "test" with which a just God confronted Abraham. If human sacrifice is immoral by its very nature, how can God's demand be considered a religious one? Little wonder that a medieval moralist, Menaḥem Meiri, commented: "This is one of the most perplexing matters in the entire Torah."[33] The dominant meaning of the *Akaydah* in the Rabbinic tradition is the "existential" lesson: the Jew of faith must be prepared like Abraham (and — according to the Midrash — like Isaac as well) to make supreme sacrifices to validate his faith — even when God's will appears incommensurate not only with man's reasoned intelligence but even with his ethical values and moral conscience.[34] " . . . Abraham silently, and under pain hardly grasped to its full extent, bore the brunt of a hardly bearable destiny. He goes ahead silently and tries to do his task without the slightest sign of self-assuredness, as sincere men in the most difficult moments of their lives always had to tread their paths alone — without knowing where the journey to Moriah would lead, with a heavy heart and even with a gnashing of teeth . . . Isaac's fate is characteristic of a situation laden with symbolic significance: that in which one is crushed as a blameless victim in a great moral conflict whose nature is entirely beyond one's grasp" (David Baumgardt).[35]

What is religion in essence if not that which we consider "holy," that is, so supremely significant that we are willing to make the ultimate sacrifices for it? As a people, the Jews have had no equal in their willingness to make supreme sacrifices for their faith. "Abraham's readiness to sacrifice his most sacred affections on the altar of his God evoked and developed a new ideal in Israel, the ideal of *martyrdom* . . . As persecution deepened during later centuries, the Binding of Isaac was ever in the mind of men and women who might at any moment be given the dread alternative of apostasy or death" (Joseph H. Hertz). Shalom Spiegel has traced the concept of the *Akaydah* as it was refracted through the many-faceted prism of Jewish suffering for which it became a historic symbol. One historic community after another interpreted the *Akaydah* in the light of its own harrowing trials, some of which — in their tragic outcome — far exceeded the mental anguish of Abraham and Isaac.[36]

Allusions to the *Akaydah* early found their way into the liturgy and in time a large number of *piyyutim* grew up around the episode. (Many phrases have been transferred from the Rosh Hashanah service to the daily morning service to accompany the recital of the

Akaydah, which is found in many daily rites.) There is even a *piyyut* celebrating the *Akaydah* attributed to Maimonides himself. Folk literature in Yiddish of the sixteenth and seventeenth centuries elaborated on the *Akaydah* story. To this day the theme inspires Jewish verse; H. Leivick, the distinguished Yiddish poet, for example, has composed a simple but moving *Akaydah* in a style reminiscent of *piyyut.* Uri Tzvi Greenberg plays upon the *Akaydah* theme in his Hebrew poem, "On Holy Steps," and Sh. Shalom has penned a cycle of *Akaydah* poems. This listing could be multiplied many times over.

Christian theological writing has also been markedly influenced by the so-called "sacrifice of Isaac" from the Gospels and Church Fathers to the currently influential religious existentialism of Soren Kirkegaard, to whom Abraham was "the Knight of Faith." Even psychoanalysis has found rich material in the ancient narrative — witness the recent work (by Erich Wellisch) "Isaac and Oedipus, A Study in Biblical Psychology and the Sacrifice of Isaac, the Akedah." According to an expert of the Library of Congress, there are more than 100,000 interpretations of the *Akaydah* in extant literature — "The fundamental distinctions between religion and ethics, laws of aesthetics, the nature of all moral and legal obligations, whole modern philosophies have come into being and have matured through an interpretation of these few lines of the Old Testament" (David Baumgardt).

The Levi Reading

לוי

The expression, "and they went both of them together," referring to Abraham and Isaac, occurs twice in the narration of their journey to the top of Mt. Moriah where the "sacrifice" was to take place. It is first used *before* Isaac learned the nature of the journey and again *after* he had been told that he is to be the offering. Familiar to all students of Rashi's classic commentary is the explanation that the repetition of the phrase indicated that Isaac went along with his father in spirit as well as in body. There can be no richer reward to a man's striving than to see his own flesh and blood take up his vision and join him in a common effort. "Happily we are not tested as was Abraham. No such sacrifices are required of us and our children. Perhaps if we as parents will give similar evidence of our loyalty and obedience to the teachings of our faith, our children will 'go on together' with us" (Louis L. Kaplan).

The Shelishi Reading שלישי

Why do we sound the horn of a ram on Rosh Hashanah? Rabbi Abbahu explained: "The Holy One, blessed be He says, 'Sound before me the horn of a ram in order that I may recall in your behalf the Binding of Isaac son of Abraham and I shall account it to you as if you had personally bound yourselves before Me.' "[37] The episode of the "ram caught in the thicket by its horns" furnishes the direct link between the Torah reading and Rosh Hashanah. In Rabbi Abbahu's statement we meet the familiar Jewish idea of *Zekhut Avot,* the "merit of the fathers."[38] Briefly, the doctrine refers to the extraordinary virtues of the Patriarchs (and, by extension, of our exemplary ancestors in general) whose surplus of righteousness is credited to the account of all Israel. When their posterity is in critical need, God often draws from this fund of merit to sway the balance of judgment in their favor. "In the traditional Jewish phraseology, the original virtue of the patriarchs is eternally redemptive and ensures the welfare of their descendants, even outweighing the latter's defects" (T. H. Gaster).[39]

The Ḥamishi Reading חמישי

Once again, in the last section of this Torah portion, we read of the birth of children. The reason for the inclusion of this prosaic passage is presumably the mention of Rebecca, who was destined to become the wife of the saintly Isaac. According to the Talmud, the three barren women, Sarah, Rachel and Hannah, all conceived on Rosh Hashanah.[40] The Sages interpreted Rosh Hashanah variously as the birthday of the Universe or as the day on which Man was created. Deeply embedded in the ideology of the festival is the hope for the rebirth of mankind through moral regeneration. Symbolic of such a regeneration is the raising up of a "new seed" of exemplary children. "In the child, God gives humanity a chance to make good its mistakes and fulfill its fondest dreams" (Mordecai M. Kaplan).

The Haftarah for the Second Day הפטרה

The Prophetic portion for the second day is taken from the book of Jeremiah, Chapter 31, verses 2-20. Jeremiah is faced with the heart-breaking task of comforting his fellow Judeans after the destruction of their holy Temple and the exile of leading elements of the population to Babylonia. He paints a dramatic picture of the exiles streaming past the historic tomb of Rachel at Ramah on the road to Babylonia. Rachel weeps disconsolately for her homeless children.[41] God comforts her, however, in some of the most moving verses of Scripture, and promises to restore His penitent people to their own border.

The climax of the touching scene comes when the prophet casts Ephraim (a synonym for Israel) in the role of a prodigal son who has transgressed against his loving father (the Almighty). When the child repents of his errors, the forgiving father gathers him once again unto his yearning heart. This masterful figure is repeated later in the *Zikhronot* prayer of the Musaf service and has become a favorite motif of Jewish folk culture. The Biblical theme, "as a father pitieth his children," recurs again and again in the High Holy Day services. The brilliant Biblical scholar, Arnold Ehrlich, observed that the father-child relationship, unlike the husband-wife relationship which the prophets elsewhere ascribe to God and Israel, is indissoluble. The affection of God for His "precious son, Ephraim" is also reminiscent of Abraham's love for Isaac ("your son, your only son, Isaac, whom you love") but the parallel with the Torah reading is to be found rather in the theme of "Remembrance" *(Zikhronot)*. The act of remembrance is performed by each of the partners to the Covenant: God remembers His debt to Israel for the sake of its trust and devotion, and Israel remembers that only by virtue of this devotion is it entitled to claim the favor of God.

In this *Haftarah,* there is a strong emphasis on "return" and "repentance." Both words are represented by *teshuvah* in Hebrew:

"turn Thou me from evil and I shall return . . . surely my exile led me to repent . . . " This marks the selection as highly appropriate for Rosh Hashanah, the occasion *par excellence* for *teshuvah.*

In the light of recent history, it is probable that the contemporary worshipper will be impressed most by the verses, " . . . and they shall come back from the land of the enemy . . . thy children shall return to their own border." These prophetic words have been fulfilled in epic proportions before our eyes. The Zionist movement, on the one hand, and the persecution of tyrants, on the other, combined to restore to their ancestral borders hundreds of thousands of Jews who had been dispersed in "the land(s) of the enemy." Moreover, many Jewish artists, intellectuals and men of affairs have reacted to their people's epic martyrdom and rebirth by returning to the spiritual fold of Israel, if not to its soil.

Many gifted but alienated sons of Israel won great renown among the nations in their chosen fields, only to suffer disillusionment and to return to serve their own folk and faith. Theodor Herzl, urbane journalist, Moses Hess, the Marxist, and Max Nordau, critic of Europe's decadent civilization, became leaders of the new Zionist movement. Franz Rosenzweig turned his philosophic gifts from Hegel to Torah and helped a bewildered generation of German Jews to re-accept their Jewish heritage; his influence is latterly being felt in American Jewish circles once far removed from the ancestral faith.

Walter Rathenau, the brilliant statesman of Weimar Germany, who had rebelled against Judaism in his youth, toward middle age took up the study of Hebrew and began a return to the faith of his fathers, guided by the master theologian, Martin Buber. Shortly before his murder by Nazi thugs, Rathenau wrote: "After an estrangement of twenty years, I am back with my people. I have come to be one of them again, to participate in the celebration of the holidays, to share the memories and hopes of a nation, to take part in the spiritual and intellectual warfare going on within the house of Israel, on the one hand, and between our own people and the surrounding civilized world on the other."

Of Max Nordau's return to Jewish loyalties, his gifted daughter has written:

I shall never forget the day, so strange to me, when I saw my father, the author of "Conventional Lies," the atheist, carrying the Scrolls of the Law, his shoulders wrapped in the *tallith.* The small Jewish community in the Spanish capital had obtained — not without difficulty — the right to open a synagogue in a back yard. They asked father to inaugurate it and he consented as a token of solidarity, as a step toward unity among the Jews. The long-forgotten words of prayer came back to his lips and in his innermost soul there must have been a deep gratitude for that unique moment of communion.

The Sermon on Rosh Hashanah דרשה

The Rabbi's sermon is to be delivered, according to custom, either immediately preceding the sounding of the Shofar[41a] or immediately following. The emphasis is not on homiletical skill but on moving the hearts of the worshippers to thoughts of *teshuvah,* penitence and return.[42] A favorite theme is the *Akaydah*, the Binding of Isaac. Another tradition suggests that the sermon on the first day deal with the theme of *Yom Ha-Din,* The Day of Judgment, and on the second day with the sounding of the Shofar. This order is preferable because the first day may fall on Shabbat, when the Shofar is not blown, whereas the second day never does (the calendar is so fixed by tradition that Rosh Hashanah never begins on a Sunday, Wednesday or Friday).[43]

In Eastern Europe, rabbis made their appearance in the pulpit for formal addresses only on rare occasions, such as *Shabbat Ha-Gadol,* before Pesaḥ, and *Shabbat Shuvah,* between Rosh Hashanah and Yom Kippur. Many rabbis were reluctant to preach and chastise in the prophetic vein; many sincere and humble scholars felt unworthy of such a role. Even the light of his age, Elijah Gaon of Vilna, felt the need of inviting a preacher like the Maggid of Dubno to come to his private study to speak words of *Mussar* (chastisement). A renowned Ḥasidic rabbi would post a critic in the audience to stop him if he said anything unworthy of his followers.[43a] In view of this scrupulous regard for humility in preaching, we can understand the words of Rabbi Pinḥas of Koretz when his glance fell upon the pulpit: "This pulpit too is judged on Rosh Hashanah — whether it is to break or to be preserved."[44]

CHAPTER SIX

THE SOUNDING OF THE SHOFAR

- TEKIAT SHOFAR
- THE SHOFAR AS A MUSICAL INSTRUMENT
- RULES FOR THE SHOFAR AND THE TEKIOT
- INTERPRETATIONS OF THE SHOFAR SOUNDS
- THE SHOFAR AND THE ETHICAL LIFE
- THE SHOFAR AS A SYMBOL OF JEWISH UNITY
- THE SHOFAR AS A SYMBOL OF JEWISH UNIQUENESS
- THE SHOFAR AS A SYMBOL OF THE JEWISH WILL TO LIVE
- THE SHOFAR AS THE AUTHENTIC VOICE OF THE SPIRIT
- THE SHOFAR AS ISRAEL'S MOST EFFECTIVE WEAPON
- THE SHOFAR AS A SYMBOL OF REDEMPTION
- THE SHOFAR IN JEWISH FOLKLORE AND SUPERSTITION

THE SOUNDING OF THE SHOFAR

Tekiat Shofar — תקיעת שופר

The Sounding of the Shofar is the oldest, most colorful and best-known ritual of Rosh Hashanah. The Torah does not mention the word *shofar* in connection with Rosh Hashanah, but neither does it mention the name *Rosh Hashanah*. Rabbinic tradition, however, early fixed the instrument implied in the phrases "Day of *Teruah*" (Numbers 29:1) and "Memorial of *Teruah*"[1] (Leviticus 23:24) as the Shofar and no other instrument.[2]

The actual ritual for *Tekiat Shofar* in the Maḥzor, though moving in its simplicity, is exceptionally brief when compared to the total worship service. Yet nothing short of a complete work could hope to do justice to the vast store of rules and regulations, customs and folklore, homilies and parables, poems and anecdotes that have accumulated through the centuries around the Shofar theme.[3] The following notes purport to do no more than summarize some of this material in the hope of indicating how the Shofar has become a symbol of the Jewish people, their historical experience and their highest aspirations, as well as the vehicle of popular folklore and wisdom.

The Shofar as a Musical Instrument

Fundamental to all the vast literature and lore of the Shofar is the fact that it was originally a simple musical instrument. Next to the shepherd's reed or flute, this crude instrument, made by boring a narrow passage through an animal's horn,[4] is probably the oldest musical instrument still in use. Moreover, in most synagogues throughout the world it is the only musical instrument ever employed in worship. As the musicologist, Peter Gradenwitz, points out, "The flute, the lyre, and the drum — none of them strong in sound — were the instruments of the people and were used to accompany their songs. The ram's horn and the trumpet, on the other hand, were the shrill and resounding instruments of Israel's cult: they point to a still primitive stage in the worship of the Lord. The trumpet, used in pairs in accordance with the most ancient belief in the power of symmetry, fulfills the task ascribed to it in all primitive communities, namely to remind God of his people in worship as well as in war (Numbers 10:1-2, 9-10)."[5]

In the Torah, the metal trumpet *(ḥatzotzerah)* is specified for the blowing of the two sounds, *tekiah* and *teruah*. The tenth chapter of Numbers describes situations in war and peace when trumpets were to be blown, and records a veritable code of trumpet calls. The most important for our purposes is the proclaiming of holy convocations, not only Shabbat and Festivals but also the New Moon *(Rosh Ḥodesh)*, for in Biblical times — unlike today — *Rosh Ḥodesh* partook of the nature of a festival. One of these New Moons, that of the seventh month, (significant also as the month of the autumnal equinox) was eventually distinguished as the New Year.[6] In the Temple of Jerusalem, as the Mishnah tells us,[7] sounds from the two trumpets were augmented by those of the Shofar to call up "a memorial" before the Lord on Rosh Hashanah. The Shofar sounded the long notes and the trumpets the short ones. This practice was derived from the coronation ritual of Israelite kings; in this instance, it is the Kingship of God which is proclaimed (see Psalms 98:6).[8]

In his careful analysis of the Biblical and Rabbinic sources that deal with the Shofar and the *ḥatzotzerah*, Sol B. Finesinger[9] concludes that, almost without exception, the passages in which the Shofar occurs belong to the earlier rather than the later strata of the Bible, while the *ḥatzotzerah* is almost never mentioned in these early passages. The Shofar is an instrument used by, and associated with, the life of the people. It generally has the effect of frightening its hearers; in some instances, it seems to be used to frighten away evil spirits or powers. The *ḥatzotzerah*, on the other hand, is used almost exclusively by the priests, and generally in connection with the Temple ritual. In the later Biblical passages, it is used for several purposes for which we find the Shofar used in earlier passages. Thus, it appears that the popular instrument (the Shofar) was displaced by the priestly ritualistic one (the *ḥatzotzerah*) as part of the centuries-old struggle between priestly and popular forces.

The problem of the relationship of the two instruments to one another is further complicated by the fact that, in the two passages of the Mishnah (Rosh Hashanah 3:3 and 3:4) where the Shofar is used in conjunction with the *ḥatzotzerah,* the Shofar is not the ordinary popular instrument but one adapted for Temple use by having its bell (i.e., mouthpiece) covered with gold, for Rosh Hashanah use, and with silver, for use on public fast days. But the displacement of the popular Shofar by the priestly trumpet was not destined to be a permanent one. The later (i.e., Talmudic) traditions for Rosh Hashanah and Yom Kippur do not know the use of the *ḥatzotzerah* at all. This would tend to show that its use disappeared after the destruction of the Temple in the year 70 C.E. and only the Shofar was used on Rosh Hashanah. Thus the triumph of the popular instrument is complete, and has remained so down to the present day, in spite of efforts in some quarters to substitute a more refined musical instrument for the Shofar in the New Year worship service.

The Bible offers eloquent testimony to the widespread use of the Shofar as a musical instrument. The sounding of the ram's horn at Joshua's siege of Jericho and at Gideon's rout of the Midianites is familiar to all, but the Shofar was also blown to proclaim the advent of peace (II Samuel 2:28). The Shofar was used throughout Biblical times to warn the people of danger.[10] The book of Nehemiah (4:14) records a dramatic instance of such usage. It was similarly employed to proclaim occasions of national humiliation (Joel 1:15). From such direct usages the prophets derived the symbolic meaning of the Shofar as a warning to the sinner to repent of his evil ways and to return to God's commandments before the day of retribution.[11]

The early use of the ram's horn to proclaim the reign of a new Israelite king[12] strongly influenced the liturgy of Rosh Hashanah.

The coronation theme looms large in the traditional Shofar sounding ceremony. The *tekiot,* divested of the crude and grotesque features found among pagans, commemorate the annual re-creation of the universe by the Eternal who reigns over it. In our liturgy, we recite the 47th Psalm to introduce the *tekiot,* with special emphasis on the verse, "God has gone up with the (sound of) *teruah*, the Lord with the Shofar sound." This Psalm may have been sung in the Temple on Rosh Hashanah;[13] it proclaims the coronation of God as King over all the nations. The Sovereignty of God is one of the major themes reiterated in the prayers of Rosh Hashanah; here we see its Biblical origins.

The Shofar was also blown in ancient Israel on Yom Kippur to signal the advent of the Jubilee year (Leviticus 25:9). Indeed, only by analogy with this law did Rabbinic tradition establish the Shofar as the proper instrument implied by the term *teruah* in the Torah passages concerning "the first day of the seventh month."[14] Many other usages are described in Rabbinic literature, some of which will be discussed later: to stir the people to repentance on fast days,[15] to proclaim the ban of excommunication,[16] and to proclaim the New Moon at the court of the Sanhedrin.[17]

Rules for the Shofar and the Tekiot

The Shofar may be made from the horn of any kosher animal except the cow or ox. Two reasons are given. First, the horn of the latter is called *keren* rather than *shofar.* The second explanation is homiletical, and more cogent: the cow and the ox are reminiscent of the Golden Calf and "the prosecutor (the idolatrous animal) cannot be made into a defense counsel."[18] In any case, a ram's horn is preferred because of its association with the Binding of Isaac, for whom a ram was substituted upon the altar.[19]

The minimum size for a Shofar is six inches, the average is ten to twelve. Some Oriental Jews use horns as much as four feet long! There is usually a simple curve to the horn though the Sephardim prefer a spiral curve. The Shofar may not be painted, but it may be gilded, and designs may be carved upon it so long as the natural sound is not changed thereby in any way. The ceremonial Shofar used in the Temple of Jerusalem on Rosh Hashanah had its mouthpiece covered with gold.[20]

By forcing the breath through the narrow passage three distinct notes may be blown on the Shofar, though the pitch and quality vary from instrument to instrument because of its primitive nature. Known collectively as *tekiot,* these notes are specifically: *tekiah,* a deep, unbroken sound ending abruptly; *shevarim,* a series of three broken sounds totalling the length of a *tekiah;* and *teruah,* a wavering sound made up of nine staccato tones equivalent in length to a single *tekiah.* A brief discussion of the musical structure may be found in the Jewish Encyclopedia, Volume XI, under the heading, "Shofar." The three notes are indicated respectively by the Hebrew letters: *tav, shin,* and *resh.* The Mishnah ordains that on Rosh Hashanah we are to sound "three blasts, thrice repeated," i.e., each of the three notes is to be sounded as an accompaniment to the three major prayers: *Malkhuyot, Zikhronot,* and *Shofarot.*[21]

The development of these three sounds is complex. The Biblical texts (Leviticus 23:24, Numbers 29:1) speak only of *teruah* for the first day of the seventh month. By analogy with the Shofar blasts at the Jubilee year (Leviticus 25:9) the Talmud ordains that the *teruah* shall be sounded thrice. It is further ordained that each *teruah* be preceded and followed by a simple *tekiah.* The exact nature of the Biblical *teruah,* however, was obscure to later generations and both our present *shevarim* and *teruah* represent attempts to approximate it.[22] The *tekiah* is variously combined with the other two sounds until a total of thirty notes has been blown. The final *tekiah* of this series is considerably prolonged and is therefore called *tekiah gedolah* (great *tekiah*). The number thirty is probably taken from the Temple ritual for the *tekiot* at the New Moon.[23]

Nor is this the entire story, for there is more than one series of thirty sounds. Once again the historical development is a complex one. Following the old Rabbinic tradition that it is meritorious to perform a *mitzvah* as early as possible, the Shofar was originally blown at dawn.[24] In the Synagogue service, the Shofar sounding originally took place in the *Amidah* of Shaḥarit. However, because of certain historical events, alluded to in the Talmud,[25] the Patriarch Rabban Simeon ben Gamaliel (II) in the second century ordained that the *tekiot* be postponed until the Musaf service. Roman occupation troops in Palestine on at least one Rosh Hashanah misconstrued the Shofar sounds as a call to revolt and slew many Jews. When, however, the Romans observed how the Jews would pray for a considerable period before blowing their Shofar, they were apparently convinced of the peaceful nature of its ritual use.

The events vaguely described in the Talmud were explained by Rashi and other commentators as referring to the Hadrianic persecution of the second century; but Jacob Mann[26] has shown that this can hardly be the case since, at that time, not only the sounding of the Shofar was prohibited but the whole Synagogue service as well. In his opinion, the situation referred to is the period immediately following the death of the Emperor Hadrian (138 C.E.) "when the rigor of the persecution was relaxed and the local Roman authorities would allow the Jews in certain pacified areas to resume their religious practices while in other places, still under the suspicion of harboring some turbulent elements of the population, watchfulness was still maintained." In either case, even after this period of danger had passed, the postponement of the Shofar sounding to the Musaf service was retained, as it is to this day.

Since, however, Musaf is the last section of the service, an earlier series of thirty sounds was ordained to follow the Reading of the Torah. That is our present practice. It is, moreover, at these earlier *tekiot* that the prescribed benedictions are recited; once having been said, they cannot be repeated at the Musaf *tekiot*. Nevertheless, the latter are deemed the more important *ritually*, since it is only in Musaf that the three special prayers for Rosh Hashanah — *Malkhuyot, Zikhronot* and *Shofarot* — have been recited since Talmudic times; and they were clearly intended to accompany and interpret the meaning of the *tekiot*.[27]

The *tekiot* of Musaf are called *Tekiot* [*d*-] *Me'umad* (i.e., *tekiot* to be sounded while standing) because they are sounded during the *Amidah*, the "standing prayer." Some communities still follow the Kabbalistic practice, introduced by Isaac Luria, of sounding thirty *tekiot* at the corresponding points during the silent recitation of the *Amidah* as well. The *tekiot* of Shaḥarit are designated *Tekiot* [*d*-] *Meyushav* (i.e., *tekiot* to be sounded while seated) because the worshippers are not obligated to stand for them. In practice, however, everyone stands for these early *tekiot* as well as the later ones.

A final development was to sound a number of *tekiot* at the conclusion of the entire service in order to complete a total of one hundred *(may'ah kolot)*.[28] There are many slight variations in the order and number of the *tekiot* from one rite or locality to another. However, the basic procedure is the same everywhere.

The Shofar is blown only by day and only by one trained in the art, a *Ba'al Tokay'a,* also referred to as *Ba'al Tekiah* or simply *Tokay'a.* The earlier *tekiot* may be sounded by the Reader of the prayers but not those of Musaf, for he must give his complete attention to his chanting of the Musaf prayer service. In most instances the ritual is performed from the *bimah*, the locale of the Torah reading; some communities, however, permit the lesser *tekiot* (e.g., on the second day) to be blown by the *Ba'al Tokay'a* at his seat. There is generally only one such expert — unless his inability to produce the prescribed notes necessitates a replacement;[29] but some divide the Musaf *tekiot* among several dignitaries as a recognition of their love for the performance of the *mitzvah.* The officiant stands, though some rites permit him to sit between certain divisions of a long series of *tekiot.*[30]

It is traditional for the *Ba'al Tokay'a* to wear a *Kittel,* which is simply a white gown reminiscent of the ancient Palestinian festive garb. The Shofar is concealed until the moment of sounding the *Tekiot.*[31] The *Ba'al Tokay'a* recites the two benedictions in a traditional chant. At this point the sounds prescribed by tradition are announced one by one by the Rabbi or a congregant familiar with the proper procedure. The purpose of having this *Makri* (Prompter) is simply to avoid error. This practice itself goes back to the Temple service.[32]

The text of the Shofar ceremony varies but slightly in the different rites although as early as Talmudic times there is dissent over the wording of the Shofar benediction.[33] The accepted text *lishmo'a kol shofar,* "to hear the sound of the Shofar" (an echo of Jeremiah 4:21) emphasized the role of the worshipper as well as that of the officiant.[34] The emphasis on "hearing" rather than "blowing" implies taking to heart the message of the Shofar. The benediction *She-heḥeyanu,* which one recites at the initial performance of a commandment prescribed for special occasions, follows.

Both benedictions are confined to the earlier *Tekiot* [*d-*] *Meyushav,* the sounds blown at the end of Shaḥarit; once having been recited, they are not repeated for the later *tekiot.*

In some rites, *piyyutim* are recited before the *tekiot.* More widespread is the recitation of appropriate verses from the Psalms both before and after the Shofar is sounded in this early series. The seven-fold recitation of the entire 47th Psalm as a prelude and the use of meditations between groups of *tekiot* are customs introduced by mystics like Isaac Luria and Jacob Emden. Rationalist authorities (like the Vilna Gaon) strongly and characteristically objected to such interruptions of the simple statutory prayers. Mystical considerations aside, the 47th Psalm is highly appropriate for Rosh Hashanah by virtue of its content alone. As Finesinger points out,[35] "Though we cannot determine with certainty the occasion of the psalm, the context clearly portrays the Kingship of God. In view of this and of the functions associated with His kingship — His subduing the nations, His sitting on the throne judging them as they are assembled around Him — it is likely that we have here a new year's psalm." The allusion in the Psalm to God's "ascending with the *teruah* . . . and the Shofar sound" most likely refers to His ascending the throne in order to render judgment. The sound of the Shofar is possibly intended to drive off Satan, the accuser, and thus insure a favorable verdict; it is this theme which especially attracted the mystics. Thus we find, in the meanings this Psalm has had for Jews, two notions about the Shofar, one primitive and the other advanced. The struggle between these two levels of meaning underlies the entire history of the Shofar in Jewish consciousness.

Luria also introduced the recitation after Psalm 47 (which contains God's name seven times) of seven additional verses from the Bible, beginning "*Min ha-maytzar* . . . out of the straits." The initial letters of the last six verses in this series spell out a mystical message, *KeRA SaTaN*, "cut off Satan (the accuser)."

Following the thirty *tekiot* after Shaḥarit, one or more verses from the Psalms — depending on the various rites — are recited. Common to all is the verse, "*Ashray ha-am yode'ay teruah* . . . happy is the people who know the sound of the trumpet blast" (Psalms 89:15).

The Shofar is sounded on the second day of Rosh Hashanah in

the same manner as on the first. If the first day is Shabbat (the second never is) the *tekiot* are postponed to the second. The Shofar is no longer sounded on Shabbat.[36] The ritual basis of this prohibition, as we shall see, is of minor importance; the main reason is historical. In ancient Palestine the Shofar was sounded on Shabbat only in the Temple and the city of Jerusalem and, after their destruction, only at the seat of the Great Sanhedrin — first in Yavneh and later in Galilee. When that supreme body went out of existence, the *tekiot* were suspended everywhere on the day of rest.[37] Accordingly, on Shabbat, the phrase *Yom Teruah* (Day of *Teruah*) is replaced in the prayers by the alternate Scriptural phrase *Zikhron Teruah* (Memorial of *Teruah*).

The purely legalistic explanation offered in the Talmud for the total cessation of Shofar sounding on a Rosh Hashanah which coincides with Shabbat leaves many questions unanswered. The reason given, namely, that some individual might carry the Shofar through the public domain (in search of an expert to instruct him in the proper technique) and thus violate the Shabbat, still does not explain why it could not have been sounded in the Synagogue. Finesinger[38] offers the following explanation, based on a historical approach to the Shofar ceremony: "Its use on the Shabbat was permitted in the Temple, because there it was a part of the ritual, probably the sacrificial ritual; and all acts connected with the sacrificial ritual were permitted on the Sabbath. But with the destruction of the Temple the necessity for this disappeared. Hence its use on the Sabbath was in time forbidden, or at least was not customary."

Finesinger also proposes an alternate explanation to that offered by the Talmud for the two names of Rosh Hashanah found in the Torah, *Yom Teruah* and *Zikhron Teruah*. Proceeding on the theory that the original Hebrew new year was on the *tenth* of the seventh month, he suggests that on this day, the day of the autumnal equinox, the Shofar was used to sound a *teruah,* perhaps as part of the popular sun-worship opposed by the priestly legislators. (It should be recalled that the only instance where the Torah specificially connects the words *shofar* and *teruah* is in Leviticus 25:9, which deals with the *tenth* day of the seventh month, the beginning of the Jubilee year.) When the *first* of the month became the day for the celebration of the new year, the priestly legislators did not immediately transfer the Shofar sounding (i.e., *teruah*) because they still hoped to suppress this vestige of the old sun-worship. But there lingered in the mind of the people a *zikaron,* i.e., a *memory* that a *teruah* had been part of a new year's celebration — the old one, of course, that used to be on the tenth. The *teruah* was not yet officially, at any rate, a ceremony of the new year's day. For this reason, the day was at first known as *Zikhron Teruah,* "Remembrance of the Shofar sound" (Leviticus 23:24). Sometime later, this first day of the month became known officially as *Yom Teruah*, "Day of the Shofar sound" (Numbers 29:1) and, since the *teruah* was now a recognized part of the ceremonies connected with the first day, the vague *Zikhron Teruah* was no longer used.

On Yom Kippur the Shofar is not sounded during the worship services except for a solitary *tekiah* at the close of the fast. The reasons for this practice will be discussed below, in the section THE SHOFAR AS A SYMBOL OF REDEMPTION.

The Shofar is also blown during the month of Elul as part of the preparation for the High Holy Day season. The practice is fancifully traced by the Midrash back to the days of Moses.[39] When he ascended Mt. Sinai to receive the second set of tablets of the Ten Commandments, the people sounded the Shofar to avoid falling again into the trap of idolatry, as they had during Moses's earlier ascension. Tradition has it that Moses went up on the first day of Elul and the Shofar was blown daily during his forty day sojourn until his return on Yom Kippur. The Shofar is not blown, however, on the eve of Rosh Hashanah, in order to distinguish between the voluntary *tekiot reshut* and the obligatory *tekiot mitzvah* of the New Year.

Interpretations of the Shofar Sounds

We have seen (in our discussion of THE SHOFAR AS A MUSICAL INSTRUMENT) that, in the early Biblical period, the sounding of the Shofar was intended to attract the attention of God so that He would listen to the entreaties of His people and deal kindly with them. Side by side with this religious interpretation, there existed the popular belief that these sounds had the power of frightening and repelling evil powers, however they may be conceived. The strength of these two viewpoints is not always the same; the more advanced explanation became the official one and is far more frequent in the ancient and medieval literature, but the popular belief persists throughout the long history of the Shofar. "Their relative strength is determined by the equilibrium of the forces of enlightenment and superstition — or, put otherwise, by the relative power of the more advanced, enlightened mind and of the more primitive, popular mind" (Sol B. Finesinger).

Attempts to ascribe symbolic significance to the notes of the ram's horn are as old as the prophets and singers of ancient Israel. They heard in the strange sounds, on the one hand, the Divine warning to the transgressor, both individual and collective, and, on the other, the triumphant proclamation of God's universal reign.

However, the roots of that luxurious flowering of homily and parable on the Shofar theme which spreads throughout Jewish thought and literature are found in the Talmud and Midrash. The clear *tekiah* is "simplicity" *(peshutah)* and contentment; the *teruah* is variously "the sound of wailing" and "the sound of moaning";[40] a third note, *shevarim*, is added to simulate the latter sound. The classic summary of the various meanings and interpretations of the Shofar sounds noted by the Sages and supported by Biblical texts was compiled by Saadiah Gaon in the tenth century. Originally a commentary on Leviticus 23:24,[41] these interpretations are preserved in the *Siddur* of Abudarham:[41a]

1. Rosh Hashanah is the anniversary of the creation of the world. On this day, God became the King of the Universe. Just as mortal kings are crowned to the accompaniment of Shofar blasts, so is the King of Kings.
2. Rosh Hashanah is the beginning of the Ten Days of Penitence. The Shofar is a last warning to make amends.[42]
3. The Shofar is a reminder of Israel's acceptance of the Torah at Mt. Sinai. It calls upon us to rededicate ourselves to the covenant of our fathers.
4. It reminds us of the chastisements of the Prophets Amos and Ezekiel whose warnings were often compared to the sound of the Shofar.
5. It reminds us of the destruction of the Temple which was

also accompanied by the sound of Shofars used in battle, and arouses our hopes of restoring the ancient glory.

6. It recalls to us the example of Isaac who was ready to offer himself upon the altar.
7. The sound of the Shofar is such that a fear seizes the hearer and he recalls his failings.
8. The Shofar announces the Day of Final Judgment.
9. It is the symbol, too, of the Messianic period which will be ushered in by "The Great Shofar." We should recall the prophetic promise of the ingathering of the exiles and strive toward that historic restoration of the people of Israel.
10. The Shofar, finally, reminds us of the resurrection of the dead and urges us to strengthen our faith in immortality.

Other philosophers and theologians have explored the Shofar theme for its universal and eternal aspects. The Alexandrian philosopher, Philo, sees a two-fold significance in the Shofar call. The first is a message specifically to Jews: to remind them of the Covenant made at the giving of the Law on Sinai when the Shofar sounded loud and clear (Exodus 19:16); this is, of course, the interpretation given in the *Shofarot* prayer in the Musaf service. The second applies universally: the Shofar, like a trumpet on the battlefield, reminds us of the eternal conflict between the constructive and destructive forces in both nature and human nature. It thus calls on all men to express gratitude to God who brings peace and reconciliation to both the natural and human orders.

Isaac Arama, author of the medieval homiletical classic, *Akaydat Yitzḥak,* sees in the three Shofar sounds varying approaches to three different types of people. The *tekiah* — simple and straightforward — is intended for the righteous, arousing emotions of strength, confidence and inner peace. The *teruah* — wailing and groaning — is aimed at the wicked, moving them to fear and trembling. The *shevarim* — broken and uncertain — is intended for the average person, neither saint nor sinner, who may find in the notes, as he chooses, a message of joy or grief, hope or despair.

The classic philosophical interpretation of the Shofar's sound is that of Maimonides:

Awake, ye sleepers; be aroused ye slumberers, and ponder

your deeds. Remember your Creator and go back to Him in penitence. Be not of those who miss reality in the search after shadows, and waste their years in seeking after vain things which cannot profit or deliver. Look well to your souls and consider your acts. Forsake each of you his evil ways and thoughts, and return to God so that He may have mercy upon you.[42a]

The medieval mystics and Kabbalists let their fancies take flight on the soaring Shofar sounds. Working especially with the Talmudic idea that the unearthly sounds of the Shofar are intended to confuse Satan, the "Prosecutor," when he comes before the Heavenly Court to accuse Israel,[43] the "seekers after secrets" endowed these same notes with specific powers to influence God and His angels on Israel's behalf. The Kabbalists and their spiritual heirs, the Ḥasidim, developed a complex array of secret meanings for each sound. An expert *Ba'al Tokay'a* was expected to be well versed in these interpretations which were called *kavanot*, meaning literally "intentions," i.e., concentration of thought. Great emphasis was placed on the mystical thoughts which occupied the mind of the *Ba'al Tokay'a* during the performance of the ritual; as the representative of the Congregation, he carried a weighty responsibility to aim his potent blasts well. Many old Maḥzorim abound at this point in petitions to various angels to carry the sounds before the Heavenly Throne.

Ḥasidic literature, too, is replete with imaginative and often moving parables concerning the Shofar and its sounds. The following is a splendid example of how an eighteenth century master of Aggadah built upon a theme of an ancient Palestinian predecessor. In the Talmud, Rabbi Abbahu asks, "Why do we blow on the horn of a ram? Because the Holy One, blessed be He, says to us: 'Blow before me on the horn of a ram in order that I may remember for you the Binding of Isaac son of Abraham and I shall deem it as if you had bound yourselves before me.' "[44] Rabbi Levi Yitzḥak of Berditchev, the Ḥasidic master, reflects the Talmudic homily in his own parable:

A king was once lost in a great forest for many years until no one remembered him at all. He begged the foresters to lead him back to his kingdom but none knew the way. One of them finally recognized the king and guided him home. There the clever forester persuaded the populace to resume their allegiance to the monarch. As a reward, the king appointed the guide as his chief minister and dressed him in royal robes. The forester accepted, on the condition that he be allowed to save his old clothing. The king was puzzled but he consented. Years later, the minister sinned against the king and was brought to trial for his life before his fellow courtiers who had always secretly hated and resented him. On the day of judgment, he appeared before the court in his old forest costume. The king was so moved by the memories aroused by the sight of these old clothes that he pardoned his erring minister and restored him to his good graces.

We Jews, explained Levi Yitzḥak, are like the peasant, for we have recognized the King of Kings. We alone took it upon ourselves to restore Him to His rightful position of sovereignty in a world which had forgotten Him. We alone knew the way of the king — the Torah. Of late, it is true, we have transgressed before Him and must appear for judgment. We are accused by our enemies and rivals but we ask mercy of the King, not for the sake of our own virtues which are so few but on the basis of *Zekhut Avot,* the merit of our ancestors. Symbolically, we put on our old clothes — in this case the Shofar, which was sounded at Sinai — in the hope that God will be moved by fond memories to render a merciful verdict on the Day of Judgment.

Even the barest sketch of the vast literature on the interpretation of the Shofar sounds must at least mention the modern commentators, in both the Old and New Worlds. The nineteenth century German rabbi and theologian, Samson Raphael Hirsch, saw allegorical meaning in the code of Shofar signals for the Israelite camp as preserved in the tenth chapter of Numbers.[45] The code indicates a *tekiah* (strong, even tone) to summon the scattered Israelites together; then a *teruah* (broken, wavering tone) for the breaking-up of the camp; finally another *tekiah* to signal the setting off together in a new direction. Hirsch derives timeless significance from these tones for the individual Jew: *tekiah* summons us to leave our diffused interests and self-centered purposes and to gather before the Lord. *Teruah* jars us into a rearrangement of our interests in accordance with the Divine will. The final *tekiah*, however, strengthens us to follow a new and even way of life before God leading to a better future.[46]

A fine summary of the Shofar's messages has recently been given by Theodor H. Gaster:

> The blowing of the ram's horn . . . was taken to recall those moments in Israel's history when it had heard, in more than a physical sense, the notes of the clarion. It recalled the trumpets and thunders at Sinai, sounds which . . . far from being a means of repelling hostile forces of nature, revealed their co-operative presence at the Giving of the Law and the Conclusion of the Covenant. Moreover, since, in Jewish teaching, memory always looks forward as well as backward, the blasts of the Shofar came . . . to pre-figure the great day when, as the prophet had foretold, God himself would drive out the power of darkness, "blow the ram's horn, and come with the whirlwinds" (Zechariah 9:14). Nor this alone; it was interpreted also as a symbol of the Last Trump and as the rallying call of Israel in its eternal battle for the Kingdom of God.[47]

The Shofar and the Ethical Life

Jewish moralists quickly seized upon the Shofar and the ritual of the *tekiot* for the purpose of expounding ethical teachings. As noted previously, the Talmud itself sets the tone when it forbids the use of the horn of cows and oxen for a Shofar on the grounds that this would be reminiscent of the Golden Calf — "The prosecutor cannot be made into a defense counsel."[48]

The Shofar is used in Jewish ethical literature metaphorically to designate a leader, especially one who claims to speak the word of God. The figure is taken from the Bible itself: God commands the prophet, "Lift up thy voice like a Shofar."[49] Consequently, rules and regulations originally ordained for a Shofar are transferred homiletically to rabbis, preachers and leaders generally.

The distinguished British scholar, A. Cohen, counsels students for the Rabbinate to apply the standards of a proper Shofar to their preaching: " . . . the Shofar should be *kafuf,* bent, curved. That may be taken as symbolic of a humble frame of mind . . . 'If it is split lengthwise it is unfit for use.' A preacher is similarly useless who is split-minded, who has not clear-cut views and definite convictions. 'If the Shofar was overlaid with gold, with the result that the original tone is changed, it is disqualified.' The application we may draw from these words is that the preacher must be independent. He must not allow his utterances to be affected by such an external influence as the power of gold . . . 'If the *Ba'al Tokay'a* reverses the Shofar and blows into it, he has not fulfilled the obligation.' He obviously acts in this way to make a parade of his extra-ordinary power and is not actuated by a pious motive. It is precisely the same with a preacher. He, too, must avoid what is vulgarly called 'showing off' in the pulpit."[50]

Homilies on the theme of sincere concentration as the prime requirement in sounding the Shofar are legion. One points out that the Shofar, being an unimproved wind instrument, possesses no inherent sound other than that imparted to it by the breath of the blower. Obviously, then, everything depends on the *Ba'al Tokay'a* himself and the purity of his motive. That is why he does not say in his benediction, " . . . to *sound* the Shofar," but " . . . to *hear* the sound of the Shofar." The Shofar sounder is not a performer. He has the same obligation as the humblest member of the Congregation to give heed to the sound and message of the Shofar.

Among the Ḥasidim it was considered the highest honor to be designated by one of the saintly Tzadikim (holy leaders of the Ḥasidic community) as his *Ba'al Tokay'a.* The founder of the movement, Israel Ba'al Shem Tov, once asked a disciple to prepare himself for the sacred task of sounding the Shofar. The student, Rabbi Wolf Kitzes, could not memorize the *kavanot*, proper intentions, and resorted to jotting down memoranda on slips of paper. But, when his great moment arrived and he put the Shofar to his fervent lips, the papers were nowhere to be found. With tear-filled eyes and trembling heart, the Ḥasid proceeded to sound the Shofar as best he could. Afterwards, the Master of the Good Name, Rabbi Israel, approached him with a smile of approval. "You have done well," he said. "You know that in a house of many rooms, many different keys are needed to open all the doors, but one good axe will open them just as well. Similarly, one broken and contrite heart will open the doors to God's Throne as well as a multitude of *kavanot.*"

In the same spirit is the anecdote told of Rabbi Levi Yitzḥak of Berditchev, one of the successors of the Ba'al Shem Tov. The Berditchever would often sound the Shofar himself, but one year he called for applicants to perform the sacred rite. Dozens of experts clamored for the honor. The Tzadik, Rabbi Levi, questioned each applicant as to his thoughts at the moment of sounding the Shofar, and each of them regaled the great saint with his erudition in all the veiled *kavanot.* But Levi Yitzḥak, unpredictable as always, was unimpressed. Then he noticed one Jew trying to make himself as inconspicuous as possible in the face of all this learning. "Who are you?" asked the Rabbi. "I am a *Ba'al Tokay'a* and I wish to sound the Shofar for you, Master," replied the shy one. The Rabbi inquired what intentions were in his mind when he sounded the Shofar and the humble Jew replied: "I do not know the secret *kavanot,* but I have four daughters, God bless them, and no money to give them for dowries. If I shall be selected to sound the Shofar, I shall ask the Holy One, blessed be He, to send me fine husbands for my poor girls." Rabbi Levi Yitzḥak looked no further.

The Shofar is a major element in the High Holy Day ritual, but those who would emphasize it to the exclusion of other basic *mitzvot* should ponder the following episodes.

When the saintly Chief Rabbi Kuk of Palestine was taken to the hospital in Jerusalem a few days before his death, during the month of Elul, 1935, he insisted on following the traditional practice of hearing the Shofar blown each morning of Elul. His physicians feared that the effects would be too much for his delicate condition but they were unable to dissuade him. Finally a colleague succeeded with the only plea capable of swaying the gentle Chief Rabbi — "The sound of the Shofar will affect the other patients." The dying man withdrew his request in the face of the greater *mitzvah* of consideration for the feelings of others.[51]

On a similar ethical plane is the story of the Ḥasid, Rabbi David of Liliov, who was spending Rosh Hashanah with his master, Rabbi Yaakov Yitzḥak, the Seer of Lublin. When the time came for sounding the Shofar, the Seer noticed that his distinguished guest was absent. It was inconceivable that the Shofar would be sounded before he was found. The searching party finally came upon Rabbi

David in the stable: the saint was busy feeding his horses. "The groom has gone to the synagogue to hear the Shofar," he explained calmly, "and no one was here to feed the horses." When Rabbi David finally came into the House of Prayer, the Seer said: "That was a fine sounding of the Shofar to which Rabbi David treated us!"

Once on Rosh Hashanah, Rabbi Levi Yitzḥak of Berditchev paused interminably with his Shofar in hand. When he saw that the worshippers were bursting with mixed impatience and curiosity, he chastened them with his explanation: "Dear friends, you have all completed your learned meditations preparatory to hearing the Shofar. Back there next to the door, however, is a poor, unlettered Jew who knows only the *alef-bet*. He is offering up his prayer letter by letter. I have delayed the sounding of the Shofar while the Almighty pieces together the prayers of this saintly man. We must wait until God is ready."

THE SHOFAR AS A SYMBOL OF JEWISH UNITY

Some scholars have derived the word *teruah* from the same root which gives the Hebrew language its word for "friend" *(ray'a)*. Tzvi Hirsch Masliansky, the famed Zionist orator, cited the opinion of a learned musician that the sound of the Shofar resembles the voice of a hen summoning her chicks to gather beneath her wings. Whether there is any validity to either of these theories is a matter for specialists, but both contain an element of truth.

The Shofar call was originally a summons for attention and group action. In the book of Nehemiah (4:14) there is a dramatic example of how the Shofar was employed in time of danger. The Governor, Nehemiah, armed his tiny band of Judaeans who were struggling to rebuild the wall of Jerusalem in the face of attacks by hostile native tribes, saying: "The work is great and large and we are separated upon the wall far from one another; wherever you hear the sound of the Shofar, hurry to that place to us; our God will fight for us."[52]

The Talmud tells us that the Shofar was used to summon the townspeople for Shabbat observance.[53] A similar practice is followed in the modern State of Israel, though a trumpet has been substituted for the Shofar. The prophet Isaiah foretold that a "great Shofar" would be sounded to herald the ingathering of Israel's scattered exiles when the Lord will redeem His people for all time (27:13).

But if the Shofar is to herald the redemption of a united people, it must, in turn, be preceded by a spirit of unity and brotherhood. The preachers of old noted that the prophet speaks of "*A* great Shofar" which the Talmud interprets correctly as, "One Shofar, says the Scripture, not two or three."[54] As long as there is a multiplicity of strident voices leading Jews in opposite directions, *Ge'ulah* (Redemption) will not come. On the other hand, even sincere, devoted and inspired leaders are not sufficient to produce a united and creative people. In this vein, the Chief Rabbi of Tel Aviv, Avigdor Amiel, explained why the blessing of the *Ba'al Tokay'a* ends with the words, "to *hear* the sound of the Shofar" rather than the more logical, "to *blow* the sound of the Shofar." He noted that we Jews have an abundance of "blowers," that is to say, visionaries and dreamers. What we need most is "listeners," people who will heed their inspired leaders and follow them.

The Shofar as a Symbol of Jewish Uniqueness

What is it about the Shofar that explains its hold upon the imagination of the Jew to the present day? Perhaps the secret lies in its very primitiveness and antiquity. Many musical instruments in ancient Israel were more melodious, more graceful and more prominent in the rituals of the Temple. Some of them — the shepherd's reed, the tambourine, the drum — were perhaps even more ancient than the Shofar. The difference is that while all of these instruments were improved according to the latest styles and techniques, the Shofar retained its archaic form and sound through the centuries. The Shofar became the symbol, among other things, of the unique historical experience of the people of Israel and of its spiritual destiny. "All good things come to Israel through the Shofar; and they will be apprised of the Messiah's coming through the Shofar sound; they conquered in battle (at Jericho) through the blast of the Shofar; they are summoned to repentance by the

Shofar; and they will be apprised of the Messiah's coming through the Great Shofar."[55]

The unique power of the Shofar was brilliantly pointed out by the gifted preacher, Tzvi Hirsch Masliansky. In one of his Rosh Hashanah sermons, he explains how as a child he was perplexed by the verse from the Psalms (89:15) which is recited after the sounding of the Shofar. It reads: "*Ashray ha-am yode'ay teruah* . . . Happy is the people that know the *teruah*." His *melamed*, or elementary teacher, was also the local *Ba'al Tokay'a* and used to blow his daily practice round every morning during the month of Elul. Unfortunately, Masliansky's teacher — like so many of his colleagues — was weak and sickly and could hardly coax the required notes out of the stubborn horn. Once a lusty Russian soldier, who had been quartered in the teacher's house, out of curiosity picked up the Shofar and sounded a tremendous blast. The child was chagrined: how can we Jews call ourselves "the people who know the sound of the *teruah*" when any strong non-Jew can do a better job than most saintly rabbis?

Years later, Masliansky discovered the answer. In the Mishnah, he learned the rule: "A person who is walking near a synagogue or lives close by and hears the Shofar being blown . . . if he directed his heart, he has fulfilled his obligation, but if not, he has not fulfilled his obligation. Though both may have heard, one heard it with a purpose and the other accidentally."[56] The important thing is not the skill of the blower but the sincere intention of both blower and listener.

The Shofar notes constitute a secret language of love by which Israel communicates its most intimate feelings to its adored God. Solomon Schechter reminded us that one does not have his love-letters written for him by strangers. The ancient Midrash anticipated the modern argument: "Is it possible that other peoples do not know how to sound the Shofar? Of course they do, but Jews know how to influence their Creator through their Shofar-sounding that He might forgive."[57]

THE SHOFAR AS A SYMBOL OF THE JEWISH WILL TO LIVE

Throughout Jewish history, the peal of the Shofar has testified to the Jewish will to survive in the face of every attempt at suppression. Even when forbidden to sound the Shofar, Jews always found a way. The Mishnah speaks of cases where it was necessary literally to take the Shofar underground: "If the Shofar was blown in a cistern or in a cellar or into a large jar . . . "[58] The authorities were forced to postpone the Shofar ritual of the Shaḥarit service until Musaf during the Roman persecutions (as we have seen in our discussion of RULES FOR THE SHOFAR AND THE TEKIOT). In the Middle Ages, whenever Jews were forbidden to blow the Shofar — as in Spain, Arabia and elsewhere — the *Ba'al Tokay'a* would often conceal himself in a pit or in a barrel or walk off into the fields so that the sound might be lost among the hills and valleys. In Yemen, Jews were for centuries forbidden to blow Shofar.

In Palestine itself, as late as 1946, Jews were still being arrested by British police for blowing the Shofar at the Wailing Wall in Jerusalem despite strict prohibition of public religious ceremonies at this site of Arab-Jewish friction. As a matter of fact, it was forbidden even to bring a religious object into the area under pain of heavy jail sentence. Yet each summer determined Jewish youths drew lots for the privilege of trying to outwit the police and smuggle the forbidden Shofar into the congested area at the end of Yom Kippur. Not a year went by without a successful attempt to sound the Shofar at Israel's holiest shrine on the most solemn of days. During the War of Liberation in 1948 the Wailing Wall, like the rest of the Old City of Jerusalem, fell into the hands of Arab Jordan. Nevertheless Jews continue each Yom Kippur to ascend nearby Mt. Zion, face the Western Wall and sound the Shofar. Indeed, on Rosh Hashanah of 1958 (5719), Israelis reported having heard the sounds of a Shofar coming from the Old City; it is presumed that this Shofar was sounded by British soldiers of the Jewish faith among the troops who had been rushed into Jordan during the preceding summer to bolster the regime of King Hussein.

When the new Republic of Israel was officially proclaimed on May 14, 1948, unprecedented celebrations were touched off all over the Jewish world and the Shofar played its part in some of these observances. When the Knesset, Israel's parliament, held its inaugural session, the arrival of President Chaim Weizmann to take the oath of office was heralded by the sounding of the Shofar; a similar rite marked the dedication of the new religious headquarters, *Haykhal Shelomo*, in 1958. Thus the ancient ram's horn has helped to mark a new epoch in the age-old struggle for the restoration of Israel and Torah to the ancestral homeland. No more appropriate symbol could have been found to give voice to the Jewish will to live as a free nation and to shape its own destinies as the "People of the Covenant."

The Shofar as the Authentic Voice of the Spirit

The Biblical account of the giving of the Torah at Sinai contains the verse: "And the sound of the Shofar went forth and waxed louder and exceedingly louder . . . " (Exodus 19:19). Israel H. Levinthal, contemporary exponent of Midrashic preaching, has interpreted the verse in the modern idiom. It is natural for a sound to weaken as it is held, but the sound of the Shofar increased in volume as it went forth. Obviously we are not dealing here with the laws of the material universe but rather with the laws of the spiritual life, which have their own validity. The voice of a spiritual ideal waxes more and more powerful and gains increasing influence as the years pass. Rabbi Levinthal's profound observation is reminiscent of the ancient Midrash[59] which held that one horn of Isaac's ram was reserved to be sounded on Mt. Sinai at the giving of the Torah; the other was destined to become the *Shofar shel Mashiaḥ*, the horn which in the fulness of time will proclaim the advent of the Messianic Age, when the life of the spirit will have its ultimate triumph.[60]

One of the most profound religious thinkers of our century was the late Chief Rabbi of Palestine, Abraham Isaac Kuk. He commented on the law in the Mishnah[61] which describes the sounding of the Shofar in the ancient Temple: "The Shofar at the New Year was made from the horn of the wild goat . . . and at the sides were two trumpets." The Shofar, he explained, is an instrument taken directly from nature and thus represents the *natural* unspoiled sanctity of life. The trumpets, on the other hand, are made artificially and symbolize the *technical* advances of man. The law which ordains that both shall be blown simultaneously aims to teach the importance of harmonizing these two basic aspects of human life — the spiritual and the material, the natural and the technical.

The only place, however, where such perfect harmony is possible for the Jew is in his own homeland, for the law applies only in the Temple of Jerusalem. For many centuries Jews have lived in an unharmonious exile and have had to sacrifice the "trumpets" of technical progress for a "Shofar" of spirituality (though even in this we are more blessed than those nations which sacrificed in the opposite direction). When Israel is reconstituted in its own land, it will be in a position to restore the ancient harmony. "Techniques must not swallow up and destroy but should be subordinated to the establishing of the universe in all the purity of its wholesome, fresh nature." Rabbi Kuk ended his homily with a final reminder that the Mishnah states, "the Shofar sounded a *long* note and the trumpets a *short* note, since the proper ceremony of the day devolved upon the Shofar." Thus, even in a restored Israel on its own soil, the Shofar of the spirit must ring longer and louder than the trumpets of technical excellence.

The Shofar as Israel's Most Effective Weapon

The *Ba'al Tokay'a* customarily recites a series of seven verses from the Bible before the Shofar benedictions. The first of these is "*Min ha-maytzar* . . . Out of my straits I called upon the Lord; He answered me and set me free" (Psalms 118:5). To explain the appropriateness of this verse, the traditional preachers resorted to a beautiful parable *(mashal)*:

A king had two sons. He sent the elder to rule over one of his vast provinces, but out of a special love he kept the younger near to him. Finally the time came to train the young prince in the art of government. Reluctantly, the king sent him to his brother, with strict instructions to send a daily communication concerning his own welfare and progress. The prince was also ordered to appear in person before the king on the coronation anniversary and, if possible, to bring his older brother with him. When the younger son arrived in his brother's domain, the latter grew jealous and feared for his own position. Instead of instructing his younger brother in the art of statecraft, he treated him like a slave and sent him on dangerous missions. Finally, with an eye to alienating father from son, he intercepted all the daily communications which the young prince sent to his father. When the coronation day approached, however, the lad managed to escape and fled to his father with the truth.

This is the meaning *(nimshal)* of the parable: the King is the Almighty; the older brother is Esau, the gentile nations, to whom God has given dominion over the choice provinces of His earthly Kingdom; the young prince is Israel, His dearly beloved, whom the King has been compelled to send out among the nations to learn the ways of government. The letters to be sent daily are the prayers and the words of Torah-study. But our envious brother-peoples have tried to suppress our learning and drown out our prayers. Yet they cannot prevent us from reaching our Father on His coronation day, Rosh Hashanah. On that day we break the bonds of our spiritual servitude and flee to the waiting arms of our merciful Father, the King of Kings. True, we have failed to bring our brother-nations with us; we scarcely manage to save our own souls. Yet, year after year, we ask our Father to forgive our disobedience, to requite our suffering and to allow us to live in security. Perhaps then we can fulfill our mission.

The acknowledged master of the *mashal*, Rabbi Jacob Krantz, better known as the Dubner Maggid, explains in his favorite technique the crucial importance of the Shofar for Israel. A city dweller while traveling in a forest is frightened by all sorts of mysterious forms and shadows. He shoots one arrow after another in a vain attempt to drive them away. In the morning he is dismayed to see that he has only a single arrow left; the others had been wasted on harmless tree stumps and rocks. He is determined not to expend his final precious weapon unless there is a real, present danger. Similarly, when the Jews lived on their own soil, they had many excellent "weapons" of faith — the holy city of Jerusalem, the Temple, sacrifices, High Priest, altars, etc. But these were all wasted on vanities and illusions. Now we are scattered among the nations and only one arrow remains in our quiver, the Shofar. We must be very careful to see that we do not expend in vain our final means of reaching our heavenly Father.[61a]

The Shofar as a Symbol of Redemption

"Proclaim liberty throughout the land and to all the inhabitants thereof." These deathless words, later inscribed on the Liberty Bell, originally constituted the law of the Jubilee year as ordained by the Torah (in Leviticus 25:9). The word "Jubilee" is derived from the Hebrew *yovayl,* meaning a ram's horn. Every fiftieth year was the occasion for liberating slaves and restoring hopelessly mortgaged family lands and it was inaugurated with the sounding of a Shofar. The Jubilee year began at the conclusion of Yom Kippur.

The ancient practice of sounding the Shofar to mark the conclusion of Yom Kippur[62] is generally explained as a reminiscence of the Shofar that inaugurated the Jubilee year. This interpretation began in the period of the Geonim. Aaron of Lunel[63] quotes the Babylonian authority, Hai Gaon, (died 1038) as saying that, since we have lost track of the Jubilee years, we sound the Shofar at the end of Yom Kippur each year. Even this Provençal scholar who reports the Geonic explanation finds it strange that we should base an annual custom upon one that was observed only once in fifty years. Aaron of Lunel explains that the purpose of this Shofar sounding is "to confound Satan" *(l-arbayv et ha-satan).*

The correct explanation for the post-Yom Kippur sounding of the Shofar is actually a simple and logical one. Louis Ginzberg[64] points out that in ancient Palestine, through the days of the second Temple, a Shofar was sounded on the eve of Shabbat to remind the people to desist from work and at the conclusion of Shabbat to inform them that work was now permissible. Since Yom Kippur is legally analogous to Shabbat (it is called in the Torah, *Shabbat Shabbaton*), the Shofar was also sounded prior to its inauguration and immediately following its conclusion. The practice of sounding the Shofar on the eve of the Day of Atonement died out eventually but it was retained for the close of the fast, when most people were still in the synagogue. This custom has come down to us from

Palestine but, by the time of Hai Gaon, its origin had been forgotten.

Although the association of the Shofar sounding at the conclusion of Yom Kippur with the Jubilee year is not historically accurate, it has struck a responsive chord in the hearts of the Jewish people. The interpretation of the Shofar as a symbol of liberation is in keeping not only with the Shofar of the Jubilee year but also with the Shofar of the Messiah (referred to in Isaiah 27:13). An ancient *midrash* on this verse states, "The Shofar is synonymous with freedom."[65] In many communities today the ceremony of sounding the Shofar at the conclusion of Yom Kippur is accompanied by the proclamation — once or even three-fold — "*L-shanah ha-ba'ah bi-Yerushalayim* . . . Next year in Jerusalem!" Once again, as everywhere in Jewish thought, past memories are converted into future hopes.

The Shofar in Jewish Folklore and Superstition

"To primitive peoples, New Year, or the beginning of a new month or season, is a crucial and critical time, when demons are thought to be especially rampant, eager to inflict mischief and harm. To scare them away, it is customary in most parts of the world to beat drums, sound gongs, blow trumpets, crack whips and generally create pandemonium."[66]

This primitive practice — whether or not it is connected with the origin of Shofar sounding on Rosh Hashanah — certainly underlies much of the folklore and superstition that Jews have woven about it. Talmudic literature regularly speaks of the eerie Shofar blasts as intended "to confuse (or confound) Satan," to whom tradition assigns the role of "Prosecutor" *(Kataygor)* in the drama of Divine Judgment.[67]

Folklore has assigned to this "accuser" a specific and strategic locale — within the Shofar itself. This device serves to explain the difficulty encountered by even the most saintly *Ba'al Tokay'a* in the performance of his sacred function. It is equally true that the mystical literature assigns special angels to carry the various sounds of the Shofar before the throne of God; but obviously their infernal counterpart often comes off the victor in the struggle for control of the Shofar. Popular anecdotes based upon this allegorical conflict are legion.

Even the sober and sophisticated Maḥzorim of the modern age carry vestiges of these primitive ideas embedded in their text. For example, immediately after Psalm 47 (which is still chanted seven times in good mystical fashion),[68] seven additional verses from the Bible may be found. The first of these, beginning *Min ha-maytzar*, has already been discussed (in the section, THE SHOFAR AS ISRAEL'S MOST EFFECTIVE WEAPON). The subsequent six verses were selected not only for their intrinsic merit — which is very high — but also because the initial Hebrew letters spell out the two words, *KeRA SaTaN*, that is, "cut off from Satan." The reference is, of course, to the efforts which must be made to foil the evil designs of the accusing "prosecutor" upon the Congregation of Israel. One of the most effective means of "cutting off Satan" was to catch him at unexpected moments with the eerie wail of the Shofar. Another was to blow either to the right or to the left — depending upon the local custom. But there were times when all these expedients failed. The codes of Jewish law amply testify to this frequent impasse, for they give the procedure for calling on substitutes whenever the official *Ba'al Tokay'a* finds his best efforts frustrated — "even two or three (substitutes) one after the other . . ."

Some medieval Jewish groups associated the Shofar with death. Some mystical circles maintained the custom of sounding the Shofar at the removal of the dead from the home to the burial ground, presumably to protect the living against the angel of death.[69] This custom may reflect, however, the practice recorded in the Talmud of blowing the Shofar simply to summon mourners to the funeral procession.[70] The Shofar design is found carved on Jewish tombstones in ancient Palestine; some scholars take it as a symbol of the resurrection of the dead, but others see in it nothing more than a favorite artistic motif.

CHAPTER SEVEN

THE MUSAF SERVICE

• THE MUSAF SERVICE • HINENI • THE MUSAF KADDISH
• THE MUSAF AMIDAH • REPETITION OF THE AMIDAH: AVOT
• UPAD MAY-AZ • ZOKHRAYNU L-ḤAYYIM
• MEKHALKAYL ḤAYYIM • TAYFEN B-MAKHON
• MELEKH ELYON, EL DAR BA-MAROM • U-NETANEH TOKEF
• B-ROSH HASHANAH YIKATAYVUN • THE KEDUSHAH
• V-KHOL MA'AMINIM • U-V'KHAYN TAYN PAḤDEKHA
• U-V'KHAYN TAYN KAVOD • U-V'KHAYN TZADIKIM
• V-YE'ETAYU • ATAH BEḤARTANU • U-MI'PENAY ḤATA'AYNU
• PRELUDES TO MALKHUYOT-ZIKHRONOT-SHOFAROT
• MALKHUYOT-ZIKHRONOT-SHOFAROT • ALAYNU
• AL KAYN NEKAVEH • THE MALKHUYOT VERSES
• MELOKH AL KOL HA-OLAM
• TEKIOT FOR MALKHUYOT-ZIKHRONOT-SHOFAROT
• HA-YOM HARAT OLAM—ARESHET SEFATAYNU
• ATAH ZOKHAYR • THE ZIKHRONOT VERSES
• ZOKHRAYNU B-ZIKARON TOV • ATAH NIGLAYTA
• TEKA B-SHOFAR GADOL
• AVINU MALKAYNU, ZEKHOR RAḤAMEKHA
• B-SAYFER ḤAYYIM • HA-YOM TE'AMTZAYNU
• KADDISH TITKABAL—SUPPLEMENTARY TEKIOT

THE MUSAF SERVICE

The Musaf Service מוסף

The Musaf service generally, even more than Shaḥarit, has become associated in Jewish tradition with the idea of group *(tzibbur)* worship, as distinguished from that of the individual *(yaḥid)*. Originally, Musaf was exclusively a collective worship service; later it came to be generally considered as obligatory upon the individual as well (like Shaḥarit). The one prayer that all authorities, ancient and medieval, agree must be recited only with a congregation is the Musaf of Rosh Hashanah.[1] The Talmud counsels individuals not to recite this prayer alone, in view of the decisive character of the main service on the Day of Judgment.[2] Rashi comments on this view: "An ordinary Musaf consists of passages dealing with praise of God and historical events; but the Musaf of Rosh Hashanah — containing, as it does, the *Malkhuyot, Zikhronot* and *Shofarot* prayers — emphasizes God's judgment. On such an occasion, a man should not separate himself from the community."

An insight into what the Musaf service, especially on the High Holy Days, has meant to Jews has been put into words by the gifted Austrian Jewish novelist, Stefan Zweig:

> On this disturbed planet, prayer alone offered refuge, rest and comfort. Prayer had a marvelous power: it deadened fear by recalling great promises; it put to slumber the soul's terror by means of its singing litany; on its murmuring pinions it lifted up to God the heaviness of the heart. Prayer in need was good. Common prayer was better still, for all burdens were lighter if borne in common and the good was better in God's sight if done in unison.[3]

HINENI הנני

Centuries ago, in some European town, a humble unknown Cantor — overwhelmed by the solemnity of the day and haunted by a sense of his own unworthiness to represent his fellow-Jews before the Almighty in the great service of Rosh Hashanah — paused to give voice to his innermost feelings. His supplication has been immortalized in the Maḥzor as the *Hineni* prayer. This simple entreaty is framed in the style of a *Reshut*, a humble prayer for God's indulgence. (We have already discussed the *Reshut* type of synagogal poetry at the beginning of the Cantor's repetition of the Shaḥarit *Amidah*, in Chapter Four.)

To this day, the *Ba'al Musaf* (Reader of the Musaf Service)[4] in the Ashkenazic synagogue chants this hallowed petition to its traditional melody, in a minor key. Sometimes he begins the prayer at the entrance of the synagogue and completes it as he reaches the Ark. The famous Cantor, Yossi of Slonim, is reputed to have arranged a highly dramatic setting for his *Hineni* recitation. Placing his white-robed choir on the *bimah,* he stood among the poor at the synagogue entrance. One of the choir boys would ask aloud, "Where is the Cantor?" The answer came in musical accents from the door — "*Hineni* . . . Here I am!" A second chorister would continue, "Why are you standing at the entrance?" The Cantor would reply, in the words of the prayer, "*he-ani* . . . I am poor." "Is he begging for money?" the choir asked, and Yossi replied, "*mi-ma'as* . . . (no, I am poor) in good deeds." At this point the Cantor would walk slowly up the aisle, chanting the remainder of the prayer.

The Sephardim have a different *Reshut* at this point. Some communities recite a poem based upon the third chapter of Habakkuk the prophet: "O Lord, I have heard the report of Thee, and I am afraid, etc." Others recite *Oḥilah la-El,* the poem which Ashkenazim use as a prelude to the *Malkhuyot, Zikhronot, Shofarot* prayer-group in the Cantor's repetition of the Musaf *Amidah* on Rosh Hashanah.

THE MUSAF KADDISH קדיש

The majestic melody of the Kaddish is a fitting prelude to the great *Amidah* of the Prayerbook. Each Kaddish of Rosh Hashanah is chanted according to its own special mode, though the words are identical. In much the same way the mode of cantillation of the *te'amim*, or musical notations of the Biblical text, changes depending on the particular book involved and the occasion for its intonation. The Musaf Kaddish on Rosh Hashanah is one of the musical peaks of the service.[5]

The Musaf Amidah עמידה

The silent devotion *(Amidah)*, upon which the entire Musaf service is constructed, is the longest of the entire year.[6] Yet it justly has been said that no ritual in Judaism excels it in spiritual grandeur, in beauty of language or in architectural perfection of structure. The late Chief Rabbi of Great Britain, Joseph H. Hertz, has offered a summary of the pattern of this epic literary creation: " . . . the Jew thinks not of himself, but of peace and blessedness for all mankind . . . He prays to God to hasten the time when the mighty shall be just and the just, mighty; when all the children of men shall form one band of brotherhood, when national arrogance and oppression shall have passed away, like so much smoke from the earth."

The main outlines of the Rosh Hashanah Musaf were set by the second century C.E.; Rabbi Akiba, for example, knew of all the nine blessings contained in our prayer. The unique element in the structure of the Rosh Hashanah *Amidah* is its central section. It contains a group of three special prayers, each with its own name and message, but all composed in the same pattern. The first is called *Malkhuyot* (Kingship), stressing the thought that man's spiritual welfare depends on his acceptance of God as the sole Sovereign in human life. The second is entitled *Zikhronot* (Remembrance), declaring God to be the Judge of our lives who remembers things forgotten by mortals. Finally, there is the section called *Shofarot* (Trumpets), proclaiming that God is the Ruler of history, who revealed Himself to our forefathers at Mt. Sinai amid the Shofar blasts, and Who in due time will "sound the great Shofar" for the complete redemption of Israel and of all mankind.[7]

Repetition of the Amidah: Avot חזרת הש״ץ

The Ark is opened and the congregation rises as the Cantor begins the *Ḥazarah*, or repetition, of the Musaf *Amidah*. In some synagogues the curtain before the Ark is changed to mark the transition from the Shaḥarit to the Musaf service.

The opening benediction of every *Amidah* is called *Avot*[8] (literally "fathers") referring to the three patriarchs of Israel. The name is descriptive of the contents: God is praised as "the God of Abraham, Isaac and Jacob" as well as "our God." The faith of the Jew issues not alone from his personal search for and encounter with the Divine but simultaneously from the collective spiritual experience of all Israel. Implicit in *Avot* is the Rabbinic doctrine of *Zekhut Avot*, the "Merit of the Fathers," which is so prominent in the High Holy Day prayers, especially in the themes of *Zikhronot* (Remembrance) and the Binding of Isaac. "The piety of the fathers is often pleaded in behalf of their descendants, and the Messianic hope is here attached to this 'piety.' The idea binds the generations of Israel together with a threefold cord of love, duty and hope" (Israel Abrahams).

As befits its prominent position, *Avot* is chanted to a special melody, different from that of its exact counterpart in the Shaḥarit. Bowing low, the Ḥazzan begins in a low-toned, wordless style; then, slowly and deliberately though in a festive mood, he intones *Barukh Atah*. Suddenly he raises his voice in a piercing *Adonai*. The Cantor always chants these opening words alone but, in the remainder of the benediction, the choir or congregation, as it were, intuitively joins with the Cantor, especially in the wordless sighs that punctuate this opening passage.[9]

Upad May-az אפד מאז

Following the opening passage of *Avot, piyyutim* are inserted into the *Amidah*. The sacred poems of the Synagogue which are inserted into the *Amidah* are called *Kerovot* (as we have seen in the discussion of THE PIYYUTIM, in Chapter Two). The *piyyutim* which make up the *Kerovah*-cycle are prefaced here as always by the ancient *Reshut, Mi-sod ḥakhamim.* The *Kerovah*-cycle for the *Amidah* of the Musaf service in the Ashkenazic rite was composed by Eleazar Kallir; it is designated by the opening words of the poem which begins the cycle, *Upad may-az.* Like Kallir's *Kerovah* for the *Amidah* of the Shaḥarit service *(At ḥil yom pekudah), Upad may-az* and the other poems of this cycle are recited only on the first day of Rosh Hashanah. *Upad may-az* follows a simple alphabetical acrostic design.

The poem is based upon a charming legend told in the Midrash. According to the theory that the creation of the universe began on the 25th of Elul, Adam was created on Rosh Hashanah. On that very same day, he committed the sin of disobedience, and was judged and pardoned by the Divine tribunal. This first Day of Judgment was then established for all time; the Holy One blessed be He said to Adam: "Let this be a sign for your descendants. Just as you have stood before Me in judgment on this day and have been pardoned, so shall your descendants stand before Me in judgment on this day and they shall be pardoned."[10]

This vivid legend indicates the strong emphasis which our ancestors placed on the role of Rosh Hashanah as an indispensable element in man's redemption. By means of bold homiletical interpretation they projected their own experience of penitence and forgiveness back to the very creation of the universe. Indeed, in another Aggadah, the Sages declare that *teshuvah*, "repentance," predates Creation itself, and, like the Torah, formed part of the Divine plan by which the universe was fashioned.[11]

ZOKHRAYNU L-ḤAYYIM זכרנו לחיים

Rabbi Jacob ben Asher, author of the *Tur*, an important code of Jewish practice, finds a direct connection between the petition, *zokhraynu l-ḥayyim,* and *Avot,* the opening benediction of the *Amidah* into which it was inserted in post-Talmudic times.[12] The word *zokhraynu*, "remember us," refers back to the words in the *Avot* prayer, *zokhayr ḥasday avot,* "Who remembers the good deeds of our forefathers;" the word *l-ma'ankha*, "for Thy sake," refers back to the words *l-ma'an shemo*, "for the sake of His name."[13]

Thus we base our plea to be "remembered in the book of life" on the merits of the patriarchs, *Zekhut Avot*, lovingly translated as "original virtue" by Solomon Schechter.

In the Bible, while there is frequent appeal to the lives and spiritual achievements of the patriarchs, the emphasis is on *Brit Avot*, the "Covenant of the Fathers." "A Covenant calls for continued mutual obligations . . . each Jew finds his way to God by fulfilling the obligations required of him, by his actions and his way of life" (David Aronson). The doctrine of *Zekhut Avot* is a creation of the Rabbinic sages.[14]

A beautiful re-interpretation of the Rabbinic concept of *Zekhut Avot* has been given by Milton Steinberg: "Though mankind never achieves a perfect society, one exempt from God's judgment, the goodness wrought by the successive generations somehow add up to one another . . . Always and unfailingly, the goodness of the past is available to any given present on demand, whereas the evil is lost beyond recapture."[15]

MEKHALKAYL ḤAYYIM מכלכל חיים

The juxtaposition of "the living" and "the dead" in this second benediction of the *Amidah* recalls the familiar Talmudic statement that on Rosh Hashanah "the books of the living and the books of the dead are opened" before the Heavenly Tribunal.[16] Commentators have long been puzzled over the relevance of "the books of the dead" at the judgment of the living. One explanation holds that a defendant in court is judged in the light of his total background and history. If, for example, a criminal stems from a lawless environment, his record does not appear as heinous as that of a man who has enjoyed all the advantages of a fine family and education. Therefore, the "books of the dead," i.e., our family history, are also opened on our annual Day of Judgment, the better to evaluate our personal records.[17]

TAYFEN B-MAKHON תפן במכון

This *piyyut* petitions God to judge us from "His seat of mercy," in the light of His intimate knowledge of human nature — "We are assembled like warriors in the day of battle, yea, we are at war with the evil within ourselves."

"Since war begins in the minds of men, it is in the minds of men that defenses of peace must be constructed" — this profound insight of the United Nations Economic and Social Commission applies to conflicts not only between nations but between individuals and even within the individual personality. Our forefathers so vividly felt the reality of this "adversary within the gates" that they did not hesitate to personalize it, as in this *piyyut.* He who would find God must struggle against the selfishness and greed which — to use Schechter's phrase — prevent the channels of Divine grace from flowing as freely and as fully as intended by the Merciful Father. "We must call upon the reserve powers of God's beneficent love to effect a true cleansing of the soul and to behold a greater vision. God is always near but He is near only to 'those who call upon Him in truth.' Man must take the initial step in reaching out for God's mercy and blessing" (Max Arzt).

This poem is the second part of the poem-cycle (i.e., *Kerovah*) which began with the *piyyut, Upad may-az.* In structure it follows, through the initial letter of each line, the inverted Hebrew alphabet acrostic (known as *TaSHRak).* Like all the parts of Kallir's *Kerovah*, it is recited on the first day of Rosh Hashanah only.

MELEKH ELYON, EL DAR BA-MAROM אל דר במרום

This *piyyut* is designated (by Israel Davidson) as part six of the *Kerovah*-cycle by Kallir which began with the poem, *Upad may-az.*[18] It has virtually the same structure and theme as its parallel poem, *Melekh elyon, amitz ha-menusa* (see Chapter Four, THE SHAḤARIT SERVICE). In both poems, the original text has been abridged: each stanza beginning *Melekh elyon,* "Supreme King," was once followed by a contrasting stanza beginning, *Melekh evyon*, "poor (i.e., mortal) king." But only two sample stanzas of the latter group (the first and the last, beginning with the letters *bet* and *tav*, respectively) have been preserved,[19] toward the end of the poem. Consequently, the alphabetical acrostic now reads *alef, gimmel, heh, za'yin*, etc.; the letters missing from this alphabetical acrostic were employed with the *Melekh evyon* verses. The latter were deleted either in order to shorten the lengthy poem or to satisfy Christian censors who interpreted the *Melekh evyon* passages as derogatory to the founder of their faith.

The burden of these parallel poems — as of so many of the High Holy Day *piyyutim* — is the contrast between "Highest Divinity" and "Lowly Humanity."[20] Granted that this is a major motif in Judaism, the worshipper should bear in mind that it does not accurately reflect the Jewish concept of the relationship between God and man. The prayers of the Maḥzor also emphasize the more positive aspects of the Jewish idea of man. The problem of man's capacities revolves about the two poles of divinity and dust already indicated by the eighth Psalm. The Ḥasidic sage, Rabbi Bunam, expressed the eternal paradox to his disciples thus: "Each one of you must have two pockets, so that he can reach into the one or other, according to what he needs. In one pocket are the words, 'For my sake was the world created;' in the other, 'I am dust and ashes.' "[20a]

Milton Steinberg has succinctly phrased for the modern mind this paradoxical teaching of Judaism:

> What is man? A creature of dust; a thing of transience whose days fly by faster than the weaver's shuttle; a fragile being, crushed sooner than a moth; a body, sustaining and reproducing itself after the manner of beasts; a vessel filled with shame and confusion, impelled by pride and self-love, driven by passions . . . But he is also more and other. The handiwork, the child, the mirrored image of God; fashioned after and instinct with Him, he displays, though in infinitely less degree and with innumerable flaws, the powers ascribed to and associated with Divinity: the ability to think and create, the awareness of the good and beautiful, the capacity for love and compassion, and freedom of the will.[21]

U-NETANEH TOKEF ונתנה תקף

By common consent, this moving meditation is the outstanding *piyyut*[22] of the Rosh Hashanah liturgy; certainly it is the best known and most beloved among Ashkenazic Jews (it has even been reprinted in some Sephardic prayerbooks).[23] Much of its solemnity its origin. The oldest source is the thirteenth century work, *Or Zarua* by Rabbi Isaac of Vienna, who quotes Rabbi Ephraim of Bonn: A certain Rabbi Amnon of Mayence was friendly with the Archbishop who pressed the leader of the Jewish community to accept Christianity and reap the certain rewards of this world as well as the next. In a moment of weakness, the Rabbi yielded but was immediately stricken with remorse and repented of his act.

When he was brought before the ecclesiastical authorities, Rabbi Amnon decreed his own punishment — a barbarous mutilation which was promptly executed. Rosh Hashanah was then at hand. Amnon, dying of his wounds, begged his disciples to carry him into the synagogue. The Ḥazzan was about to intone the solemn *Kedushah* but Amnon stayed him, saying, "Pause that I may sanctify God's Holy Name." He then recited his own composition, *U-netaneh tokef,* expiring at the words, "*u-shemaynu karata bi-shemekha* . . . and our name hast Thou linked with Thine own."

The legend has it that three days after his martyrdom, Rabbi Amnon appeared in a dream to Rabbi Kalonymos ben Meshullam, the eminent Mayence *payyetan*,[24] and taught him the prayer which the latter set down for later generations. Israel Davidson, however, points out that *U-netaneh tokef* has all the earmarks of a much earlier origin — "its simplicity of style and lucidity of expression are reminiscent of the most ancient prayers."[25] Questions of authorship aside, this *piyyut* is a masterful example of the art of weaving many Biblical and Talmudic allusions[26] into a soul-stirring poetic creation. An example of such skillful composition is the symbolism of God as the shepherd, tithing his flock by passing them through a narrow gate and marking each tenth one.

The scene of the poem is the Heavenly Court in session, an image already familiar from the Bible (as in Psalm 50). The Almighty is judge and arbiter, witness and scribe, remembering things forgotten and sealing our destiny. It has been noted that this allegory reflects the three major themes of the Rosh Hashanah Musaf: *Malkhuyot* ("*U-vo tinasay malkhutekha* . . . Thereon is Thy *dominion* exalted"); *Zikhronot* ("*V-tiftaḥ et sayfer ha-zikhronot* . . . Thou unfoldest the *records*"); and *Shofarot* ("*U-v'shofar gadol yitaka . . .* The great *Shofar* is sounded").[27] The phrase, *kedushat ha-yom,* "the holiness of the day," in the opening verse of *U-netaneh tokef*, is an allusion to the joining of the prayer-group *Malkhuyot-Zikhronot-Shofarot* to the fourth benediction of the *Amidah,* whose name in the Rabbinic literature is *Kedushat Ha-Yom,* "The Sanctification of the Day."

The musical rendition of *U-netaneh tokef* marks the high point of the cantorial repertoire for Rosh Hashanah. It features a wide range of modes and motifs, major and minor. In it, we hear the majestic music of the Heavenly Court, the peal of the Shofar at which even the angelic hosts tremble, the soothing pastoral of the shepherd mustering his flock. Then the mood changes again into the tearful supplication of "who shall live and who shall die" and the humble sigh of "man's origin is dust and he returneth to the dust." Finally, the music soars into the promise of "But Thou art ever our living God and King."

B-Rosh Hashanah Yikatayvun בראש השנה יכתבון

With these awesome phrases,[28] the prayer *U-netaneh tokef* reaches a peak of dramatic urgency. The plaintive recitation of the Cantor confronts each worshipper with a vision of his possible fate in the year ahead. The theme of man's destiny resting ultimately in the hand of his Creator recalls the prayer of Hannah in the *Haftarah* for the first day of Rosh Hashanah: "It is the Lord Who causeth death and giveth life . . . The Lord maketh poor and maketh rich; He bringeth low, He also lifteth up."[29]

Yet, no matter what the verdict may be, the gates of mercy are never closed. "Repentance, prayer and righteousness" can always hold them open to "avert the severe decree."[30] These words have become, as it were, a formula that sums up not only the message of the Days of Awe but of Judaism generally. "Our character is determined not by what happens to us but by what we do in the face of circumstances. A moral person responds; a spiritually inanimate individual only reacts" (Max Arzt). If "the severe decree" is construed as death — as many commentators take it — the phrase must be rendered, " . . . avert the severity of the decree" (in any case, this is the literal meaning of the Hebrew text). Death is inevitable, but the tragedy of a meaningless life can be averted. "The true alternative lies in whether we shall live in resentful opposition to death or in gracious acceptance of its inevitability" (Ernst Simon).

Significantly repentance, *teshuvah,* is mentioned first. Repentance is "a cardinal doctrine in Judaism — its doctrine of salvation," wrote George Foot Moore, the preeminent Christian authority on Rabbinic Judaism.[31] We might add the observation of a Jewish scholar of Christianity, Claude G. Montefiore: "The whole doctrine of Repentance is emphatically a Jewish teaching and its full development is purely the work of Rabbinical Judaism."[32]

The emphasis upon the efficacy of repentance, prayer and righteousness is in complete accord with the classic Jewish belief in the freedom of the will under the providence of God. "Everything is foreseen yet freedom of choice is given"[33] is Rabbi Akiba's classic phrasing of life's eternal paradox. The great issues of human destiny are in the hands of the Creator yet mortals are never mere puppets. There is always an imponderable and indeterminate "arena of moral decision." Man's godlike endowment of personality makes human behavior, unlike that of nature's other creatures, refreshingly unpredictable. The third century Palestinian sage, Ḥanina ben Pappa, taught that before a child is conceived, God has already ordained "whether he shall be strong or weak, intelligent or dull, rich or poor. But whether he shall be wicked or virtuous is not pronounced. Nor can even God predetermine this since all things are in the hands of Heaven except the fear of Heaven."[34]

The philosophic formulation of this cardinal teaching was phrased in classic form by Maimonides:

> Free will is granted to every man. Give no room in your minds to that which is asserted by heathen fools, and also by many of the ignorant among the Israelites themselves, namely, that the Holy One, blessed be He, decrees that man from his birth should be either a righteous man or a wicked man. Since the power of doing good or evil is in our own hands, and since all the wicked deeds we have committed have been committed with our full consciousness, it befits us to turn in repentance and to forsake our evil deeds, the power of doing so being still

in our hands. Now this matter is a very important principle; nay it is the pillar of the Law and of the commandments.[35]

The Kedushah קדשה

Some commentators see in the phrase, "*Mi-mekomo hu yifen b-raḥamim* . . . From His sacred abode may He turn in mercy," a reference to the familiar Talmudic legend of God's two thrones, the Throne of Judgment *(Kissay ha-Din)* and the Throne of Mercy *(Kissay ha-Raḥamim)*. On Rosh Hashanah, God might be expected to occupy His Throne of Judgment; but, as a favorable response to our prayers of repentance, we ask Him to "turn in mercy," to occupy the Throne of Mercy.[36] Jewish theology teaches that the two qualities of Judgment and Mercy are not mutually exclusive but are blended in God's very nature. The Midrash states that God originally created the Universe on the principle of *Din* (Judgment). However, when He saw that the human race would not long exist if Judgment were to be the only criterion, He decided to temper Judgment with Mercy *(Raḥamim)*.[37]

Such is the intimate, poetic theology of Rabbinic Judaism. In the modern philosophical idiom, we have Hermann Cohen's analysis of God's judgment.[38] The essence of God is a tension between *Din* (Judgment) and *Ge'ulah* (Redemption). What polytheism calls "fate" and "luck," monotheism calls Judgment and Redemption. These two qualities are never exercised separately but always in combination wherever man's fate is involved, as on the High Holy Days. Rosh Hashanah represents the element of Judgment while Yom Kippur is characterized by the quality of Redemption. Together the two festivals symbolize this mystic unity of God's Justice and Love.

V-khol Ma'aminim וכל מאמינים

This poem is one of the most beloved *piyyutim* of the High Holy Days (like many other Rosh Hashanah poems it is repeated on Yom Kippur). A leading contemporary scholar[39] attributes its authorship to Yannai, one of the earliest poets of the Synagogue.

Others trace its authorship to Rabbi Yoḥanan Ha-Kohen of the ninth century. The structure is a double alphabetical acrostic. The opening phrase, "*Ha-oḥayz b-yad* . . . He holds in His hand" — sometimes given as the name of the poem — is understood by some commentators to refer back to the closing words of the preceding prayer, as if they formed a single phrase: "O King of *justice* (Who) holds in His hand the measure of *judgment*."

The refrain, "*V-khol ma'aminim* . . . And all believe," sounds the great theme of the poem, faith in God's wondrous powers. The crisis of Western civilization in our time can be understood as the desperate struggle to rediscover the sources of the faith that underlies our ideals and institutions. For it is this faith which is the surest defense against despair and cynicism at home and tyranny abroad. Louis Finkelstein, chancellor of the Jewish Theological Seminary of America, wrote in his Rosh Hashanah message of 1942, at the high tide of Nazi power and conquest:

> Nothing which has happened in the whole course of history reflects more completely the mercy and lovingkindness which are at the core of the Universe than the tragic events of our day. The world which denied the teachings of the Prophets and Sages, and substituted the standards of power for those of right, has come to grief. An insane egotism of individuals and groups which yesterday seemed destined to set a permanent stamp on mankind is today revealed as contradictory to the nature of things. We are witnessing this revelation. Despite our lethargy, we have become the instruments of a great spiritual recovery. The moral and spiritual truths which ordinarily are discernible only to the greatest poets and philosophers are being spelled out in the events of our time, so that the simplest cannot fail to understand. Reluctant to accept the word of the Prophets, we insisted on the tragic fulfillment of the lesson. But it is the manifestation of the Divine purpose that once the lesson has been driven home, we have the strength to confront its consequences.

U-V'KHAYN TAYN PAḤDEKHA ובכן תן פחדך

Like each *Amidah* of Rosh Hashanah and Yom Kippur, the Musaf contains the three brief *U-v'khayn* prayers. The origin and significance of this prayer-group, as well as its relationship to the Rosh Hashanah liturgy in general, have been discussed in the commentary on the Arvit and Shaḥarit services (Chapters Three and Four, respectively).

The first of the three prayers is a plea for the recognition of God's supreme sovereignty by all the peoples of the world. "It is the Creator's will," said R. Berekhiah, "that on Rosh Hashanah the hearts of all mankind shall be directed to Him in unison."[40] The prototype of *U-v'khayn tayn paḥdekha* was composed by the author of the Apocryphal book of Ben Sira (Ecclesiasticus) — "Save us, O God of all; send Thine awe upon the nations . . . let them know Thee as we also have known Thee . . . "[41] Indeed the roots of this universalism reach back to the creation of man as told in the early verses of Genesis and its fruits enrich every expression of Jewish ethics, law and theology down to the present day.

U-V'KHAYN TAYN KAVOD ובכן תן כבוד

Though we pray on Rosh Hashanah for universal brotherhood we do not neglect to add a petition for the glory of Israel. The Jewish conception of society envisioned men as members of national groups rather than Man in the abstract. Thus, even for the Messianic age, the Hebrew prophets foresaw the continued existence of the nations of the earth, albeit with new moral standards of national existence drawn from the example of Israel. Our Sages declared that the redemption of mankind will not come about until Israel is fully liberated: "The return of Israel to its own land and the restoration of its pristine glory is part of the world's salvation."[42]

Such a prayer for honor and status — not only for individual Jews but for the group as an historic entity — is entirely consistent with Biblical faith. Clear-thinking and unprejudiced Christians have seen the truth of this more readily than many a Jewish intellectual. Alfred North Whitehead, perhaps the greatest mathematical philosopher of the twentieth century, paid eloquent tribute to the enormous Jewish contributions to Western civilization in science, literature and religion. But the greatest contribution of all, he said, is that Jews continue to be a living people: "The Jews supply ideals beyond conventional habits and the light of Jewish genius must not be allowed to be quenched, otherwise the light of the world also will flicker and perish."[43]

U-v'khayn Tzadikim ובכן צדיקים

This ancient prayer is distinguished by a remarkable ethical scrupulousness. Note that whereas "the righteous . . . the just . . . and the pious" are personified, there are no corresponding phrases such as "the iniquitous . . . the wicked . . . the tyrants." Instead, the abstract terms "iniquity . . . wickedness . . . tyranny" are used. This is no accident, as has been well pointed out by Seligmann Baer in his distinguished commentary on the Prayerbook: "Such a change in wording would make it a prayer against the individuals who commit evil; but it is not fitting to pray in this way nor is it ethical to do so. Let us pray for the destruction of evil rather than that of the doers of evil." Baer is only making explicit the lesson of the famous Talmudic incident in which Rabbi Meir cited against his enemies a verse of the 104th Psalm, "May the wicked cease from the earth." Beruriah, his learned and pious wife, corrected him by showing that the Hebrew words really mean, "May *wickedness* cease from the earth."[44]

This ethical distinction has momentous implications for our troubled times, for one of the darkest dangers to the peace and security of our world is the confusion of evil-doers with evil itself. Nations and groups within nations have found it useful to portray their rivals as the incarnation of evil, but the truly pious know that evil is not confined to any one group of individuals, much less to any one nation. Indeed, evil is to be found everywhere and in every heart and the struggle to root it out, to be effective, must start close to home.

V-YE'ETAYU ויאתיו

Solomon Schechter wrote about this remarkable *piyyut*: "In its iconoclastic victory of monotheism over all kinds of idolatries, ancient as well as modern, (it) might best be described as the 'Marseillaise of the people of the Lord of Hosts,' a Marseillaise which is not followed by a Reign of Terror but by the Kingdom of God on earth."[45] Scholars have been unable to identify the poet but all agree that it is a very ancient poem, dating perhaps from the seventh century. Some see in it references to the iconoclastic (idol-smashing) uprising of that period in Constantinople ("their idols overthrown . . . ") which must have struck the Jews as a partial fulfillment of Biblical prophecies.[46]

The alphabetical acrostic of this *piyyut,* traced through the third letter of the opening word in each phrase, is so skillfully done as to escape the notice of the casual reader.[47] The closing words of the hymn, chanted in many synagogues to a joyous traditional melody, are *keter melukhah*, "the crown of kingship." This phrase is equivalent to the name of the great poem *Keter Malkhut* by Solomon Ibn Gabirol, which is recited by some individuals after the service of *Kol Nidre* night. In the eighth canto of Gabirol's work, one reads lines strongly reminiscent of *V-ye'etayu*:

> Thou art God,
> And all beings are Thy servants, Thy worshippers;
> Thine honor is not diminished
> By those who serve other gods,
> For they all aim to come to Thee.[48]

ATAH BEḤARTANU אתה בחרתנו

In the Talmud, this benediction, the fourth in the *Amidah*, is termed *Kedushat Ha-Yom*, "the Sanctification of the Day," because the name of the specific festival whose holiness is proclaimed was inserted into it. Therefore, the Sages (following the tradition of Rabbi Akiba[49]) honored this benediction with the special prayers that distinguish the Rosh Hashanah *Amidah* from that of Shabbat and the Festivals, namely, *Malkhuyot*, *Zikhronot* and *Shofarot*. *Atah beḥartanu* is found in all the rites.[50]

The religious significance of *Atah beḥartanu* lies in its restatement of the Biblical teaching of "The Chosen People."[51] It asserts both Israel's privilege and duty as the recipient of the festival, a sign of God's love. The same thought is contained in the Kiddush. The Torah benediction clarifies the purpose of Israel's election by praising God, "Who has chosen us from among all peoples by giving us His Torah." A fine summary of the "Chosen People" concept has been given by Morris Silverman in the Sabbath and Festival Prayer Book of the Rabbinical Assembly of America and United Synagogue of America:

> The traditional idea of "The Chosen People" involves obligations rather than privileges. It is a form of *noblesse oblige*, imposing upon the House of Israel the responsibility to lead a life of holiness and righteousness. This moral responsibility is also clearly expressed in the admonition of the Prophet Amos, "You only have I known of all the families of the earth, therefore, I will punish you for all your iniquities" (Amos 3:2). This integral relationship between the concept of "The Chosen People" and the religious and moral responsibilities of the Jew is emphasized in the Prayer Book which invariably links "The Chosen People" with the Torah, the Sabbath and the *Mitzvot*. The moral and spiritual values of Judaism, through the medium of which our people may continue to make a contribution to mankind, are consistently emphasized. The fact that the great religions of the western world and the ideals of democracy are rooted in the spiritual heritage of Israel bears eloquent testimony to the validity of this doctrine.

U-MI'PENAY ḤATA'AYNU ומפני חטאינו

Rosh Hashanah and Yom Kippur share this prayer with the other festivals;[52] nevertheless, it contains an interesting variation on the theme of repentance which characterizes the Days of Awe. Although the destruction of the Temple of Jerusalem and the Exile were considered the greatest catastrophes of Jewish history, our ancestors blamed no one but themselves for the national humiliation.[53]

Our prayer echoes the Talmudic teaching, "Our Temple was destroyed because of rancor, jealousy and self-sufficiency."[54] That the Jews could adopt such a spiritual attitude toward defeat not only distinguished them among the nations but endowed them with the power to develop repentance into a program of active faith — a faith that is beginning to find its fulfillment in the contemporary restoration of Zion.

Another intriguing association of this prayer with Rosh Hashanah is its alleged authorship by Rav,[55] who composed many of the prayers for that day. It is suggested that Rav's personal experience of self-exile from Palestine to Babylonia is reflected in the text ("Because of our sins we were exiled from our land"). The theme of *Malkhut,* God's Kingship, is prominent in this prayer: "Our Father, our King, speedily reveal the glory of Thy kingdom unto us; shine forth and be exalted over us in the sight of all men."

The full text of *U-mi'penay ḥata'aynu* is found for the first time in the ninth century Babylonian prayerbook, *Seder Rav Amram*;[56] but some of its basic elements are included in the earlier Palestinian work, Soferim.[57] Since Rav Amram's time, all rites include *U-mi'penay ḥata'aynu,* but the ancient Palestinian rite differs considerably.[58]

היה עם פיפיות — אוחילה לאל
PRELUDES TO MALKHUYOT-ZIKHRONOT-SHOFAROT

The core of the Rosh Hashanah Musaf service consists of a group of three monumental prayers entitled respectively *Malkhuyot, Zikhronot* and *Shofarot.*[59] (These prayers will be discussed in detail in the pages that follow.) The Maḥzor contains two poetic preludes to this group of prayers. Each of these poems is called a *Reshut*, the name given to the Cantor's personal plea for God's indulgence and assistance before the recitation of an important element of the service (an example of a *Reshut* is the prayer, *Hineni,* discussed at the beginning of this chapter).

The first prelude, "*He'yay im pifiyot* . . . inspire the lips," is not treated here as a *Reshut* because it is not a prayer *by* the Cantor but *for* the Cantor, the "Emissary of the Congregation"

(Sheliaḥ Tzibbur). The East European custom was for the Cantor to remain silent while the worshippers individually recited the prayer on his behalf. In some communities today, the Rabbi recites it; in others, the Cantor chants the prayer alone or in unison with the congregation.

The second prelude, "*Oḥilah la-El* . . . I will hope in the Lord," is the Cantor's personal meditation. The Sephardic rite differs from ours in that *Oḥilah la-El* is recited as a prelude to the entire repetition of the *Amidah* (also on Yom Kippur for Musaf and Ne'ilah). In the Ashkenazic tradition, both preludes are recited between *Alaynu* and *Al kayn nekaveh*; some modern editors, however, prefer to print *Alaynu* and *Al kayn nekaveh* as a single unit, following the two preludes.

Both of these preludes, or *Reshuyot*, are of great antiquity and show evidence of the importance, even in early times, of the skilled *Sheliaḥ Tzibbur*. *He'yay im pifiyot* is first mentioned by the great Ashkenazic authority, Maharil (about 1400), but it is undoubtedly many centuries older and probably originated in Palestine.[60] *Oḥilah la-El* is definitely of Palestinian origin[61] and may even be a composition of the earliest known *payyetan*, Yose ben Yose.[62] Indeed, the language of *Oḥilah la-El* is strongly reminiscent of the well-known *Reshut, Mi-sod ḥakhamim*, which is the Cantor's prelude to the poems *(Kerovot)* at the beginning of the *Amidah* (see Chapter Four, THE SHAḤARIT SERVICE)[62a]

מלכיות, זכרונות, שופרות
MALKHUYOT - ZIKHRONOT - SHOFAROT

The three monumental prayer-structures, *Malkhuyot, Zikhronot* and *Shofarot*, portray God, in turn, as Sovereign of the Universe, as Divine Judge, and as Lawgiver and Redeemer. These prayers were already well-known to the authorities of the Mishnah, though they did not receive their final formulation until much later. Tradition ascribes their authorship to the pre-Maccabean "Men of the Great Assembly" but the Talmudic authorities clearly assign their final editing to the School of Rav (third century Babylonia).[63] The

Talmudic name for this triad, *Tekiata d-bay Rav* (or *Tekiata d-Rav*), has reference to the practice of sounding the Shofar at the conclusion of each of the three sections; indeed, the function of these prayers may well have been to interpret the meaning of the Shofar sounds.

The present structure of *Malkhuyot, Zikhronot* and *Shofarot* consists — in each case — of an introductory prayer or prologue, a constellation of Biblical verses,[64] and a finale climaxing in a benediction which summarizes each of the three themes. At first, however, they consisted simply of the Biblical verses: each of these was designated either as *malkhut* (because it contained some form of the root *m'l'kh*, "reign"), *zikaron* (where the key word is some form of *z'kh'r*, "remember") or *shofar* (verses which speak of the ram's horn). There was some difference of opinion in Rabbinic times about how many verses of each type were required, but the prevailing practice is to cite three verses each from the Torah, Writings and Prophets (in that order) and a concluding verse from the Torah, for each of the three sections. At an early time, each of these collections from Scripture was provided with a prayer climaxing in a benediction which recapitulated the central theme respectively of *Malkhuyot, Zikhronot* or *Shofarot.* Later Rav added a prologue *(Alaynu, Atah zokhayr* and *Atah niglayta*, respectively) to each set of Biblical verses. These are of varying quality, ranging from the classic majesty of *Alaynu* to the relatively prosaic *Atah niglayta.* Since the appearance of Rav Amram's prayerbook in ninth century Babylonia, the various rites of the far-flung Jewish communities have preserved a remarkable agreement on the wording of the *Malkhuyot*, et al. in all their parts.

Throughout the ages, the prominence of the *Malkhuyot-Zikhronot-Shofarot* has elicited attempts to summarize their spiritual significance. The earliest is that of the Talmud itself: "The Holy One, blessed be He, says: 'On Rosh Hashanah recite before me *Malkhuyot*, in order that you may proclaim my *Kingship* over you; *Zikhronot*, in order that your *Remembrance* shall rise before me for good; how shall you do this? — through the *Shofar*.' "[65] The three-fold structure suggests that God is *Sovereign* in the *present, Judge* of the *past*, and *Redeemer* in the *future.* A variation on this theme is the thought that the three prayers portray the past, present and future of Israel.

The medieval theologian, Joseph Albo, sees in the threefold prayer three fundamental teachings of Judaism: the existence of God, His providence and retribution, and revelation.[66] A modern theologian, Hermann Cohen, explained them as three critical stages in the historical process: universal-government, universal-judgment, and universal-redemption.[67]

The *Malkhuyot*, et al. are not recited on Yom Kippur. However, there is a Rabbinic tradition that they were recited on Yom Kippur whenever it coincided with the inauguration of the Jubilee year.[68]

Alaynu עלינו

The prologue to the *Malkhuyot* prayer-structure is the great *Alaynu*.[69] The *Alaynu* prayer was borrowed from this place of its origin, about the thirteenth century, to become the closing prayer of every synagogue service.[70] Although a medieval tradition[71] ascribes its authorship to Joshua at his entry into the Promised Land, it is clearly the work of Rav, the third century Babylonian sage, who employed much ancient Palestinian material to create one of the masterpieces of world liturgy.

Much of the solemn beauty of *Alaynu* derives from the sublime concept of the Kingdom, or the Kingship, of God to which it gives expression. As Solomon Schechter pointed out,[72] the Kingship of God has two meanings. There is the "visible" Kingdom, which has both universal and national aspects, and which each Jew can build by devotion to the Torah. There is also the "invisible" Kingdom, which "is mainly spiritual, expressive of a certain attitude of mind, and possessing a more individual character." Both Kingdoms, however, are of this world. Furthermore one of the key ideas of Jewish theology is that God's Kingship has need of Israel's acceptance; just as "parent" implies "child" and vice versa, so "king" implies "people," and "redeemer" implies "redeemed."[73]

An unusual feature of the *Alaynu* recitation, which dramatizes the total allegiance of the Jew to the King of Kings, is the act of prostrating oneself, Oriental style, at the words *"Va-anaḥnu kor'im*

. . . We bend the knee."[74] This is a rare survival of the ancient Palestinian custom; in the Western synagogue of our day, even this act has been widely relegated to the officiants, or to the Cantor alone. In Eastern Europe, it was customary to cover the synagogue floor with straws or boughs lest there be any suspicion of bowing to any images which might be in the flooring (a pagan practice prohibited by Leviticus 26:1).

Franz Rosenzweig has a moving analysis of this dramatic display of allegiance in his "The Star of Redemption":

> What distinguishes the Days of Awe from all other festivals is that here and only here does the Jew kneel. Here he does what he refused to do before the king of Persia, what no power on earth can compel him to do, and what he need not do before God on any other day of the year, or in any other situation he may face during his lifetime. And he does not kneel to confess a fault or to pray for forgiveness of sins, acts to which this festival is primarily dedicated. He kneels only on beholding the immediate nearness of God, hence on an occasion which transcends the earthly needs of today.[75]

Al Kayn Nekaveh — על כן נקוה

This concluding passage of *Alaynu* is the Prayerbook's classic expression of the Jewish faith in the inevitable recognition of the one true God by all mankind. "The establishment of the Kingdom of the One and Only God throughout the entire world constitutes the Divine Plan of Salvation toward which, according to Jewish teaching, the efforts of all the ages are tending" (Kaufmann Kohler). Moreover, the prayer envisions this ultimate achievement as a process of conversion in the hearts and minds of men. Thus, the text reads, "Thou wilt remove the abominations from the earth and all idolatry will be destroyed;" but — speaking of the evil-doers — it says, "all the wicked of the earth shall be turned to Thee." This is in accord with the Biblical teaching: "As I live, saith the Lord, I have no pleasure in the death of the wicked, but that the wicked turn from his way and live" (Ezekiel 33:11).

The Malkhuyot Verses מלכיות

The closing words of *Al kayn nekaveh* form the first of the "Kingship" or *Malkhuyot* verses — "The Lord shall reign forever and ever."[76] There are ten such verses in all: three from the Torah, three from the Writings (all of them from the Psalms), and three from the Prophets; the tenth and final verse of the series is *Shema Yisrael* (from the Torah again). Although the word *melekh* itself in absent in any form, the *Shema* was interpreted from Roman times on as a proclamation of allegiance to *Malkhut Shama'yim*, the "Kingdom of Heaven."[77] This connotation was made explicit by the special responses that were created for it: *Barukh shem kevod malkhuto l-olam va-ed* (for public recitation) and *El Melekh ne'eman* (for private prayer).

The multiplication of Biblical verses to establish an idea may seem redundant to Western tastes but it is characteristic of Rabbinic literature. As an elaborate coronation pageant in words, the Rosh Hashanah liturgy repeats the word *melekh* in all its variations, from the opening word of the Shaḥarit service through this great climax.

Melokh Al Kol Ha-olam מלוך

This majestic plea for the Kingship of God on earth — attributed to Rav — serves a dual function. First, it is the conclusion of *Malkhuyot*. Second, it provides the specific benediction for the festival, the *Kedushat Ha-Yom,* in the *Amidah* of the Musaf service. Commenting on this prayer, Solomon Schechter wrote:

> We can easily lecture on the history of this prayer, and even make a guess as to its date and authorship, but we should certainly fail were we to try to make one understand what the Kingdom of God on earth really meant for the saints of Israel, whose life was nothing else than a preparation for entering into the Kingdom. The ideal for which so many noble men and women suffered martyrdom . . . was the blissful vision of love triumphant, righteousness triumphant, truth triumphant.[78]

Tekiot for Malkhuyot-Zikhronot-Shofarot תקיעות

Following the *Malkhuyot* section — and similarly after *Zikhronot* and *Shofarot* — the Shofar is sounded, except on Shabbat (as is the case with all the *tekiot*). There is no special benediction over the Shofar sounds nor any uniform ritual, as in the case of the thirty *tekiot* sounded after the Shaḥarit service. Nevertheless, these latter sounds are the more significant in that they serve to dramatize and interpret the profound meanings of *Malkhuyot-Zikhronot-Shofarot.*[79]

The relative importance of these *tekiot* is indicated by the name *Tekiot me'umad* (*tekiot* to be heard while standing); the congregation is not obligated to stand at the earlier *Tekiot meyushav* (those to be heard while seated). In actual practice, however, we stand for all the *tekiot*. The twelfth century Provençal authority, Ibn Yarḥi, reports that the rabbis shortened the number of these latter *tekiot* out of consideration for the congregation, wearied by the long service.[80]

The old Babylonian custom was to sound the Shofar at the conclusion of *Malkhuyot*, et al. during the silent recitation of the *Amidah* as well; this is still standard practice among Sephardim and even among Ashkenazim of the Ḥasidic tradition, following the Kabbalist, Isaac Luria.

היום הרת עולם — ארשת שפתינו
Ha-yom Harat Olam — Areshet Sefataynu

After the Shofar is sounded for each of the *Malkhuyot, Zikhronot* and *Shofarot* sections, two brief poems are recited. The first is *Ha-yom harat olam.* Biblical in style and inspiration, it appears in all the rites — indicating its great antiquity. The Sephardim include it in the silent recitation of the *Amidah* as well. The second brief poem is "*Areshet sefataynu* . . . May the entreaty of our lips . . ." It is found as early as the ninth century *Seder Rav Amram* but is today included only in the German-Polish (Ashkenazic) and the Romanian rites. *Areshet sefataynu* is omitted on Shabbat along with the *tekiot* to which it makes direct reference.[81]

Ha-yom harat olam presents some difficulties in interpretation. *Harat* has been rendered "assize," referring to the Day of Judgment theme. The popular rendering, however, is "conception" or "birth (day)" — denoting the Creation of the world. The date of the Creation is the subject of a well-known running controversy in the Talmud.[82] Rabbi Eliezer taught that the world was created on the twenty-fifth of Elul, while Adam was fashioned on the first of Tishre, i.e., on Rosh Hashanah. Rabbi Joshua, on the other hand, held to the less popular view that the world was created in Nisan. (The controversy reflects the problem of multiple New Years in Jewish law.) Rabbi Eliezer's teaching gave rise to the tradition that Adam was created, sinned, was judged and was absolved — all on Rosh Hashanah. He was then given the Divine consolation: "Let this be a sign unto your descendants. Just as you have stood in judgment on this day and have been pardoned, so shall it be with your descendants on each Rosh Hashanah."[83]

This tradition of Rosh Hashanah as the birthday of man is uniquely Jewish. Abraham Joshua Heschel points out that, whereas pagan myths are concerned with the *site* of Creation, their shrines often claiming sanctity on this account, Judaism sanctifies the *time* of Creation.[84] Understood in this light, Rosh Hashanah carries the momentous message that the human personality, the "crown of Creation," also possesses limitless capacities for renewal. Thus God is quoted by the Sages: "My children, I look upon you as if today (Rosh Hashanah) I had created a new creature."[85] Rabbi Elimelekh of Lizensk said, "Every man is created twice: first, when he is born; second, when he repents his past and takes on new courage to live in ways more acceptable to God."

Atah Zokhayr אתה זוכר

As *Malkhuyot* interprets the majestic motif of God's "Kingship," so *Zikhronot* elaborates on the more ancient theme of *zikaron*, i.e., Rosh Hashanah as the Day of "Memorial" or "Remembrance." On the New Year, man remembers the creation of the universe; God remembers the deeds of His creatures; the people of Israel remembers its destiny as the Divine witness.

The motif of "Remembrance" has had a complex development from its Biblical beginnings to the present, a history which has yet to be clearly traced. Its origins are in the baffling name given to the "first day of the seventh month" (in Leviticus 23:24) — *shabbaton zikhron teruah*, "a day of rest, remembrance (or memorial) of the trumpet sound." The relationship of "memorial" or "remembrance" and "trumpet sound' is spelled out in the tenth chapter of the book of Numbers. There the use of the trumpets as a means of communication in the Israelite camp is explained; indeed, a code of trumpet sounds — *tekiah* and *teruah* in their several combinations — is preserved. Although the Shofar sounds for Rosh Hashanah are derived by Rabbinic tradition from these trumpet sounds, it should be recalled that the Torah speaks of a non-ritual *teruah* when it says, " . . . and ye shall be *remembered before the Lord* and ye shall be *saved from your enemies*" (Numbers 10:9). The transition to the later Rosh Hashanah type of "remembrance" is indicated in the subsequent verse, "In the day of your gladness, and in your appointed seasons and in your new moons, ye shall sound *(u-teka'tem)* the trumpets over your burnt offering . . . and they shall be to you *a memorial before your God*."[86]

The prayer *Ya'aleh v-yavo* (which has been discussed in Chapter Four, THE SHAḤARIT SERVICE) echoes these Biblical verses plus later developments in the concept of "memorial before your God." Whether it originated as a Rosh Hashanah prayer or not, *Ya'aleh v-yavo* represents a step in the evolution of the "remembrance" idea which reaches its fruition here in the *Zikhronot* prayer-group. The Ashkenazic rite omits *Ya'aleh v-yavo* in the Musaf service, but the Sephardim feature it prominently as part of *Zikhronot* itself.[87]

The Biblical verses for *Zikhronot* stress the Covenant of the Patriarchs *(Brit Avot)* which has bound God and Israel together since the origins of our people. This theme is elaborated in the closing benediction by a reference to Abraham's supreme act of faith, the *Akaydah*, "Binding of Isaac."

In our version of *Zikhronot* (dating from the third century School of Rav) the "remembrance" theme, though given a historical dimension, remains intensely personal. The memory of God encompasses all that He has ever created or wrought throughout time. He is mindful of man's every deed, open or secret; He knows even our innermost thoughts and motives.

Atah zokhayr deals, however, not only with judgment of the individual but of nations as well. "On this day, judgment is pronounced upon the nations for war or peace, for famine or plenty." The so-called "sovereign states" must also submit their records to review by the Authority on high. Israel H. Levinthal has pointed out that the Hebrew word for "state" *(medinah)* is formed from the word for "justice" or "judgment" *(din)*. The development in recent years of weapons capable of the total destruction of mankind underscores the urgency of heeding the prophetic warning that "power politics" must be raised to a higher power, the Sovereignty of God, if man is to survive and fulfill his humanity.

The Zikhronot Verses זכרונות

As in the *Malkhuyot* section, ten verses are cited from the three divisions of the Bible; the final verse, from the Torah, is included in the closing benediction. These texts introduce an important dimension into the ancient theme of "remembrance." It is the Biblical concept of *Brit Avot*, the Covenant of the Patriarchs.[88] A covenant calls for continued mutual obligations. When a Jew prays that God "remember His covenant with our fathers," he must accept the implication that he must find his way to God by fulfilling the obligations required of him. "The idealism of our forbears reveals the possibilities inherent in us; man is capable of rising to great spiritual heights if he bears in mind his spiritual ancestry and the demands of 'noblesse oblige' " (Max Arzt).

The most familiar of the *Zikhronot* verses is the touching quotation from the prophet Jeremiah (31:20), "Is not Ephraim my darling son . . . ?" The text of *Ha'vayn yakir li Ephraim* has been a favorite of cantors who, throughout the centuries, have attempted to express its delicate beauty and deep passion through the medium of song. The rendition of these words remains a highlight of the cantorial repertoire in the traditional synagogue. Rabbi Levi Yitzḥak of Berditchev, prominent among the Ḥasidic preacher-cantors, together with his son, developed exceptionally moving melodies and gestures in rendering the verse. *Ha'vayn yakir li Ephraim* also appears in the *Haftarah* for the second day of Rosh Hashanah; indeed, the fact that it so beautifully illustrates the "remembrance" theme may be the original basis for the selection of this *Haftarah*.[89]

ZOKHRAYNU B-ZIKARON TOV זכרנו בזכרון טוב

The epilogue to *Zikhronot* recapitulates the theme of *Brit Avot*, the Covenant of the Patriarchs, and introduces the concept of *Akaydat Yitzḥak,* the "Binding of Isaac."[90] The covenant renewed by God with Abraham as a reward for his exhibition of supreme loyalty is movingly invoked. The opening sentences of this prayer are also quoted to introduce the *Parashat Ha-Akaydah*, the Biblical passage narrating the Binding of Isaac, in those prayerbooks which include the latter in the daily Shaḥarit service.

Toward the close of this summation of the *Zikhronot* occurs the phrase *"zokhayr kol ha-nishkaḥot* . . . (Thou) rememberest all forgotten things." This phrase was the original closing benediction for *Zikhronot* in the earliest period.[91] The Ḥasidic master, Moshe Leib Sassover, explained these unusual words as follows: "Your way, Sovereign of the Universe, is to remember only that which man forgets." When a Jew performs a meritorious deed and then forgets it (out of true piety) God holds it in remembrance; if, on the other hand, having performed a *mitzvah*, the Jew continually alludes to it (out of pride), God does not wish to remember the deed. Similarly with transgressions: those which the sinner callously forgets, God recalls; those which the transgressor, stricken with remorse, keeps ever close to his consciousness, God does not wish to remember.

A penetrating summary of the Remembrance theme on Rosh Hashanah has been penned by Theodor H. Gaster:

> The central theme of New Year's Day is the power of Memory itself. Memory defies oblivion, breaks the coils of the present, establishes the continuity of the generations, and rescues human life and effort from futility . . . The act of remembering is thus in itself redemptive. If, on the one hand, it involves a chastening

assessment, it involves, on the other, a comforting reassurance. New Year's Day is at once a day of judgment and a new beginning. If it looks backward, it does so only on the way forward; and its symbol is the trumpet of an eternal reveille.[92]

To mark the conclusion of *Zikhronot* (as of *Malkhuyot* and later *Shofarot)* the Shofar is sounded followed by two brief *piyyutim, Ha-yom harat olam* and *Areshet sefataynu.*

Atah Niglayta — אתה נגלית

Shofarot, the final section of the triad of prayer-structures which climaxes the Rosh Hashanah worship service, has the briefest and simplest prologue of the three. It is devoted entirely to a reminiscence of the Shofar sounds which accompanied the revelation of the Torah at Mt. Sinai, because this is the first reference to the Shofar in the Torah.[93] In the Biblical verses that follow, additional associations of the Shofar with Israel's spiritual history are evoked: as the symbol of our joyful thanksgiving to God (illustrated by the entire 150th Psalm) and as the herald of the Messianic deliverance.[94]

The final paragraph presents the Shofar entirely in its Messianic role. Even the concluding Torah verse (Numbers 10:10), "On the day of your gladness . . . " is construed as part of the restored Temple service, following the in-gathering of the exiles to Zion.[95] *Shofarot* thus underscores the attributes of God as both Lawgiver and Redeemer.

The closing benediction is expanded from the simpler *"Shomay-'a teruah* . . . He hears the Shofar sound," which is cited in the Mishnah as part of the *Shofarot* prayer for public fast days.[96] Following the benediction, the Shofar is again sounded, and the *piyyutim, Ha-yom harat olam* and *Areshet sefataynu*, are recited, as before.

Teka B-shofar Gadol — תקע בשופר גדול

As we have noted, the closing passage of *Shofarot* is an expression of the ancient hope for the Restoration of Israel to its land

and Sanctuary.[97] The drama of Jewish history reverberates with Shofar sounds from the climactic act of Revelation to the closing scene of the hoped-for Redemption. "The Shofar signifies freedom," said the Sages[98] and freedom meant for the generations of Diaspora just what this paean of hope envisions.

The fervent prayers of two millennia were at least partially fulfilled with the re-establishment of the third Jewish State in May, 1948 (fifth of Iyyar, 5708). When, in many communities throughout the world, the Shofar was sounded to celebrate the proclamation of independence of *Medinat Yisrael*, those familiar with the Rosh Hashanah liturgy found the ritual wholly appropriate. The words of our prayer have been literally brought to life by the incredible "Ingathering of the Exiles" which has been the first priority of the new State; at its peak, the immigration into war-scarred Israel reached the fantastic average of a thousand souls per day! One of the first legal acts of the State was to promulgate the "Law of Return" which provides that any Jew in the world may petition *Medinat Yisrael* to aid him to settle there that he may exercise his right of automatic citizenship.

Avinu Malkaynu, Zekhor Raḥamekha — זכור רחמיך

This brief petition, though included in the earliest known prayerbook, the ninth century *Seder Rav Amram Gaon*, and mentioned by Maimonides and other medieval authorities, has dropped out of many rites. It originally belonged to the familiar group of four interpolated petitions for God's "remembrance" known collectively as *May-ayn Zikhronot,* namely, *Zokhraynu l-ḥayyim,* et al. It was specifically part of the third member of this group, namely, "*U-khetov l-ḥayyim tovim* . . . Inscribe for a happy life . . . ," until the two elements became separated by phrases of the statutory *Amidah.* Our practice is to recite *Avinu Malkaynu, zekhor raḥamekha* only during the Cantor's repetition of the *Amidah,* whereas *U-khetov l-ḥayyim* is included in the silent recitation as well. The surprising result of this practice is that the truncated *U-khetov l-ḥayyim* remains the only one of the four "facsimile" *Zikhronot* which lacks any mention of remembrance.[99] (A full description of the *May-ayn Zikhro-*

not group may be found in the outline of the *Amidah* for the Arvit Service, in Chapter Three.)

B-SAYFER ḤAYYIM בספר חיים

"We pray not for mere existence but for *life*, the kind of life in which the King of the Universe delights. We want to live 'for Thine own sake,' O living God" (Max Arzt). The spiritual challenge which Rosh Hashanah poses for us is how to raise time to the level of life, a life that will be purposeful because it is consecrated to noble ends. Man's life is fleeting, ephemeral, but when it is linked with God it takes on permanent significance.

The Ba'al Shem Tov, founder of the Ḥasidic movement, has a beautiful interpretation of this prayer (the fourth and final member of the *May-ayn Zikhronot* group):

> "Inscribed in the Book of Life." This must be understood in a spiritual sense. When a man clings to the love of God, and, putting his trust in His infinite mercy, takes upon himself the yoke of the Kingdom of Heaven, he therewith inscribes himself in the Book of Life. But when a man is a slave to his passions, and so far loses his belief in the all-embracing love of God that he fails to repent and return to his Father in heaven, this despairing of the love of God is equivalent to his being inscribed — God forbid — in the Book of Death.

HA-YOM TE'AMTZAYNU היום תאמצנו

Our Maḥzorim preserve here only seven lines of this ancient litany which must originally have included a verse for each letter of the alphabet.[100] The author is unknown but it is written in the style of Eleazar Kallir, one of the earliest Palestinian poets.

A popular devotional commentary [101] has this unusual explanation for the poem: "This prayer was established for the penitent. Since it is not permissible to include it in the main part of the service (prayers for forgiveness are not allowed on Rosh Hashanah), it was placed here at the end." Since we are all penitents, it behooves the congregation as a whole to ask for "strengthening of the spirit" that we may return to God wholeheartedly.

However, the mood of *Ha-yom te'amtzaynu* in the modern synagogue is not a penitential one. It is chanted in a lively, clipped rhythm that contrasts sharply with the sustained solemnity of the main body of the service.

קדיש תתקבל
Kaddish Titkabal — Supplementary Tekiot

In many synagogues it is customary (though not obligatory) to sound a final round of *tekiot* at the conclusion of the Musaf service — either before *Kaddish titkabal*, during its recitation, or following the Mourner's Kaddish. One explanation of this practice is an old tradition that a total of one hundred individual notes *(May'ah Kolot)* should be sounded on the Shofar each day of Rosh Hashanah. The number of *tekiot* sounded at this point represents the difference between the number previously sounded (according to the particular rite followed) and the total of one hundred. The number of supplementary *tekiot* is usually thirty. Another tradition sets the total at seventy, which was held to be the number of Shofar sounds at the giving of the Torah. These traditions were particularly cherished by Kabbalists and mystics to whom numbers were of special significance. Others saw in the *May'ah Kolot* a reference to the Midrashic teaching that a woman in labor groans ninety-nine times in the pangs of death but, with the hundredth, gives birth to life.[102] Whatever the historical origin may have been, these final *tekiot* serve the very useful function of allowing the late-comers to fulfill their obligation "to hear the Shofar" even though they have missed the earlier *tekiot*.

The *Kaddish titkabal* itself is frequently recited to a joyful melody in keeping with the festive mood of Rosh Hashanah that reasserts itself as the long Musaf comes to an end.

A curious parallel to, if not the origin of, these supplementary *tekiot* is the practice called for by the *Seder Rav Amram*[103] and by a number of medieval authorities to sound one final *teruah gedolah* "in order to harass Satan, the accuser of Israel." Hai Gaon traces this custom to the Talmudic report that at the seat of the Sanhedrin in Yavneh a deafening Shofar blast ended the Rosh Hashanah services.[104]

CHAPTER EIGHT

THE MINḤAH SERVICE

• THE MINḤAH SERVICE • THE AMIDAH
• ZOKHRAYNU L-ḤAYYIM • THE U-V'KHAYN PRAYERS
• MELOKH AL KOL HA-OLAM • SHALOM RAV
• AVINU MALKAYNU • ALAYNU • AL KAYN NEKAVEH
• THE CONCLUSION OF ROSH HASHANAH

THE MINḤAH SERVICE

THE MINḤAH SERVICE מנחה

The Minḥah service for Rosh Hashanah contains no prayers, poems or hymns which are not already contained in the previous services of the festival with the single exception of *"U-va l-tziyon go'ayl . . .* A redeemer shall come unto Zion." Nor is this exclusively a Rosh Hashanah prayer, since it comes from the daily Prayerbook. According to Rabbinic tradition, Minḥah was established by the patriarch Isaac;[1] hence, on Rosh Hashanah, this brief service indirectly also recalls the motif of *Akaydat Yitzḥak*, the "Binding of Isaac."

When Rosh Hashanah falls on Shabbat, the Torah is read, as on every Shabbat afternoon. The passage is Deuteronomy 32: 1-12. These are the opening verses of *Ha'azinu*, the next to last weekly portion in the annual Torah cycle; the portion is read in its entirety on *Shabbat Shuvah*, the "Sabbath of Repentance" between New Year and Atonement.

The *Amidah* recurs in Minḥah without the insertion of *piyyutim*. The worshipper is afforded an opportunity to ponder again the profound content and simple dignity of the classic benedictions which represent the older, Talmudic stage of the Rosh Hashanah worship, prior to the interpolation of the newer synagogal poetry.

THE AMIDAH עמידה

In the Minḥah service for Shabbat (or a Festival which coincides with Shabbat) the Torah is read first and the *Tefillah* (or *Amidah*) follows immediately. This juxtaposition recalls a question that has puzzled commentators, namely why do we stand for the *Tefillah* and not for the Reading of the Torah? Rabbi Jonathan Eibeschuetz, an illustrious teacher of the eighteenth century, gave the following explanation. In prayer, God approaches — as it were — before we even begin and it is only fitting that we rise to greet Him as it is written, "Seek the Lord where He may be found."[2] In Torah study, on the other hand, the Divine Presence is felt only after we have sat down to study. This comment is additional testimony to the personal character and to the essential dignity of Jewish prayer. Each individual communes with his God directly and immediately.

On the High Holy Days, when the congregational aspect of prayer is so heavily underscored, it is important that Jews be reminded of the personal element. Congregational prayer was a post-Biblical development; the prayers found in the Bible are chiefly individual and intimate. Contrary to older sociological theories, individual prayer preceded group worship. "It is true that a Jew never worships as an isolated individual but as a part of the people Israel. Yet it is within the heart of every individual that prayer takes place. It is a personal duty, and an intimate act which cannot be delegated to either the cantor or the whole community" (Abraham Joshua Heschel).

ZOKHRAYNU L-ḤAYYIM זכרנו לחיים

"All of the varying aspects of the day, as they are conceived in Jewish thought, are epitomized in (this) great formula . . . Here is the remembrance; here is the kingship; here is the judgment. But here also is the resonant, dominant note that New Year is a new beginning, and that on this day all these things coalesce into a triumphant affirmation of life" (Theodor H. Gaster).[3]

Rabbi Jacob ben Asher suggested that *zokhraynu l-ḥayyim* is based upon the verse in Ezekiel 18:23, "Have I any pleasure at all that the wicked should die, saith the Lord God, and not rather that he should return from his ways and live?" In the Hebrew both verses have the same number of words (eleven). Another Biblical antecedent is the phrase in Isaiah 4:3, ". . . all who are inscribed for life in Jerusalem."

The fascinating history of the struggle of *Zokhraynu l-ḥayyim* and its three companion petitions (known collectively as *May-ayn Zikhronot*) to gain a foothold within the *Amidah* has already been discussed in the comments on this prayer in Chapters Four and Seven.

The U-v'khayn Prayers

ובכן

Each member of this triad of prayers begins with the word *U-v'khayn*,[4] an introductory particle meaning "now" or "and so." Abudarham and Jacob ben Asher quaintly connect this word with that used by Queen Esther as she resolved to go before King Ahasuerus, though uninvited, in order to plead for her people: "And so *(U-v'khayn)* I will go unto the king" (Esther 4:16). Similarly do we appear on these Solemn Days before the supreme King to ask for a merciful judgment.

The next passage, beginning *"V-timlokh* . . . Thou shalt reign," is not a new prayer but a continuation of the *U-v'khayn* group. The final triumph of God's Kingdom will begin with the vindication of the righteous over the wicked in this world and will then extend throughout all time and space, with Zion as its spiritual focus.

Melokh Al Kol Ha-olam

מלוך

This benediction, designated "Sanctification of the Day" *(Kedushat Ha-Yom)*, summarizes the sublime ideal of Rosh Hashanah, the dream of a world faith rooted in the teachings of Israel's prophets.

The genius of Talmudic thought translated the prophetic ideal into exact law. Realizing that a strict adherence to the entire Jewish tradition was impossible for the masses of the heathen world, the Sages defined "The Seven Commandments of the Sons of Noah." These basic moral precepts — (1) the establishment of courts of justice; (2) the prohibition of blasphemy; (3) of idolatry; (4) of incest; (5) of bloodshed; (6) of robbery; (7) of eating flesh cut from a living animal — were considered binding upon all mankind from the dawn of civilization. Non-Jews who lived up to these minimum fundamentals of "natural religion" did not thereby become full converts to Judaism but they were considered to be followers of the one God. As such they were respected by all Jews and were deemed eligible for the same Divine rewards. An important extension of this principle was made in medieval Jewish law which held that Christians and Moslems were not heathens and idolators but believers in one God, spiritual brethren of the Jews themselves. The commentators on the Talmud, notably Maimonides, are explicit on this point.

The attitude of Jews toward their neighbors, however, did not end at the legal frontier. Saadiah Gaon, outstanding religious leader of world Jewry in the tenth century, counseled his adherents: "All creatures are His creatures and we may not say that He has taken to Himself one to the exclusion of the other or to a greater degree than another . . . We hold that He is the God of all mankind . . . and the worth of each man and his lot are equally precious before Him." In the more recent pietistic movement of Ḥasidism, concern for the spiritual welfare of the non-Jew was prominent. Rabbi Pinḥas of Koretz said: "We should also pray for the wicked among the nations; we should love them too. So long as we do not pray like this, so long as we do not love like this, the Messiah will never come." Rabbi Israel of Koznitz prayed: "Lord of the world, I beg of you to redeem Israel; and if you do not want to do that, then redeem the gentiles."[5]

Shalom Rav שלום רב

The closing of the final benediction of the *Amidah* (in the Ashkenazic rite) during the High Holy Day season differs from that used on all other days of the year. The usual benediction ends "*ha-mevaraykh et amo Yisrael ba-shalom* . . . Who blesses His people Israel with peace." The High Holy Day text, "*osay ha-shalom* . . . Who makest peace," is the original Palestinian form of the blessing.

Like similar variations in the statutory benedictions on the High Holy Days, this one may be construed purely as a nostalgic throwback to an ancient form. On the other hand, it is possible that the simpler "Who makest peace" was deemed more congenial to the universalistic emphasis of Rosh Hashanah and Yom Kippur.

Judaism was the first civilization (certainly in the Western world) to conceive the possibility of a permanent and universal state of peace. It never tolerated the glorification of war as an instrument of policy, much less as a national virtue. Jews were taught that the beating of swords into plowshares and spears into pruning hooks would signal the triumph of the Kingdom of God. Noting that in the *Amidah* the benediction of Peace follows that of Gratitude *(Modim)* and Divine Service *(Retzay)*, Samson Raphael Hirsch commented, "Only that peace has lasting worth which is the fruit of a common gratitude and a common devotion to God's Torah."

The spiritual continuity of Jewish history has been dramatically demonstrated by the declaration of Prime Minister David Ben Gurion, made while the new State of Israel was still in the grip of the Arab war which attended its birth, and basic to her foreign policy thereafter:

> The future of the Jewish people must not remain constantly dependent upon its armed might. We will have to fight on. Nevertheless the future is not based upon the military but upon creative ability, labor, colonization and reconstruction, upon scientific and technical achievement. Our spirit must be the spirit of the Prophets!

Avinu Malkaynu אבינו מלכנו

All of the petitions of the *Avinu Malkaynu* prayer are chanted aloud but the final verse is said silently.[5a] One of the most illustrious of all Jewish preachers, Rabbi Jacob Krantz, the Maggid of Dubno, created a brilliant parable based on this curious fact. On the High Holy Days, he observed, a Jew can be compared to the village storekeeper who came to a warehouse in the big city in order to purchase stock for the coming year. He ordered everything in sight in large quantities while the employees made a great fuss over the excellent account. When the bill was presented to him, however, the purchaser grew pale. He begged to see the manager. Drawing near, he whispered in the latter's ear the following sorry declaration: "I'm sorry to say I have no cash. Do me a favor and let me have this order on credit."

This is the situation of the Jew on the Days of Awe, explained the Dubner Maggid. In our *Avinu Malkaynu* prayer we order plentifully from the Divine storehouse of blessings, singing aloud:

> "Our Father, Our King, renew unto us a year of good . . . send a perfect healing to the sick . . . inscribe us in the book of happy life . . . fill our storehouses with plenty."

But when we come to the end of the order, we grow weak. We know it is time to render payment and we have no cash in the form of "good deeds," so we whisper into God's ear, as it were:

> "Our Father, Our King, be gracious unto us and answer us for we have no merit."

Alaynu עלינו

Alaynu calls to mind not only the sublime Jewish conception of God as the Sovereign of the universe; it also carries with it moving associations of tragic persecution and martyrdom.[6] Ironically, this universalist prayer became the victim of a slanderous accusation and, as a result, was virtually mutilated out of fear of the official censors in medieval Europe. The accusation was levelled chiefly against the first paragraph which was absurdly misconstrued into an attack upon the founder of Christianity — this despite the fact that the disputed phrases, "for they bow down to vanity and emptiness and pray to a god that saveth not," are from the book of Isaiah, composed many centuries before the rise of Christianity. The form of the *Alaynu* prayer had been fixed by Rav in third century Babylonia, where there were no Christians at all! The Ashkenazic communities reluctantly deleted the passage which the authorities found objectionable; it is preserved, however, in the Sephardic rite, since the Islamic neighbors of the Sephardic Jews saw nothing to criticize in this beautiful prayer. The famous French manual of prayer,

Maḥzor Vitry, which first mentions the use of *Alaynu* as a daily prayer, also comments that it is to be recited silently — probably because of Christian animosity.[7]

Its declaration of the ultimate Kingship of God has made *Alaynu* a fitting death-song for those who were often called upon to defy the kingship of mortal men, choosing rather to sanctify the name of God with their lives — *al Kiddush Ha-Shem.* The last words of the *Alaynu* ("the Lord shall be One and His name One") are reminiscent of the Shema, that other companion piece to martyrdom. Joseph Ha-Kohen, in his "Vale of Tears," first mentions the use of *Alaynu* as a martyr song. During the persecution of the Jews of Blois (France) in 1171, where many scholars of the Torah died at the stake, an eye-witness wrote that the death of the saints was accompanied by a solemn song which resounded through the stillness of the night, causing the churchmen who heard it from afar to wonder at the melodious strains, the like of which they had never heard before. It was later ascertained that the martyred saints had used the *Alaynu* as their death-song.

In Ashkenazic synagogues, the music for the *Alaynu* of Rosh Hashanah is majestic rather than tragic; yet the martyr motif has persisted to the present. Eric Werner has recently incorporated the melody into his "Hazkarah Symphony," memorializing the martyred victims of Nazidom.

Al Kayn Nekaveh   על כן נקוה

The playwright Henrik Ibsen said that the Jews taught him "how to wait." If it is true that Israel is the most patient of peoples, the reason lies in such traditional expressions of hopeful waiting as *Al kayn nekaveh.* To wait, but not to sit with folded hands. Such faith as Israel acquired and retained in the face of every adversity called for acts of faith. The pious felt themselves obliged to become (in the picturesque Talmudic phrase) "partners of the Holy One, blessed be He" in the work of completing the Creation and of *tikkun ha-olam*, "establishing the world" under the Kingship of the Almighty.

The Messianic ideal has never ceased to inspire Jewish poets, even in the secularized atmosphere of the twentieth century. H. Leivick, the ranking Yiddish poet, has taken the motif of the "Redeemer in Chains" as his favorite theme. Writing in the black days of 1940, he restated the ancient Messianic tradition for his own generation, so prone to despair:

Tanks and airplanes come
But the Messiah does not come upon them . . .
The Messiah will not come save in a fashion
Foretold by all our most ancient dreamers.
The Messiah will not come save as the lowly come,
Riding humbly on a donkey's back.
Therefore do not profane Messiah's name, oh brothers,
And do not say the present unclean times
Are Messianic times — oh, do not say it!

But guard the wonder of the grain of sand
And the faint flutter of the blade of grass
Which with great patience awaits the Messiah's tread,
Which waits and knows, even as you know, brothers,
That the Messiah will not come save as the lowly come
Riding humbly on a donkey's back.[8]

The Conclusion of Rosh Hashanah

Following Minḥah on the first day of Rosh Hashanah (or, if that day be Shabbat, on the second afternoon) it is a widespread custom to perform an ancient ceremony known as *Tashlikh.* This custom calls for the symbolic casting of one's sins into a river or stream. The name *Tashlikh* is derived from the passage in the book of Micah (7:18-20) which is recited at the ceremony and which contains the word *V-tashlikh, "and Thou wilt cast* all their sins into the depths of the sea." The passage begins with the words, "Who is like unto Thee that pardoneth iniquity and passeth by the transgression of the remnant of His heritage? He retaineth not His anger forever because He delighteth in mercy."

Tashlikh is mentioned for the first time in *Sefer Maharil* by Rabbi Jacob Moelin (1365-1427), the greatest authority of his age and one of the chief architects of the Ashkenazic ritual.[9]

The Ma'ariv (or Arvit) service which marks the transition from Rosh Hashanah to the ordinary weekday worship, retains in the *Amidah* a few vestiges of the festival worship (e.g., *Zokhraynu l-ḥayyim* and the other *May-ayn Zikhronot* as well as *Avinu Malkaynu*). The reason is that the days between New Year and Day of Atonement are included in the *Aseret yemay teshuvah,* "The Ten Days of Penitence."[10]

The festival is officially concluded with the recitation of *Havdalah* at the end of the Ma'ariv service. The blessing is recited only over wine, and not over a candle and spices as at the termination of Shabbat.

Among the Ḥasidim, the farewell to Rosh Hashanah was marked by keen nostalgia. Naḥman of Bratzlav used to say:

> For me the key festival *(ikar)* is Rosh Hashanah. No sooner does it pass than I incline my ear to listen for the rapping (of the Sexton) awakening Jews to the *Seliḥot* service of the following year. For there is no time in reality; the entire year passes by as in the twinkling of an eye."[11]

APPENDIX

GLOSSARY OF HEBREW TERMS

Where feasible, each word is first defined literally and then explained as it is used in the book. Only terms that are used more than once in the book are explained here; terms used only once are defined in context.

ADONAI—The Lord; the name of God which connotes His quality of mercy.

AGGADAH—Narration; the non-legal part of Rabbinic literature consisting of legends, folklore, philosophy and religious thought.

AHAVAH—Love; a poem elaborating on the passage in the prayerbook that speaks of the Torah as a token of God's constant love for Israel.

AKAYDAT YITZḤAK—The Binding of Isaac, narrated in Genesis, Chapter 22.

ALIYAH (plural, *Aliyot*)—Going up; the honor of being called up to recite the benedictions over the Torah or to raise and roll the Torah scroll.

AMIDAH (plural, *Amidot*)—Standing; the silent devotion which is one of the essential elements of the service. Also known as *Shemoneh Esray* or *Tefillah*.

ARVIT—The evening service, often called Ma'ariv.

ASHKENAZIC—German; refers to the customs and rites of the Western, Central and East European Jewish community. Cf. Sephardic.

AVODAH—Service; the section of the Yom Kippur service which recalls and describes the procedure of the sacrifices offered in the Temple on that day. Also the seventeenth benediction of the daily *Amidah*.

AVOT—Fathers; refers to the patriarchs Abraham, Isaac and Jacob. The name of the first benediction of the *Amidah*.

BAKASHAH (plural, *Bakashot*)—Request; a prayer or poem of supplication.

BERAKHAH (plural, *Berakhot*)—Benediction; a basic unit of the statutory prayers.

BIMAH—Platform; the place from which the service is conducted.

DIN—Justice; strict judgment.

ELOHIM—God; the name which connotes His quality of strict judgment.

GAON (plural, *Geonim*)–Eminence; title of the heads of the Talmud academies of Babylonia.

GEMARA–Study; the body of Jewish law and lore developed after the Mishnah and which, together with the Mishnah, makes up the Talmud.

GE'ULAH–Redemption; poem elaborating on the passage in the prayerbook which speaks of Israel's redemption at the Red Sea.

GEVUROT–Mighty deeds; the name of the second benediction of the *Amidah.*

HAFTARAH (plural, *Haftarot*)–Conclusion; selection from the Prophets which is read after the reading from the Torah on Sabbaths, Festivals, and Fasts.

HALAKHAH–Rule; an accepted decision in Jewish law. A general term for the Rabbinic legal literature beginning with the Mishnah.

HALLEL–Praise; Psalms 113-118 which are recited on the Festivals, New Moon and Hanukkah as a service of praise and thanksgiving.

ḤAMISHI–Fifth; the fifth person called to the Torah reading.

ḤASIDISM–An important pietistic movement which arose in Eastern Europe in the eighteenth century.

HAVDALAH–Separation; the ceremony that marks the end of Shabbat and the Festivals.

ḤAZZAN–Cantor.

KABBALAH–Tradition; the teachings of Jewish mysticism.

KABBALAT OL MALKHUT SHAMA'YIM–Accepting the yoke of the kingship of heaven; theological doctrine of acknowledging the universal sovereignty of God.

KADDISH–Sanctification; the prayer which marks the end of a unit of the service. In one of its several forms, it is used as The Mourner's Prayer.

KARAITES–Scripturists; an eighth century sect which denied the authority of the Talmud and based itself only on the Bible.

KAVANAH–Intention; sincerity, concentration or devotion in prayer.

KAVANOT–Intentions; in the mystical tradition, the prescribed thoughts on which the worshipper strove to concentrate.

KEDUSHAH–Sanctification; name of a prayer based on the "Thrice-Holy" (Isaiah 6:3) recited responsively during the repetition of the *Amidah.* Also occurs in the *Yotzayr* section of Shaḥarit and in the prayer *Kedushah d-Sidra.*

KELAL YISRAEL–The historic community of Israel; a term used for the entire Jewish people as distinct from the various parties within it.

KEROVAH (plural, *Kerovot*)–Probably means approach or offering; a cycle of poetic interpolations into the benedictions of the *Amidah.*

KIDDUSH–Sanctification; the benediction pronounced over the wine for the Sabbath and Festivals.

KITTEL–The white garment traditionally worn on the High Holy Days and other festive occasions.

KOHEN—Priest; person descended from the house of Aaron, who is called first to the Torah reading.

KOL NIDRE—All vows; the declaration that begins the Yom Kippur Eve services. Yom Kippur Eve itself is often designated by this term.

LEVI—Levite; a descendant of the tribe of Levi, who is called up second to the Torah reading.

MA'ARIV—The evening service, also called Arvit.

MAFTIR—Concluder; the person called for the last section of the Torah reading and for the reading from the Prophets which follows. Also refers to the Torah passage itself.

MAḤZOR (plural, *Maḥzorim*)—Cycle; the Prayerbook for High Holy Days and other Festivals.

MAKRI—Prompter; the person who calls the notes for the sounding of the Shofar.

MALKHUT—Kingship or kingdom; the attribute of God's universal sovereignty which is the major theme of the Rosh Hashanah liturgy. The fuller term is *Malkhut Ha-Shem,* the Kingship or Kingdom of God; a parallel term is *Malkhut Shama'yim,* the Kingship or Kingdom of Heaven.

MALKHUYOT—Kingship verses; a section of the Rosh Hashanah Musaf service originally composed of Biblical verses whose theme is the kingship of God.

MATBAY'A SHEL TEFILLAH—Coin of prayer; term used to describe the official rubric of the service around which the liturgy developed.

MIDRASH—Study, interpretation; the non-legal Rabbinic literature contemporary with the Mishnah and Talmud. The plural, *Midrashim,* are collections of homiletical commentary on the books of the Bible.

MINHAG (plural, *Minhagim*)—Custom; local rite, as in the variant liturgical usages.

MINḤAH—Meal offering; the afternoon service.

MISHNAH—Repetition, teaching; the earliest and basic collection of Rabbinic law, edited about 200 C.E.

MUSAF—Addition; the additional service on Sabbaths, Festivals and the New Moon.

NE'ILAH—Closing; the last of the five services of Yom Kippur.

NUSAḤ—Pattern; the correct text of a prayer. Also the traditional melody of a prayer or Biblical cantillation.

PAROKHET—Curtain; the curtain of the Holy Ark.

PAYYETAN (plural, *Payyetanim*)—Poet; composer of liturgical poetry.

PIYYUT (plural, *Piyyutim*)—Liturgical poem.

PESUKAY D-ZIMRA—Verses of song; the psalms which compose the preliminary part of the morning service.

RAḤAMIM—Mercy; the attribute of God which tempers His strict judgment.
RESHUT (plural, *Reshuyot*)—Permission; a poetic prelude in which the Cantor requests the indulgence of the congregation and the aid of God before beginning to recite the *piyyutim.*
REVI'I—Fourth; the fourth person called to the Torah reading.

SELIḤAH (plural, *Seliḥot*)—Forgiveness; a penitential poem, the most frequent form of liturgical poetry in the Yom Kippur services.
SEPHARDIC—Spanish; refers to the customs and rites of the Spanish-Portuguese community (and of those communities influenced by it) and of Oriental Jewry.
SHAḤARIT—The morning service.
SHALOSH REGALIM—The Three Pilgrimage Festivals, Pesaḥ, Shavuot and Sukkot.
SHELIAḤ TZIBBUR—Messenger of the congregation; Cantor.
SHELISHI—Third; the third person called to the reading of the Torah.
SHELOSH ESRAY MIDDOT—The thirteen attributes; refers to the thirteen terms praising God's compassion which are found in Exodus 34:6-7. Frequently recited in the High Holy Day liturgy, especially on Yom Kippur.
SHEMA—"Hear, O Israel, the Lord our God, the Lord is One." The initial verse of the group of three passages from Scripture (Deuteronomy 6:4-9 and 11:13-21, Numbers 15:37-41) which are recited morning and evening. These words have become the central affirmation of Jewish faith and the core of the daily liturgy.
SHEMONEH ESRAY—Eighteen; refers to the weekday form of the *Amidah* which originally contained eighteen benedictions.
SHEVARIM—One of the notes sounded on the Shofar; it consists of three broken sounds totaling the length of the *teruah.*
SHOFAR—Ram's horn.
SHOFAROT—Shofar verses; a section of the Rosh Hashanah Musaf service composed originally of Biblical verses which refer to the Shofar in Jewish history.
SIDDUR—Order; the prayerbook.

TALMUD—Learning, study; the body of Jewish law and tradition recorded in the Mishnah and Gemara. Found in two recensions, the Palestinian (Yerushalmi) and the Babylonian (Bavli).
TEFILLAH—Prayer; in Rabbinic literature it refers to the *Amidah.*
TEFILLAH SHEL ḤOVAH—Obligatory prayer; as opposed to the later, optional poetic additions *(Piyyut).*
TEKIAH—One of the notes sounded on the Shofar; it consists of a deep unbroken sound ending abruptly. The plural, *tekiot,* refers to the Shofar sounds generally, whether *tekiah, shevarim* or *teruah.*
TERUAH—One of the notes sounded on the Shofar; it consists of a wavering

sound made up of nine staccato tones equal in total length to a single *tekiah.*

TESHUVAH—Return; the doctrine of repentance. May also refer to a responsum, i.e., a reply to a question in Jewish law.

TORAH—A Jewish value-concept of many meanings. The Pentateuch; also the Bible, Talmud and the entire religious literature based upon them.

VIDDUI—Confession; a recurring prayer in the services of the Day of Atonement.

YAMIM NORAIM—The Days of Awe; the High Holy Day season.

YOM HA-DIN—The Day of Judgment; name for Rosh Hashanah, used chiefly in the liturgy.

YOM HA-ZIKARON—Day of Remembrance; one of the names for Rosh Hashanah used in the liturgy.

YOM TERUAH—Day of sounding the horn; Biblical name for Rosh Hashanah, found in Numbers 29:1.

YOTZROT (singular, *Yotzayr*)—Poems elaborating on the section of the morning service called *Yotzayr* (Creator).

ZEKHUT AVOT—Merit of the fathers; the Rabbinic doctrine that the good deeds of the patriarchs help their descendants find favor before God, especially in judgment.

ZIKHRON TERUAH—Remembrance of sounding the horn; Biblical name for Rosh Hashanah, found in Leviticus 23:24.

ZIKHRONOT—Remembrance verses; a section of the Rosh Hashanah Musaf service composed originally of Biblical verses which refer to God's remembering Israel and His creatures generally.

A GUIDE TO TRANSLITERATION AND EDITORIAL USAGE

At best, transliteration of Hebrew into English represents an approximation of the original. A universally accepted system of transliteration has not yet come into being; the most one can hope to achieve, for the present, is a system that is internally consistent yet accurate and readily comprehensible.

In this volume, an attempt has been made to formulate a transliteration system as simple and easily comprehended as the proper structure and character of the Hebrew language will allow. Our system is based on that adopted by the United Synagogue Commission on Jewish Education, with some minor modifications intended to aid the comprehension of the general reader. In our treatment of the *sheva* and *tzayray,* we follow the usage of a previous publication of the National Academy for Adult Jewish Studies of the United Synagogue of America, *The Service of the Heart,* by Evelyn Garfiel. The equivalents listed below have been consistently followed except for the special cases noted and except where we have quoted verbatim from a source that uses a different transliteration system.

1. Consonants

ל	כ	כּ	י	ט	ח	ז	ו	ה	ד	ג	ב	בּ
l	kh	k	y	t	ḥ	z	v	h	d	g	v	b

ת	תּ	שׂ	שׁ	ר	ק	צ	פ	פּ	ס	נ	מ
t	t	s	sh	r	k	tz	f	p	s	n	m

The א and ע are represented by their vowels only.

The ה at the end of a word is represented by an *h.*

2. Vowels

◌ָ, ◌ַ	◌ֹ, וֹ, ◌ָ	וּ, ◌ֻ	◌ֶי, ◌ֶ	◌ִי, ◌ִ
a	o	u	e	i

◌ֵי, ◌ֵ are represented by *ay,* with the exception of certain words where we have accepted the spelling in such general use as to have become familiar to the reader, such as *bet* (pronounced *bayt*), *El* (pronounced *Ayl*), *Kol Nidre* (pronounced *Kol Nidray*), *Levi* (pronounced *Layvi*), *Rabbenu* (pronounced *Rabbaynu), resh* (pronounced *raysh), sefer* (pronounced *sayfer)* when used with titles of books, and *Yisrael* (pronounced *Yisra'ayl).*

Long and short vowels are not differentiated.

Ḥatafim are represented by the value of the corresponding full vowel.

Two consecutive vowels are separated by an apostrophe, as in *ya'aleh, te'amtzaynu* (except for commonly accepted words like *tekiah, Taanit*).

The apostrophe is also used to clarify the original Hebrew form where the transliteration is ambiguous, as in *shama'yim.*

3. Sheva

This sound, when it is vocalized at all, is nearer the *e* in the French word *le* than it is to any English vowel. In order not to make our transliteration system too technical, we have represented it simply by the letter *e.*

4. Dagesh

Dagesh Lene (kal) is represented as shown in the transliteration of consonants. *Dagesh Forte (ḥazak)* is not represented, except in words where the doubled letter has become widely accepted through usage, as in the words Rabbenu, *Tzibbur, ḥayyim.*

5. Definite Article

The definite article is represented by *h* with the vowel called for by grammatical rules, to be followed by a hyphen, e.g., *ha-, he-* (except for such a commonly accepted spelling as Rosh Hashanah).

6. Relative Pronoun

The relative pronoun is represented by *sh* and is treated in the same manner as the definite article, e. g., *she-anah.*

7. Prepositions and the Conjunction

The prepositions בּ, כּ, לּ, מ and the conjunction ו are treated in a manner similar to the definite article. However, where the conjunction is combined with a preposition, the former is followed by a hyphen and the latter by an apostrophe, as in the words, *u-v'khayn, u-mi'penay.*

8. Italics

Hebrew words and phrases are italicized, with the exception of terms which have become familiar through general usage. Since the general aim of this Commentary is to present as lucid a text as possible, we have dispensed with italics for the Hebrew names of the Sabbath and the Festivals; the names of the worship services, Shaḥarit, etc.; the names of the most familiar prayers and rituals, such as Shema, Kiddush, Kaddish; the terms Siddur and Maḥzor, when used in a general sense rather than as part of titles, etc.

In citing sources and references, we have dispensed with italics for the books of the Bible, Mishnah, Gemara and Midrash. However, the names of all medieval and modern works cited are italicized, in keeping with accepted editorial procedures.

9. Capitalization

Wherever they are referred to in the text or in the notes, the names of individual comments and chapters in this Commentary are printed in capital letters.

INDEX OF MAḤZOR PAGE REFERENCES

The index which follows lists alphabetically the various elements of the service commented upon in this volume and the pages where the comments appear. The columns to the right list page numbers in the following Maḥzorim where these elements are to be located (where a prayer covers several pages, only the initial page is listed):

ADLER-DAVIS=*Service of the Synagogue, New Year,* text prepared by Herbert Adler, prose translation by Arthur Davis (London: George Routledge and Sons, Ltd., New York: Bloch Publishing Co., 1922).

BIRNBAUM=*High Holyday Prayer Book,* translated and annotated by Philip Birnbaum (New York: Hebrew Publishing Co., 1951).

BOKSER=*High Holyday Prayer Book,* edited and translated by Ben Zion Bokser (New York: Hebrew Publishing Co., 1959).

POOL*=*Prayers for the New Year* according to the custom of the Spanish and Portuguese Jews, edited and translated by David De Sola Pool (New York: Union of Sephardic Congregations, 1937).

SHAPIRO, VALLENTINE=*The Complete Festival Prayers, Volume One: Service for the New Year,* English translation by the Rev. D.A. De Sola (London: Shapiro, Vallentine and Co., 1958).

SILVERMAN=*High Holiday Prayer Book,* compiled and arranged by Morris Silverman (Hartford: Prayer Book Press, 1951).

*Although the parallel prayer in the Sephardic rite often differs markedly from the Ashkenazic, we have included its page reference inasmuch as the Sephardic usage is discussed in the comment on that prayer.

Section of the Service	Pages in the Commentary	Pages in Selected Maḥzorim					
		Adler-Davis	Birnbaum	Bokser	Pool	Shapiro, Vallentine	Silverman
ADERET MAMLAKHAH	74	99	219	—	—	124	80
ADONAI, ADONAI	87	114	277	142	200	147	97
ADONAI MELEKH	76	203	255	129	—	271	87
ADONAI ORI	54	39	45	59	—	45a	24
AL KAYN NEKAVEH (in Arvit)	52	22	43	55	86	28	22
AL KAYN NEKAVEH (in Musaf)	155	156	381	201	238	208	160
AL KAYN NEKAVEH (in Minḥah) ..	174	22	455	237	282	28	202
ALAYNU (in Arvit)	51	22	43	55	86	27	22
ALAYNU (in Musaf)	154	153	377	197	238	205	159
ALAYNU (in Minḥah)	173	22	455	236	281	27	202
AMIDAH (in Arvit)	47	15	31	46	75	19	11
AMIDAH (in Musaf)	136	131	327	174	233	169	125
AMIDAH (in Minḥah)	168	15	439	228	270	19	185
AMITZ HA-MENUSA (see Melekh Elyon)							
ARESHET SEFATAYNU (see Ha-yom Harat Olam)							
ATAH BEḤARTANU	149	152	373	195	236	203	154
ATAH HU ELOHAYNU	73	98	217	125	—	122	79
ATAH NIGLAYTA	162	160	389	206	244	214	169
ATAH ZOKHAYR	158	158	385	203	241	211	164
AVINU MALKAYNU (in Shaḥarit) ..	82	111	271	139	192	143	94
AVINU MALKAYNU (in Minḥah)....	172	111	449	233	277	143	94

Section of the Service	Pages in the Commentary	Pages in Selected Maḥzorim					
		Adler-Davis	Birnbaum	Bokser	Pool	Shapiro, Vallentine	Silverman
AVINU MALKAYNU, ZEKHOR RAḤAMEKHA	163	164	397	210	—	219	172
BAREKHU	40	10	23	42	69	14	6
B-FI YESHARIM	59	80	169	109	168	98	60
B-ROSH HASHANAH YIKATAYVUN	143	239	361	189	—	192	148
B-SAYFER ḤAYYIM (in Shaḥarit)	82	111	269	138	189	143	94
B-SAYFER ḤAYYIM (in Musaf)	164	166	405	211	249	225	173
EḤAD ELOHAYNU	89	115	281	144	—	149	98
EL DAR BA-MAROM (see Melekh Elyon)							
ELOHAI NETZOR	68	94	209	121	190	117	76
EMET VE-EMUNAH	43	13	27	44	72	17	9
GADELU L-ADONAI ITTI	90	115	281	144	202	149	98
HAFTARAH FOR THE FIRST DAY	96	121	295	152	209	156	104
HAFTARAH FOR THE SECOND DAY	102	219	305	157	217	293	111
HALF KADDISH (in Arvit)	46	14	29	46	74	3	10
HALF KADDISH (in Shaḥarit)	60	81	171	110	173	3	60
HA-MA'ARIV ARAVIM	41	11	23	42	69	14	6
HA-MELEKH	58	80	169	109	—	98	60
HA-YOM HARAT OLAM — ARESHET SEFATAYNU	157	157	383	203	240	210	161
HA-YOM TE'AMTZAYNU	164	166	405	212	249	225	173
HE'YAY IM PIFIYOT (see Preludes to Malkhuyot et. al.)							

Section of the Service	Pages in the Commentary	Pages in Selected Maḥzorim					
		Adler-Davis	Birnbaum	Bokser	Pool	Shapiro, Vallentine	Silverman
HINENI	135	130-A	325	173	—	VI	124
KADDISH (see also Half Kaddish, Mourner's Kaddish, Musaf Kaddish)							
KADDISH TITKABAL (in Arvit)	49	20	41	53	82	11	16
KADDISH TITKABAL—SUPPLEMENTARY TEKIOT	165	167	407, 417	213	250	11	174
KADOSH ATAH	79	108	265	136	184	136	91
KADOSH, KADOSH, KADOSH	63	85	189	113	177	105	67
KEDUSHAH OF THE AMIDAH (in Shaḥarit)	77	107	261	134	184	132	90
KEDUSHAH (in Musaf)	145	148	363	190	234	194	149
KEVODO IHAYL	64	85	189	—	—	105	68
KIDDUSH	50	21	47	54	89	26	19
L-EL ORAYKH DIN	77	106	261	134	—	130	89
MAFTIR	94	120	293	151	208	155	103
MALKHUYOT VERSES	156	156	381	201	239	208	160
MALKHUYOT-ZIKHRONOT-SHOFAROT	152	154	377	201	238	208	159
MEKHALKAYL ḤAYYIM (in Shaḥarit)	72	97	213	124	183	120	79
MEKHALKAYL ḤAYYIM (in Musaf)	139	143	351	186	234	185	140
MELEKH AMON	63	177	177	—	—	237	64
MELEKH AZUR	62	81	173	—	—	100	61

Section of the Service	Pages in the Commentary	Pages in Selected Maḥzorim					
		Adler-Davis	Birnbaum	Bokser	Pool	Shapiro, Vallentine	Silverman
MELEKH ELYON, AMITZ HA-MENUSA	75	201	251	127	—	269	85
MELEKH ELYON, EL DAR BA-MAROM	140	145	355	187	—	190	141
MELOKH AL KOL HA-OLAM (in Shaḥarit	80	109	265	136	187	138	92
MELOKH AL KOL HA-OLAM (in Musaf)	156	157	383	202	240	209	161
MELOKH AL KOL HA-OLAM (in Minḥah)	170	17	445	231	274	22	187
MINḤAH SERVICE	168	172	425	221	260	231	179
MI-SOD ḤAKHAMIM (see Reshuyot)							
MIZMOR SHIR L-YOM HA-SHABBAT	40	9	21	40	64	12	3
MOURNER'S KADDISH	53	22	45	58	85	13	23
MUSAF KADDISH	135	131	327	174	232	3	125
OḤILAH LA-EL (see Preludes to Malkhuyot et. al.)							
OR OLAM (see Yotzrot)							
PENTATEUCH READING FOR THE FIRST DAY	90	117	287	148	205	151	100
PENTATEUCH READING FOR THE SECOND DAY	98	216	299	154	214	289	109
PRELUDES TO MALKHUYOT-ZIKHRONOT-SHOFAROT	151	155	379	198	233	206	156
REPETITION OF THE AMIDAH (in Shaḥarit)	68	95	209	122	183	118	77

Section of the Service	Pages in the Commentary	Pages in Selected Maḥzorim					
		Adler-Davis	Birnbaum	Bokser	Pool	Shapiro, Vallentine	Silverman
REPETITION OF THE AMIDAH: AVOT (in Musaf)	137	142	349	186	233	184	139
RESHUYOT: MI-SOD ḤAKHAMIM	69	95	209	122	—	118	77
RETZAY	81	109	267	137	187	140	92
RIBBON HA-OLAM	88	114	279	142	201	147	97
ROSH HASHANAH GREETINGS	55	24	47	—	88	—	178
SHALOM RAV	171	18	447	232	276	24	189
SHE-HEḤEYANU	51	21	49	54	90	27	19
SHEMA	41	11	23	43	70	15	7
SHIR HA-MA'ALOT, MI-MA'AMAKIM	59	—	171	110	—	—	—
TAYFEN B-MAKHON	139	143	351	—	—	186	140
TEKA B-SHOFAR GADOL	162	161	393	208	246	216	170
TEKIAT SHOFAR	106	126	315	166	219	164	117
TEKIOT FOR MALKHUYOT-ZIKHRONOT-SHOFAROT	157	157	383	203	240	210	161
TIK'U VA-ḤODESH	44	14	29	46	—	19	19
U-MI'PENAY ḤATA'AYNU	150	153	375	196	237	203	154
U-NETANEH TOKEF	141	146	361	188	—	191	147
UPAD MAY-AZ	137	142	349	—	—	184	139
U-V'KHAYN PRAYERS (in Shaharit)	78	107	263	135	184	134	90
U-V'KHAYN PRAYERS (in Minhah)	170	15	443	229	272	20	186
U-V'KHAYN TAYN KAVOD	147	151	371	194	236	201	152
U-V'KHAYN TAYN PAḤDEKHA	147	151	371	194	235	200	152
U-V'KHAYN TZADIKIM	148	151	371	194	236	201	152

Section of the Service	Pages in the Commentary	Pages in Selected Maḥzorim					
		Adler-Davis	Birnbaum	Bokser	Pool	Shapiro, Vallentine	Silverman
V-ATAH KADOSH (see Yimlokh Adonai							
VA-TITEN LANU	79	108	265	136	186	136	91
VA-TODI'AYNU	49	16	33	48	77	21	12
VA-YEHI BI-NESO'A HA-ARON	86	114	277	142	200	146	97
V-HA-ḤAYYOT YESHORAYRU	65	87	191	—	—	106	69
V-KHOL MA'AMINIM	145	149	367	192	—	197	150
V-SHAMRU	44	14	29	46	73	18	10
V-SHINANTAM L-VANEKHA	67	88	195	115	179	108	70
V-YE'ETAYU	149	151	373	194	—	201	153
YA'ALEH V-YAVO	80	108	265	136	186	137	91
YIGDAL	55	23	55	61	87	30	25
YIMLOKH ADONAI—V-ATAH KADOSH	73	98	217	124	—	122	79
YOTZROT: OR OLAM	61	81	171	110	—	99	61
ZEKHOR RAḤAMEKHA (see Avinu Malkaynu)							
ZIKHRONOT VERSES	160	158	387	204	241	212	165
ZOKHRAYNU B-ZIKARON TOV	161	159	387	205	243	213	165
ZOKHRAYNU L-ḤAYYIM (in Shaḥarit)	71	97	213	124	183	120	79
ZOKHRAYNU L-ḤAYYIM (in Musaf)	138	143	351	186	233	185	140
ZOKHRAYNU L-ḤAYYIM (in Minḥah)	169	15	439	228	270	19	185

THE STRUCTURE OF THE KEROVAH

In our discussion of the main types of *Piyyut* in Chapter Two of the Commentary, a brief sketch of the *Kerovah* form of synagogal poetry was included. There we spoke of the origins of the *Kerovah* and the meaning of the name itself. However, more detailed knowledge of how these poem-cycles we call *Kerovot* are inserted in the Shaḥarit and Musaf *Amidot* is required in order to follow the classical design of the traditional Ashkenazic service on Rosh Hashanah and Yom Kippur. The following is an attempt to present a simplified outline of the *Kerovah*-cycles used on Rosh Hashanah; it is based on the analysis of Israel Davidson in his monumental *Thesaurus of Medieval Hebrew Poetry (Otzar Ha-Shirah v-Ha-Piyyut),* and his *Maḥzor Yannai,* pp. xxvi-xxxviii.

In its complete form, the *Amidah* of Shaḥarit for the first day of Rosh Hashanah contains a ten-part *Kerovah* composed by Eleazar Kallir which begins with the poem, *At ḥil yom pekudah,* and is therefore designated by this name. This first part, known technically as a *Magen,* is inserted at the end of the first benediction which concludes, *Magen Avraham.* The second poem in this series begins, *Ta'alat zu k-ḥafaytz l-hat'il;* it is designated *Meḥayyay* because it is inserted toward the end of the second benediction which concludes, *Meḥayyay ha-maytim.* The third poem in this chain, *Even ḥug metzuk neshiah* is called a *Meshulash* ("Three-fold"); this name is a reference to the triple repetition of the word "holy" which follows shortly thereafter in the third benediction. The *Meshulash* poem is linked to part four of the *Kerovah* chain by the two Biblical verses, *Yimlokh Adonai l-olam,* etc. (Psalms 146:10) and *V-Atah kadosh yoshayv tehilot Yisrael* (Psalms 22:4). These two verses present a number of difficulties. First, there is no connection between the verses themselves nor between them and the *piyyutim* that precede or follow. Second, to the latter verse all printed editions append the words *El na,* without any apparent connection.

Davidson attempts to resolve these problems as follows. Psalms 146:10 *(Yimlokh Adonai,* etc.) is not an isolated quotation nor is it to be taken as the heading of the *piyyutim* that follow. In fact, it is the conclusion of a group of Biblical verses of a Messianic character regularly found at this point in the *Kerovah*-cycle in manuscript fragments (such as Yannai's *Kerovot).* "The printers, however (Davidson explains), have often omitted all the other verses and let this verse stand by itself, causing thereby the prevalent miscomprehension that it is the heading of the following *piyyutim.*"

As for Psalms 22:4 *(V-Atah kadosh yoshayv,* etc.), Davidson holds that this verse was not part of the original *Kerovah* structure and results from a complete miscomprehension by copyists through the centuries. The words *Atah kadosh* and *El na* were originally used only as rubrics for the two elements of part four of the *Kerovah,* just as *Magen, Meḥayyay* and *Meshulash* designate the first three parts respectively. The fourth part of the *Kerovah*-cycle takes the place of the third benediction of the *Amidah,* which begins *Atah kadosh (Kadosh Atah* in the Palestinian rite); therefore this *piyyut* is designated *Atah Kadosh.* The second element of part four in the classical *Kerovah* is always to be followed by the ancient prayer, *El na l-olam tu'aratz,* and was therefore designated by the rubric *El na.* The whole section then received the double designation *Atah kadosh — El na.* Davidson concludes: "The copyist, however, failing to see the significance of these catchwords, took *Atah kadosh* as an abbreviated form of Psalms 22:4 and generously supplied the rest of the verse, letting the words *El na* stand."

We return to the outline of the ten-part *Kerovah* by Kallir entitled *At ḥil yom pekudah.* Part four (which we have been discussing) is here the familiar poem, *Atah hu Elohaynu ba-shama'yim u-va'aretz.* It is designated (as we have seen) *Atah Kadosh,* after the opening words of the third benediction. The *Atah Kadosh* poem always concludes with the familiar formula, *Ḥai v-kayyam nora u-marom kadosh.* Part five has no designation; in this *Kerovah* it begins *Aderet mamlakhah.* Part six likewise has no special name; here it begins *Aym asher b-tzedek.* The same is true of parts seven, eight and nine — in this *Kerovah* of Kallir for the Shaḥarit of the first day Rosh Hashanah, the poems are respectively: *A'apid nayzer ayom,* etc.; *Adiray ayumah,* etc; and the universally beloved *L-El oraykh din.*

The tenth and final poem in this *Kerovah*-cycle begins, *Melekh b-mishpat ya'amid aretz,* and is designated by the term *Silluk. Silluk* is a word derived from Aramaic and means literally "ascent" (Hebrew, *aliyah),* because it is always introduced by the formula,"*U-v'khayn u-l'kha ta'aleh kedushah . . .* Now, let our *Kedushah* ascend to Thee, etc." The most famous *Silluk* in the Ashkenazic rite is *U-netaneh tokef,* found in the Musaf service for Rosh Hashanah and Yom Kippur. The *Silluk* is a "completing stanza" which links the *Kerovah* to the *Kedushah* prayer. For the sake of completeness, we might note at this point that some maḥzorim include in the *Kerovah*-cycle, *At ḥil yom pekudah,* the poem, *Etayn l-fo'ali tzedek.* This poem, however, belongs to the *Kerovah*-cycle by R. Simeon ben Isaac ben Abun for the Shaḥarit *Amidah* of the second day, as we shall see. By the same token, some maḥzorim print Kallir's *Atah hu Elohaynu* and *L-El oraykh din* in the second day's service as if they were part of R. Simeon's *Kerovah, Atiti l-ḥanenakh.*

Before proceeding to outline the other *Kerovot* for Rosh Hashanah, we must note one additional link in the chain of the classical *Kerovah* structure, namely, a prelude to the entire cycle which is designated *Reshut* (more accurately *Netilat Reshut*). In the *Reshut*, the *Sheliaḥ Tzibbur* seeks permission of the congregation to represent them in prayer, pleads his own unworthiness for such an awesome responsibility, and entreats Divine aid prior to his chanting the poems of the *Kerovah*. Similarly, *Reshuyot* are recited before the *Malkhuyot-Zikhronot-Shofarot* on Rosh Hashanah and before the *Avodah* on Yom Kippur. A relatively late *Reshut, Hineni,* is recited before the silent *Amidah* of Musaf on the High Holy Days.

The oldest *Reshuyot* are of unknown authorship and probably antedate Yannai and Kallir. They are: *Mi-sod ḥakhamim,* used as a prologue to the *Kerovah;* and *He'yay im pifiyot* and *Oḥilah la-El,* which serve as prologues to *Malkhuyot* in the Musaf *Amidah* of Rosh Hashanah and to the *Avodah* of Yom Kippur. The Sephardic rite introduces *Oḥilah la-El* prior to the entire Musaf, i.e., outside the benedictions themselves, in accordance with traditional Sephardic usage.

Yannai and Kallir did not provide *Reshuyot* to their *Kerovot,* but later copyists and *payyetanim* made up for this lack. Yekuthiel ben Moses of Speyer composed a *Reshut* to Kallir's *At ḥil yom pekudah* which begins *Yarayti biftzoti.* This poem, containing the name of the author in its acrostic structure, has become very popular in Ashkenazic synagogues.

The same ten-part structure employed by Kallir in his *At ḥil yom pekudah* was followed by Simeon ben Isaac ben Abun of Mayence in his *Kerovah* for Shaḥarit of the second day of Rosh Hashanah, which was incorporated into the Ashkenazic Maḥzor. Rabbi Simeon prefaced his *Kerovah* with a *Reshut* of his own composition (as is evident from the acrostic structure) and it is this prelude which gives the entire *Kerovah* its name, *"Atiti l-ḥanenakh . . .* I have come to entreat Thee." An outline of the ten parts of this *Kerovah* follows:

1. *Magen: Imratekha tzerufah*
2. *Meḥayyay: Tamim po'olekha*
3. *Meshulash: Shulaḥti b-mal'akhut*
4. *Atah Kadosh: Shemo mefa'arim*
5. (no designation) *Eder va-hod*
6. (no designation) *Etayn l-fo'ali tzedek*
7. (no designation) *Shavti v-ra'oh*
8. (no designation) *Melekh elyon, amitz ha-menusa*
9. (no designation) *Kol shinanay shaḥak*
10. *Silluk: Asher mi ya'aseh k-ma'asekha*

As in the case of Kallir's *Kerovah* for the first day, few congregations today recite all the parts of Simeon ben Isaac's *Kerovah* for the second day. The trend in most recent editions of the Maḥzor is to select the more popular poems for each of the two days. As we have noted above, some poems are interchanged between these two *Kerovot* in the printed editions.

For the Musaf service of Rosh Hashanah, a *Kerovah* is recited only on the first day. The *Kerovah* in this case is once again by Eleazar Kallir; it begins with the poem, *Upad may-az,* and is so designated. The outline of its full ten parts follows:

1. *Magen: Upad may-az*
2. *Meḥayyay: Tayfen b-makhon*
3. *Meshulash: Af oraḥ mishpatekha*
4. *Atah Kadosh: El emunah b-orkekha din*
5. (no designation) *Ometz adiray kol ḥayfetz*
6. (no designation) *Melekh elyon, El dar ba-marom*
7. *Kedushah: V-ḥayyot asher hayna*
8. (no designation) *V-amekha telu'im*
9. (no designation) *V-Atah ezon*
10. (no designation) *Tehilot kevodekha*

All Ashkenazic editions of the Maḥzor insert the magnificent poem *U-netaneh tokef* after part six of the *Kerovah, Upad may-az.* On the second day of Rosh Hashanah, when no *Kerovah* is recited in the Musaf service, *U-netaneh tokef* is the first *piyyut* to appear in the Musaf. The author is unknown. This beloved poem is technically designated *Silluk,* which is — as we have seen — a "completing stanza" linking the preceding sections of a *Kerovah* to the *Kedushah.*

Detailed discussion is provided in the Commentary proper concerning those elements of the three *Kerovot* outlined above which have retained a wide appeal in the contemporary synagogue. The *Kerovot* for Yom Kippur will be dealt with in the second volume of this Commentary. The central role held by the *Kerovah* in the liturgy of the New Year is filled by the *Seliḥah* in the Yom Kippur Maḥzor. A detailed analysis of the *Seliḥah* will therefore be provided in the Yom Kippur volume.

ACKNOWLEDGMENTS

Unless otherwise stated, all quotations in the text from the following authors are to be found in the works listed below:

Israel Abrahams: *A Companion to the Authorised Daily Prayer Book* (London: Eyre and Spottiswoode, Ltd., rev. ed., 1922).

Max Arzt: *A Modern Interpretation of the Rosh Hashanah Musaph Service* (Scranton: Temple Israel, 5693-1932). In addition, Dr. Arzt has graciously made available to the present writer considerable unpublished material.

Theodor H. Gaster: *Festivals of the Jewish Year* (New York: William Sloane Associates and Toronto: George J. McLeod, Ltd., 1953).

Joseph Herman Hertz: *Authorised Daily Prayer Book, With Commentary and Notes* (New York: Bloch Publishing Co., rev. ed., 5712-1952).

Morris Silverman: *High Holiday Prayer Book* (Hartford: Prayer Book Press, rev. ed., 1951).

Grateful acknowledgement is expressed to these publishers and to the publishers of works cited in the Notes for permission to quote from their publications.

The author wishes to express his deep appreciation to the Rabbinical Assembly of America and the United Synagogue of America for permission to quote from their *Sabbath and Festival Prayer Book* (New York, 1946); and to the Jewish Publication Society of America for permission to use translations of Biblical passages from *The Holy Scriptures* (Philadelphia, 1917) and to quote from those of its publications mentioned in the Notes.

NOTES

When a book is cited for the first time, the name of the author, the publisher, and the place and date of publication are given; thereafter, the work is referred to simply by title and author. If the same work is repeatedly cited for a given author, the abbreviation *op. cit.* (*opere citato,* "in the work cited") is used with the author's name.

Abbreviations used:

HUCA–Hebrew Union College Annual
JQR —Jewish Quarterly Review
REJ —Revue des Etudes Juives

INTRODUCTION

1. Quoted in Nahum N. Glatzer: *Franz Rosenzweig, His Life and Thought* (Philadelphia: Jewish Publication Society, 1953) p. 251.
2. *Seminary Addresses and Other Papers,* (Cincinnati: Ark Publishing Company, 1915) p. 26.
3. "Modernizing the Jewish Prayerbook," in *Commentary* (May, 1954).

CHAPTER ONE: THE SIDDUR AND THE MAḤZOR

1. *Yivo Annual of Jewish Social Science,* Vol. I (1946) p. 101.

1a. The original name for the Siddur was *Seder, i.e., Seder Ha-Tefillot,* "The Order of Prayers." Maimonides includes the text of the liturgy in his *Code* under the title, *Seder Tefillot Kol Ha-Shanah.* The oldest prayer text extant is the ninth century *Seder Rav Amram.*

2. It was suggested by Leopold Zunz and Samuel David Luzzatto that *maḥzor* is derived from the Syriac *ḥudra* (= *maḥzarta*); see Luzzatto's Introduction to *Maḥzor Benay Roma,* pp. 14-15. See also Zunz: *Ritus,* pp. 19-20. A good popular discussion of the nomenclature may be found in Judah Rosenthal's essay, "L-Toldot Ha-Maḥzor" in *Sefer Ha-Shanah Li-Yehuday Amerika* (New York,

1946) pp. 354-55.

3. *Maḥzor Yannai* was known for many centuries only through its mention by medieval writers until it was dramatically reclaimed from the Cairo Genizah and published by Israel Davidson in 1919. The more conventional designation in Geonic times for collections of *Piyyutim* is *Ḥazzanut*. The Karaite, Kirkisani, uses the Arabic word *Ḥazanah* in connection with the *piyyutim* of Yannai. For the role of Yannai in the creation of the great *payyetanic* tradition, see Chapter Two, THE PIYYUTIM.

4. Cf. Abraham Berliner: *Randbemerkungen zum taeglichen Gebetbuche,* II (Berlin, 1912) p. 61; the same work in Hebrew translation, *Ketavim Nivḥarim,* I (Jerusalem: Mosad Ha-Rav Kuk, 1945) p. 128; Ismar Elbogen: *Der juedische Gottesdienst* (Frankfurt am Main: J. Kauffmann Verlag, 2nd rev. ed., 1924) pp. 6-7.

5. The present-day Sephardim use neither of the terms, *Siddur* or *Maḥzor,* in the same sense as the Ashkenazim. They call the daily prayerbook *Tefillot* and the Festival prayerbook, *Mo'adim.* What Ashkenazim call the *Maḥzor* for the the High Holy Days, the Sephardim designate *Tefillot l-Rosh Hashanah* and *Tefillot l-Yom Kippur.* In the old Sephardic usage, *Maḥzor* referred to collections of prayer for the entire year. There is today considerable variation in nomenclature from one Sephardic community to another.

6. The term *Yamim Noraim,* which has become so widely adopted in recent centuries, is nowhere mentioned in the Rabbinic or Geonic literature. The earliest occurrences are among the twelfth and thirteenth century Tosafists: R. Eliezer ben Joel Halevi; his pupil, R. Isaac of Vienna (*Or Zarua, Piske Bava Kamma,* 444); and R. Mordecai ben Hillel, a descendant of Raviah (*Mordekhai* on Bava Kamma, VI, 149). These references are cited by Chaim Tchernowitz in *The Jewish Forum* (May, 1952) p. 72. The term is already well known to Maharil in the fifteenth century (see *Minhagim,* end of *Hilkhot Rosh Hashanah,* Sabbionetta edition, 53b). Maharil, it may be noted, was a great admirer of Mordecai ben Hillel.

7. A fascinating exception is the *minhag* of the three communities of the Italian Piedmont (Asti, Fossano and Moncalvo) which preserved down to our own time their old French rite for *Yamim Noraim* even though they adopted the Ashkenazic rite of their neighbors during the rest of the year. See I. D. Markon: "Ma'amar al Maḥzor Minhag A-F-M" in *Jewish Studies in Memory of G. A. Kohut* (New York, 1935).

8. See, for example, Mishnah Tamid 5:1 for the order of the daily morning prayers in the Temple, remarkably similar to the service of the Synagogue. For a popular survey of the influence of the Temple ritual upon Synagogue worship, see E. Levy: *Yesodot Ha-Tefillah* (Tel Aviv: Bitan Hassefer, 3rd ed., 5715-1955).

9. The Decalogue was also prominent in the earliest worship services but was suspended for public use, possibly as a reaction to the Christian heresy which taught that only the Ten Commandments had been revealed at Sinai (see Berakhot 12a). Solomon Zeitlin ("The Morning Benedictions and the Reading in

the Temple," in *JQR*, April, 1954) disputes this view; he suggests that it was the *discrepancies* in the two versions of the Decalogue found in the Torah (Exodus 20 and Deuteronomy 5) which constituted the danger referred to in Berakhot 12a. The likelihood of confusion was minimal in the Temple proper but not so in the provinces. Among the recent discoveries in the Judean desert near the Dead Sea are phylacteries containing the Ten Commandments. See J. Mann's interesting note on "The Decalogue In The Liturgy," in *HUCA*, IV (1927) pp. 288-89.

10. Berakhot 33a; Megillah 18a.

11. Yer. Shabbat I, 13. Cf. *Tur Oraḥ Ḥayyim*, and *Bet Yosef*, section 603.

12. For a fuller account of the liturgical contributions of Rav and Samuel, see Elbogen, *op. cit.*, pp. 262-64; W. Jawitz, *Mekor Ha-Berakhot* (Berlin, 1910) pp. 32-39.

13. Zunz, in his pioneering work, *Die Ritus der Synagogalen Gottesdienst,* gives a comprehensive listing of medieval commentators on the Maḥzor and *Piyyut.*

14. Yehudai Gaon, in eighth century Babylonia, permitted the use of a written text on Yom Kippur and fast days but not on other festivals. A legal inquiry concerning the propriety of a blind man serving as precentor indicates the habitual use of written texts by the time of Natronai Gaon in the ninth century. Cf. L. Ginzberg, *Geonica,* I (New York: Jewish Theological Seminary, 1909) pp. 120-21. See also *Saadiah Studies,* ed. Neuman-Zeitlin (Philadelphia, 1943) pp. 316 ff.

15. *Op. cit.*, I, p. 121. For a description of the contents of Natronai's "Order of Benedictions" see *op. cit.*, II, pp. 109-10.

16. *Op. cit.*, I. p. 122.

17. *Ibid.*, p. 175.

18. Joshua Bloch identified a Maḥzor for Yom Kippur in the Library of the Jewish Theological Seminary as printed in 1475 (by Marrano Jews). This would make it the oldest printed Maḥzor. The first Ashkenazic Maḥzor was printed in 1521; a Maḥzor for *Yamim Noraim* and *Shalosh Regalim,* according to the Polish rite, appeared in Prague in 1522.

19. A fascinating sidelight on the role of the Maḥzor in Jewish life is afforded us by the fact that, in twelfth century France, Maḥzorim illustrated with figures of animals and birds were in use. See Tosafot on Yoma 54a.

20. See Chapter Two, THE PIYYUTIM.

21. *Seminary Addresses and Other Papers,* p. 89.

22. Translated by Morris Silverman in *High Holiday Prayer Book,* p. iii.

CHAPTER TWO: THE PIYYUTIM

1. Pesikta 28, ed. Buber (Lyck, 1868) 179a; Leviticus Rabbah 30, ed. Margulies, p. 690; Song of Songs Rabbah on 3:6 (end), and on 1:1; Ecclesiastes Rabbah on 1:13. The use of a Greek term indicates that this poetic form dif-

fered from those previously in use; see J. Schirmann: "Hebrew Liturgical Poetry and Christian Hymnology" in *JQR*, vol. XLIV, no. 2 (October, 1953) p. 131. This monograph includes an excellent resume of previous research concerning the origins of *Piyyut*. Another useful work in English for general background in *Piyyut* is M. Wallenstein's *Some Unpublished Piyyutim from the Cairo Genizah* (Manchester: Manchester Univ. Press, 1956), especially Chapter 1, "The Nature and Composition of Piyyut."

2. For a masterful presentation of this thesis, see Shalom Spiegel: "On Medieval Hebrew Poetry" in *The Jews: Their History, Culture and Religion*, ed. Louis Finkelstein (Philadelphia: Jewish Publication Society, 1949).

3. Some authorities (e.g., S. D. Luzzatto, Wolf Jawitz) preferred to see Babylonia as the land of origin. See Ginzberg: *Ginze Schechter*, II (New York: Jewish Theological Seminary, 1929) p. 526, for a critical examination of the Geonic sources that seem to indicate a Palestinian origin.

4. *Authorised Seliḥot for the Whole Year*, ed. A. Rosenfeld (London: I. Labworth and Co., 2nd ed., 1957).

5. Israel Davidson: *Thesaurus of Medieval Hebrew Poetry* (New York: Jewish Theological Seminary, 1924-1933, plus Supplements up to 1937), an indispensable reference book for all research in *Piyyut*.

6. Spiegel, for example, reveals a contemporary political issue of the Spanish Jewish community in a *piyyut* by Yehudah Halevi. See *op. cit.*, pp. 544-45.

7. Cf. Solomon B. Freehof: *The Small Sanctuary* (Cincinnati: Union of American Hebrew Congregations, 1942) p. 243.

8. A possible reference to *Piyyut* in an earlier period is found in Yer. Ḥagigah 77b. See also note 16 below. A curious legend, found in *Maḥzor Vitry* and attributed to Rashi, ascribes several well-known *piyyutim* (e.g., *Atah konanta*) to the apostle Peter. See J. H. Greenstone: "Jewish Legends About Simon-Peter" in *Historica Judaica*, XII, no. 2 (October, 1950).

9. Cf. Elbogen: *op. cit.*, p. 280, also p. 206.

10. J. Schirmann argues for an earlier date than any scholar has yet advanced, perhaps as early as the fourth century (in Palestine). See *op. cit.*, pp. 123-61.

11. The term *Ḥazzan* is not used here in the sense familiar to Ashkenazim today. It appears to have special reference to the precentor on Festivals, as against the term *Sheliaḥ Tzibbur*, the precentor on ordinary occasions. It is especially frequent among Oriental Jewries. Cf. Elbogen, *op. cit.*, pp. 284-85. In addition to *Piyyut* and *Ḥazzanut*, another designation in the early literature is *Pizmon* – possibly derived from the word "Psalm." Later, *Pizmon* was used to designate a rhymed *piyyut* with a brief refrain, frequent in the *Seliḥot*.

12. Schirmann (*op. cit.*, p. 140) contends that *piyyut* is actually contemporary with and parallel to the Midrash: "It is also certain that the *Kerovot* represent a counterpart of the so-called Midrash literature. Their appearance occurs at the same time and their development runs parallel; both are manifestations of the same spirit."

13. Yer. Berakhot IV, 3, fol. 8a; cf. also Berakhot 29b.

13a. *Sefer Ha-Ittim*, ed. Schorr, p. 252.

14. As Louis Ginzberg pointed out, all Jewish sources that preserve this tradition are Babylonian, not Palestinian.

15. *Pirkoi ben Baboi,* a Geonic fragment recovered from the Cairo Genizah, quotes Yehudai Gaon, the great Babylonian authority of the eighth century, to the effect that the Jews of Palestine introduced *piyyutim* (the text there uses the term *ma'amadot*) during the period of persecution when the ruling power *(Edom)* forbade the recitation of the Shema and the *Tefillah.* Louis Ginzberg, however, doubts the authenticity of this tradition. See his *Ginze Schechter,* II, p. 526.

16. Rabbi Eleazar, son of Rabbi Simeon bar Yoḥai, is referred to as a scholar, *payyetan* and *darshan* (preacher) in Leviticus Rabbah 30, ed. Margulies, p. 690, note 5 and parallel passages listed in note 1 above. Some medieval rabbis erroneously identified him with Eleazar Kallir (see note 31 below).

17. Cf. the secret epistle sent from Palestine to Babylonia concerning the fixing of the calendar during the reign of Constantine II and the co-emperor Gallus in 353 C.E., as recorded in Sanhedrin 12a. During World War II, Jews in Nazi death camps and slave labor units employed similar devices to communicate with fellow Jews on the outside.

18. Davidson: *Maḥzor Yannai* (New York: Jewish Theological Seminary, 1919) pp. xix-xx. Saul Lieberman disagrees with Davidson on the grounds that a major phenomenon such as *Piyyut* does not arise because of a single historical episode or as a stratagem devised for emergencies. In his view, *Piyyut* originated in Palestine long before the edict of Justinian, but existed only as an academic exercise. During the Byzantine persecution, however, the authorities introduced these learned poems into the established worship in order to maintain, in some measure, the study of the Law.

19. In the earliest period (before Yannai) the practice of weaving the author's name acrostically into the *piyyut* was not widely used. Even in the later period, name acrostics are not invariably reliable for authorship; Zulay has shown that Saadiah and Hai sometimes honored friends by working their names into *piyyutim.*

20. Yer. Berakhot III, 4 (end). Coincidentally, the next Amora mentioned there is named Yannai. Cf. note 25 below.

21. The dating here (as elsewhere for the early *payyetanim*) follows Spiegel's chronology. Elbogen dates him as "not later than 600-650" (*op. cit.,* p. 307). Schirmann dates Yose in the fourth century (*op. cit.,* pp. 142ff.)

22. See J. Mann in *HUCA,* II, p. 291 and note 61. Berliner ascribes to Yose ben Yose also *Oḥilah la-El,* the ancient prelude to *Malkhuyot-Zikhronot-Shofarot.* See his *Ketavim Nivḥarim* I, p. 129.

23. J. Schirmann, however, contends that the *Kerovah* existed for several centuries before Yannai gave it its classic, definitive form. See *op. cit.,* p. 139.

24. Elbogen places him about the year 700. Brody puts him in the first half of the seventh century; Davidson in the second half. Schirmann, on the other hand, places Yannai about the year 400. Cf. note 25. For more complete discussion of Yannai see Elbogen, *op. cit.,* pp. 309-10; Davidson: *Maḥzor Yannai;*

Menaḥem Zulay: *Piyyute Yannai* (Berlin: Schocken, 1938); I. Brody's article in *Jewish Encyclopedia*, XII, p. 586; and J. Schirmann: *op. cit.*, pp. 143ff. Spiegel differs with Davidson on the authorship of *Maḥzor Yannai*, contending that, though some of the compositions of the original Yannai are included, the collection is the work of a certain Yannai ben Naḥum Albardani, a Bagdad *ḥazzan*-poet of the eleventh century.

25. See his monograph, "Ḥazzanut Yannai" in *Sinai* (Jerusalem, Shevat, 1939-5699) pp. 221-50. Lieberman concludes that Yannai did not use the Babylonian Talmud. Indeed, though there are many parallels between Yannai's poetry and Palestinian sources – notably from the School of Rabbi Ishmael – and, in a general way, with the Palestinian Talmud and Midrashim, there is no evidence that Yannai had used these writings as sources. It might even be conjectured that Yannai actually recorded some of these oral teachings for the first time in his *piyyutim*. According to Lieberman, the date of Yannai is open; he might even be contemporary with the Amora, Rabbi Yannai ben Simeon, who is mentioned in Midrash Tanḥuma (*Yitro*, III) in connection with the singing of praises to God by the Israelites at the Red Sea. Cf. J. Schirmann, *op. cit.*, p. 144.

26. By the Karaite writer, Kirkisani, a contemporary of Saadiah.

27. See Zulay, *op. cit.*, p. 328. Cf. further discussion on V-KHOL MA'AMINIM in the Musaf service of Rosh Hashanah, Chapter Seven.

28. Following Spiegel's chronology. Elbogen dates Kallir about 750. Others would revise his date in accordance with the earlier dating of Yannai.

29. See Ibn Ezra's commentary on Ecclesiastes 5:1. Interestingly, in the same passage, he extols two *bakashot* of Saadiah Gaon as embodying the best principles of Hebrew composition in the Biblical style and setting forth the poet's ideas clearly and concisely.

30. See *Orlogin*, VI (Tel Aviv, 1952) pp. 145 ff. Until his untimely death, Zulay was director of the renowned Schocken Institute for Research in Medieval Hebrew Poetry in Jerusalem. Zulay's researches in the language of the *payyetanim* earned him a place on the authoritative *Va'ad Ha-Lashon*, the Language Academy of Israel. Moreover, Zulay was convinced that Saadiah Gaon actually hoped to revive Hebrew as a living language in Babylonia and encouraged *Piyyut* toward that end.

31. E.g., by Rabbenu Gershom of Mayence and Rabbenu Jacob Tam, who held him to be the son of Rabbi Simeon bar Yoḥai! See note 16 above.

32. Cited by Joseph Marcus in a eulogy for Menaḥem Zulay, published in *Hadoar*, Vol. XXXVI (August 26, 1955).

33. Ginzberg shows that Naḥshon is the only Gaon who can be said to have opposed *Piyyut* in principle, and even this source is open to question. See *Ginze Schechter*, II, pp. 508f.

34. Saadiah includes one of his own *Avodah* compositions in his famous *Siddur*, though he modestly explains that its chief virtue was its relative brevity.

35. See Elbogen in *Saadia Anniversary Volume: Texts and Studies II* (New York: American Academy for Jewish Research, 1943) pp. 258-60. Cf. preceding

note.

36. This authorship was proposed by the English historian, Joseph Jacobs, but has not found acceptance among specialists.

36a. *The Earth Is The Lord's* (New York: Abelard-Schuman, 1950) p. 27.

37. For this reason the *Kerovah*-type of *piyyut* in the Musaf is sometimes designated *Shivah* or *Shivata,* because it is interwoven with each of the seven benedictions of the Musaf *Amidah* for Shabbat and Festivals. See Davidson: *Ginze Schechter,* III, p. 2. Cf. his *Maḥzor Yannai,* p. xxxviii. In ancient times *Kerovot* were even composed for the *Amidah* of certain special weekdays (consisting, in the Palestinian rite, of eighteen benedictions) and were accordingly known as *Shemoneh Esray.*

38. Even on Yom Kippur, Sephardim do not insert any *piyyutim* in the first two benedictions, only a few *piyyutim* in the third benediction (notably by Yehudah Halevi) and *Seliḥot* in the fourth benediction. See Lewis N. Dembitz: *Jewish Services in Synagogue and Home* (Philadelphia: Jewish Publication Society, 1898) pp. 410-11.

39. See Zulay's introduction to his *Piyyute Yannai,* pp. xiii-xvi. Indeed the name *Kedushta* is sometimes used as a synonym for *Kerovah.* Cf. Davidson: *Maḥzor Yannai,* p. xxvii. Elbogen suggests that the *Kedushah* of the *Amidah* itself is, in form, essentially a simple *piyyut.* See *op. cit.,* p. 215.

40. Schirmann contends (*op. cit.,* p. 140) that the *Kerovah* was not influenced by the Midrashic literature but was actually a parallel development. Indeed the Aggadic Midrashim contain pieces which are utterly *piyyut*-like. Cf. W. Jawitz: "Ha-Piyyutim Ha-Rishonim" in *Hoffmann Festschrift* (1910), Hebrew part, pp. 69-82 (cited by Schirmann, *ibid.,* note 35).

41. Samuel Feigin noted that the root word in Assyrian is associated with worship. Cf. M. Seidel in *Devir,* I (Berlin, 1923) pp. 34-35, for further conjectures on the etymology of *Kerovah.* I am indebted to Professor Leon J. Liebreich of the Hebrew Union College-Jewish Institute of Religion for this point and for a number of other fruitful suggestions as indicated in the Notes.

42. Yer. Berakhot IV, fol. 8b. The aramaic verb *krv* can mean "lead in prayer" as in the passage, "they noted that the Reader of the synagogue led in prayer *(d-kariv)* and said . . . " (Midrash Psalms on Psalms 19:1).

43. Cf. Davidson: *Maḥzor Yannai,* p. xxviii, note 34.

44. The medieval authorities derived this curious name homiletically from the initial letters of the verse in Psalms 118:15, "*Kol Rinah Vi-yeshuah B-ohelay TZadikim* . . . the voice of rejoicing and salvation in the tents of the righteous." In point of fact, however, *Kerovetz* is simply the old French pronunciation of *Kerovot!*

45. The age-old controversy over modifying the statutory prayers has its roots among the Tannaim themselves. Rabbi Yose held that anyone who departs from the forms established by the Sages has not fulfilled his obligation properly, and Rabbi Meir opposed this conservatism (Berakhot 60b). Characteristically, the Babylonian Talmud accepts the view of Rabbi Yose (Eruvin 46b) and the Palestinian Talmud follows Rabbi Meir (Yer. Berakhot VI, 2).

46. It should be noted that the Vilna Gaon objected to the interpolation of *Yotzrot* into the obligatory prayers of the Three Festivals and recited them apart from the service proper (similar to the Sephardic practice). On Rosh Hashanah and Yom Kippur, however, he recited them in the regular course of the service on the ground that additions to the original Talmudic ritual had already been permitted by the post-Talmudic authorities. For the conflicting views of the Palestinian and Babylonian authorities of the Geonic period on *Piyyut,* see Ginzberg: *Ginze Schechter,* II, pp. 508 ff.

47. The *piyyutim* were also favorite targets of the learned Christian clergy during the medieval period, especially among apostates from Judaism. See Zunz: *Ritus,* p. 176 ff. It is a curious coincidence that one of the important sources of information for the origins of *Piyyut* is another apostate — to Islam — namely, Samuel ben Judah ibn Abun of Fez. See Elbogen, *op. cit.,* p. 283.

48. See P. Selvin Goldberg: *Karaite Liturgy* (Manchester: Manchester Univ. Press, 1957) p. 108. Zunz (in his *Ritus,* pp. 160-161) lists *piyyutim* taken over by the Karaites from the Rabbanites. The opponents even cast their literary disputes in *piyyut* form. See Ginzberg: *ibid.,* p. 491.

49. Elbogen, *op. cit.,* p. 305. It might be noted here that A. Z. Idelsohn, a great admirer of the much-abused Kallir, wrote of him that he "did more for the revitalization and expansion of the Hebrew language than all the Spanish-Hebrew poets put together." See his *Jewish Liturgy and Its Development* (New York: Henry Holt and Co., 1932) p. 37. Shalom Spiegel has devoted a lifetime of research to Kallir's vast poetic output. A list of unusual Hebrew word-formations used by *payyetanim* from the Cairo Genizah is found in Davidson: *Ginze Schechter,* III, pp. 325-33.

50. *Abudarham Ha-Shalem,* ed. Wertheimer (Jerusalem: Usha, 1959) p. 71, reports an instructive case in point concerning the dilemma of Meir Halevi Abulafia (the great opponent of Maimonides). He was asked why he continued to sit in synagogues without protest while *piyyutim* were being interpolated into the benedictions of the Shema, which was against his principles. He replied, "It is not true that I could have protested . . . for I determined to follow another principle, 'Do not disturb the Jewish populace (when) it is preferable for them to sin unwittingly rather than willfully!' "

51. *Die Synagogale Poesie des Mittelalters,* pp. 70-71.

52. *Studies in Judaism,* Second Series (Philadelphia: Jewish Publication Society, 1908) pp. 18-19.

53. The process of deleting, abridging and critical selection of the accumulated mass of *Piyyut* has actually been going on for many centuries. Maharil, a leading authority of Ashkenazic Jewry (1365-1427), speaks of his making changes "in the prayers of the *Yamim Noraim*" (his is one of the first recorded uses of this designation for Rosh Hashanah and Yom Kippur). Rabbi Samson ben Zadok, faithful recorder of the practices of his master, Rabbi Meir of Rothenburg, speaks of abridging in a number of places (see Zunz: *Ritus,* p. 141). The former generations, like their descendants, were quite conscious of the length of the services. This concern was even greater on Yom Kippur when their homes were left in

danger of fire and hostile neighbors for long periods of time. Often only token verses of *piyyutim* were recited; this practice is reflected at many points (especially in Ne'ilah) in our own Maḥzor.

In modern times this process was accelerated. The Ḥasidic movement tended to give the "silent treatment" to much of the old *Piyyut;* the same was true of the Mussar (ethical) school of Lithuanian Jewry. The Haskalah movement not only began a critical study of the *piyyutim* but excised many from the services. The first truly modern congregation, Adat Yeshurun of Amsterdam, in 1796 began the process of distinguishing basic prayers from *piyyutim* which culminated in the complete rejection of *Piyyut* by the 19th century Reformists. It is interesting that S. Holdheim, leader of Reform Judaism in Germany, based this policy on the familiar objections of the medieval Geonim. Adapted from J. Rosenthal: "L-Toldot Ha-Maḥzor" in *Sefer Ha-Shanah Li-Yehuday Amerika* (New York, 1946) pp. 369-70.

54. A. M. Haberman: *B-Ron Yaḥad* (Jerusalem: Mosad Ha-Rav Kuk, 1945).

55. Cf. Simon Halkin's *Modern Hebrew Literature: Trends and Values* (New York: Schocken Books, 1950). Note especially Chapter X: "Religious Motifs in Modern Hebrew Poetry."

56. Notably the Sabbath Prayerbook and High Holiday Prayerbook issued by The Jewish Reconstructionist Foundation of New York in 1945 and 1948, respectively.

CHAPTER THREE: THE ARVIT SERVICE

1. Genesis Rabbah 22:28.

2. Leviticus Rabbah 29:1.

3. See Chapter Two, The Piyyutim. Maharil (38b) reports that *Ma'aravot* were recited on Rosh Hashanah only in Worms. The explanation for the omission of the poetry elsewhere on Rosh Hashanah evening is that the pious were wont to fast on the eve of the New Year (cf. Yer. Nedarim VIII, 2) and the services were therefore not prolonged. In Worms, however, as the *Roke'aḥ* explains, the fast had to be completed after sunset and the service was therefore prolonged with poetical insertions (i.e., *Ma'aravot*) while in other communities the fast did not have to be so prolonged. See Idelsohn: *op. cit.*, pp. 40 and 357, note 23; cf. p. 215.

Ma'arivim (= Ma'aravot) were also included in the Rosh Hashanah evening ritual of Troyes; also in *Maḥzor Vitry*, p. 576, and in *Maḥzor Romania* (see Idelsohn: *op. cit.*, p. 372, note 18). This type of *piyyut* is also to be found in the Prayerbook according to the ritual of English Jewry before 1290. See *JQR* (old series), IV (1892) p. 40 and cf. p. 29, cited by Idelsohn, *ibid.*

4. Under the influence of the Kabbalist, Isaac Luria, who — though himself an Ashkenazi — introduced many Sephardic usages.

5. In accordance with Rosh Hashanah 30b. See Mueller in his edition of Soferim, p. 262, note 3.

5a. Quoted in Hertz: *Prayer Book,* p. 109.

6. Rosh Hashanah 16a.

7. Louis Ginzberg conjectured that the three words, *El Melekh ne'eman,* may be a remnant of a somewhat longer benediction which was said prior to the private recitation of the Shema. See his *Geonica,* I, p. 138.

8. *Some Aspects of Rabbinic Theology* (New York: Macmillan, 1910) p. 64 and note 3; cf. also p. 96. It should be noted that not only the *Keri'at Shema* proper but its escort of benedictions *(Birkhot Ha-Shema)* also stresses the theme of *Malkhut Shama'yim,* e.g., *v-khulam mekabelim alayhem ol malkhut shama'yim zeh mi-zeh.*

9. See L. Finkelstein in *JQR,* XXXIII, p. 36, for a fascinating theory concerning the origin of the practice of the silent recitation of *Barukh shem kevod malkhuto l-olam va-ed,* as well as the exceptional case of Yom Kippur.

10. Yer. Berakhot, end of chapter one. Cf. Exodus Rabbah 22:4.

11. Rosh Hashanah 10b-11a.

12. Rosh Hashanah 8a-8b; also 34a.

13. See Elbogen: *op. cit.,* p. 147. Berliner, however, points out that "in Jerusalem to this day" no verse at all is recited at this point, in accordance with the Talmudic dictum that nothing should separate *Ge'ulah,* the benediction after the Shema, from the *Amidah.* See *Randbemerkungen,* II, p. 62 (= *Ketavim Nivḥarim,* I, p. 129). The authorities opposed the interpolation of these "signature verses" for Shabbat and Festivals but eventually *V-shamru* for Shabbat and Lev. 23:24 for the Festivals were permitted. Saadiah Gaon was the first compiler of a Siddur to include the verse *Tik'u va-ḥodesh.*

14. Leviticus Rabbah 29:5. Pesikta 23, ed. Buber, 154a, and the notes where *piyyutim* derived from this text are listed. Cf. also Midrash Psalms on Psalm 81.

15. *Aderet Eliyahu* on Psalms 81:4.

16. See J. Morgenstern: "The Three Calendars of Ancient Israel" in *HUCA,* vol. I, pp. 13-78; the additional notes to this article in *HUCA,* vol. III, pp. 77-107; "The Gates of Righteousness," *HUCA,* vol. VI, especially pp. 18-19, 32, 35, 37.

17. Yer. Rosh Hashanah I, 3.

18. *Sefer Minhagim* of R. Isaac Tyrnau (beginning of *Minhag Shel Rosh Ḥodesh Elul*). Also *Mateh Moshe* on this prayer.

19. This change is recommended by the *Levush* and other authorities.

20. Cf. Isaiah 5:16 which is interpreted by the Sages (Berakhot 12b) as referring to the Ten Days of Penitence spanned by Rosh Hashanah and Yom Kippur.

21. The thought is already found in Nehemiah 9:5. Wolf Heidenheim, in his historic edition of the Ashkenazic Maḥzor, notes that in Frankfurt am Main *l-ayla* was doubled only in the Shaḥarit and Musaf services, but not in Minḥah and Arvit nor in the Mourner's Kaddish.

22. Berliner conjectures that the two-fold *l-ayla* was separated by the superfluous *u* as a safeguard against suspicion of heresy, as in the case of the repetition of *modim-modim* in Berakhot 5:3.

23. The Musaf *Amidah* was thereby increased from seven to nine benedictions: *Malkhuyot* was coalesced with the fourth benediction *(Kedushat Ha-Yom)* while *Zikhronot* and *Shofarot* were each provided with its own benediction. However, the tradition of limiting the benedictions to seven in the *silent* recitation of the Musaf *Amidah* persisted down to the time of Sherira and Hai, Geonim of tenth-eleventh century Babylonia. See *Otzar Ha-Geonim*, Rosh Hashanah, pp. 68 ff.

24. Saadiah, however, does not even mention the *U-v'khayn* prayers in his *Siddur*, presumably because they were associated with the rejected view of Yoḥanan ben Nuri (Rosh Hashanah 4:5) viz., that *Malkhuyot* (which the *U-v'khayn* prayers seem to parallel) should come in the third benediction of the *Amidah* rather than in the fourth. Maimonides treats them as a variant custom and leaves their recital as optional. *Seder Rav Amram* includes them both for Rosh Hashanah and for Yom Kippur. Cf. THE U-V'KHAYN PRAYERS in Chapter Four, THE SHAḤARIT SERVICE.

25. Berakhot 33b.

26. It should be noted that though Rosh Hashanah is not specified by name, it is implied as one with all other Festivals. Terms like *mo'ed* (appointed season), *ḥag* (festival), and *sason* (joy), are here applied to it, as to the Three Pilgrimage Festivals. This usage is avoided in other prayers of Rosh Hashanah where it might be equally expected (see VA-TITEN LANU in Chapter Four). Maharil noted this instance as exceptional.

What we see here is a reflection of the early period in the Palestinian liturgy before Rosh Hashanah took on a more solemn character by association with Yom Kippur. By and large, the Babylonian Geonim (notably Hai Gaon) saw Rosh Hashanah in its more somber hues; the Palestinians, in its more festive aspects. There was considerable disagreement on this point among the medieval authorities. See note 30 below, and cf. MELOKH AL KOL HA-OLAM in Chapter Four.

The unusual phrase, *ḥagay nedavah*, often translated "festivals of free-will offering," might actually be rendered, "free-will festivals," i.e., voluntarily-accepted festivals. It has reference to the second day of the Festivals instituted through the "free-will" *(nedavah)* of the Jewish people (Maharsha on Berakhot 33).

27. See David de Sola Pool: *The Old Jewish-Aramaic Prayer, the Kaddish* (Leipsig, 1909) p. 66. The Talmud also hints at this origin (Sotah 49a).

28. The opening two words of the Kaddish are based on Ezekiel 38:23. *Yehay shemay rabba*, etc. is derived from Daniel 2:20, also written in Aramaic. Probably because the Kaddish was not yet part of the daily service, the Talmud records none of the present text except for the responses *Amen* and *Yehay shemay rabba* (cf. Berakhot 3a, 21b; Shabbat 119b; Sukkah 39a; Sotah 49a).

29. The recitation of Kiddush in the Synagogue arose because of the needs of travelers who would lodge in the synagogues of ancient Palestine (Pesaḥim 101).

30. The exact text of the Kiddush on Rosh Hashanah is a subject of controversy among the medieval authorities. The issue was whether or not Rosh

Hashanah should be treated, like the other Festivals, as a *yom-tov.* Soferim XIX, 3 (ed. Higger, pp. 325-26) ordains the use of the phrase *yom-tov mikra kodesh* (as for other Festivals), in addition to *Rosh Ḥodesh, Rosh Hashanah* and *Yom teka shofar ha-zikaron.* Maimonides prescribes the phrase, *yom-tov mikra kodesh yom ha-zikaron ha-zeh (Hilkhot Shabbat* of the *Code,* 29:19.) Sephardim still use the phrases given by Maimonides. However, the more solemn interpretation prevailed among Ashkenazim, as evidenced by the substitution of *U-devarkha emet,* etc. for *U-mo'aday kodshekha b-simḥah u-v'sason,* etc. Cf. note 26 above.

31. The Torah nowhere uses the name "Rosh Hashanah" for the "first day of the seventh month." Instead it calls this day *yom teruah,* "the day of sounding the horn" (Numbers 29:1) and *shabbaton zikhron teruah,* "a solemn rest . . . a memorial of sounding the horn" (Leviticus 23:24). Rabbinic tradition reserved the latter designation for a Rosh Hashanah that fell on Shabbat, when the Shofar could only be *recalled* in the prayers but not sounded (Rosh Hashanah 29b).

The designation, *yom zikhron teruah* (used only on Shabbat), seems to be a combination of the two Biblical names. However, David Hoffmann saw in it nothing more than a printer's confusion: the correct wording here on a Shabbat is simply *zikhron teruah,* as in the Sephardic text; the word *yom* was repeated in error from the preceding *yom ha-zikaron* (see Berliner: *Ketavim Nivḥarim,* I, p. 129). The Italian rite has here the more logical *zikhron yom teruah.* It is interesting to note that, whereas Rabbinic Judaism rarely uses the name *Yom Teruah* for Rosh Hashanah (because of its limited application), the Karaites invariably employ it — though the Shofar itself plays a minor role in their Rosh Hashanah tradition. The reason is, of course, that *Yom Teruah* is the Biblical name of the festival; the Karaites accepted only the Biblical tradition but rejected the Talmudic interpretation.

32. Rabbi Isaac of Vienna, author of *Or Zarua,* an important early source for Ashkenazic liturgy, explains that the reason for the Ḥazzan's turning to face the congregation during Kiddush is that essentially he is making a public proclamation.

33. See, for example, *Tur Oraḥ Ḥayyim,* section 600, where Asher ben Yeḥiel's practice is recorded by his son. The custom of eating foods of symbolic meaning on Rosh Hashanah night is already mentioned in the Talmud (Keritot 10a, Horayot 12a).

34. The *Roke'aḥ* reports that it was first used after the Shaḥarit service. It was later extended to all the services. Some communities, however, omitted it after Minḥah since the purpose of the recitation was to remind the worshipper of God's sovereignty before he returned to his home or to work. Since one did not leave the Synagogue after Minḥah but remained for Arvit, the *Alaynu* was reserved for the close of the latter *(Magen Avraham* quoting *Tola'at Ya'akov).* For instances of daily recitation of *Alaynu* prior to the thirteenth century, see note 70 on Chapter Seven, THE MUSAF SERVICE.

35. *Kol Bo,* 16.

35a. M. Buber: *Tales of the Hasidim, The Later Masters* (New York:

Schocken Books, 1948) p. 317.

36. It is first mentioned by Isaac of Vienna, *Or Zarua,* II, p. 11b, and by the *Maḥzor Vitry,* a French work of the early thirteenth century.

37. These words plus *Amen* are the only words of the Kaddish found in the Talmud proper. The name *Kaddish* itself is not found there; its first mention comes in Soferim (XVI, 12; XIX, 1; XXI, 6). For the emphasis on *Yehay shemay rabba,* see Sifre Deuteronomy, 306.

38. Sotah 49a.

39. Shabbat 119b; cf. Midrash Proverbs X, 10; XIV, 4. Cf. also Berakhot 3a.

40. Midrash Psalms on Psalm 27.

41. Pesikta 27, ed. Buber, p. 176a.

42. This custom was introduced by the Kabbalist, Isaac Luria, an Ashkenazi who frequently utilized the Sephardic rite.

43. Maharil recommends that this or a similar salutation head all friendly letters from the first of Elul on. The custom of exchanging Rosh Hashanah cards seems to have developed through imitation of non-Jewish practices; see A. L. Hirshovitz: *Otzar Kol Minhagay Yeshurun* (3rd ed., St. Louis, 1918), p. 173.

44. Rosh Hashanah 16b.

CHAPTER FOUR: THE SHAḤARIT SERVICE

1. This practice was introduced by Rabbi Meir of Rothenburg; see *Sefer Tashbetz* (Jerusalem 1951, reprint) p. 36 (=*Kol Bo,* fol. 30b). The practice was supported by Maharil. For a more recent interpretation of the reasons behind the variations in the opening phrases, see A. L. Hirshovitz: *op. cit.,* p. 241. The passage in question does not exist in the Sephardic rite.

2. This variation goes back to the *Roke'aḥ*; it was opposed by Maharil and by Rabbi Jacob Emden, whose view is supported by the manuscripts.

3. Cited by *Kol Bo* in commenting on the phrase, *Yitzḥak yeranayn,* in the Minḥah service of Shabbat.

4. See Soferim (ed. Higger) XVIII, 11, p. 323, and Mann's note on this passage in *HUCA,* II, p. 327.

5. For musical rendering of the Kaddish in its various forms, see *Jewish Encyclopedia,* vol. VII, p. 403.

5a. *Sefer Ha-Mo'adim,* vol. I, ed. J. L. Barukh (Tel Aviv: Dvir and "Oneg Shabbat" Society [Ohel-Shem], 1950) p. 100.

5b. The first half of the "Rebbe's Kaddish" has a close parallel in a *midrash* found in Leviticus Rabbah II, 4, ed. Margulies, p. 41 (parallels to this *midrash* are given there, p. 40, note 3).

6. See Chapter Two, THE PIYYUTIM. On *Or olam* see J. Mann, *HUCA,* II, p. 291 and note 61.

7. Genesis Rabbah III, 7; Ḥagigah 12a.

8. This interpretation is based on the correct text which omits the *bet* before the word *otzar.*

9. Quoted from *Language of Faith: Selected Jewish Prayers* (New York: Schocken Books, 1947) p. 54. The translation is by Nahum N. Glatzer and Olga Marx.

10. See Chapter Two, THE PIYYUTIM.

11. Pesikta quoted in Yalkut Shimoni to Isaiah 61, section 506, and in several other places (cited by Heidenheim).

12. For the source of this fascinating legend, see *Bet Ha-Midrash* of Jellinek, vol. V, pp. 148-52.

13. See Louis Finkelstein: "La Kedouscha et les Benedictions du Schema," in *REJ* (1932); Ginzberg; *Geonica,* I, pp. 130 ff. In Jewish mystical circles, the "Thrice-Holy" gave rise to theological speculations that issued in Kabbalah, one of whose basic premises is that God's holiness is increased by Israel's daily recitation of the *Kedushah.* A vast literature grew up around such ideas. Nevertheless, one must note the remarkable restraint of the Jewish liturgy in regard to this mystical lore so popular among the rank and file. The Talmudic authorities permitted only the briefest benediction for God's holiness in the *Amidah* proper. They required a quorum for the recitation of the *Kedushah* of the *Amidah.* Many later authorities (e.g., the Geonim of Sura, Maimonides) required a quorum for *all* occasions when the "Thrice-Holy" was to be recited. On early Christian interpretation of the "Thrice-Holy" see J. Mann in *HUCA,* IV, pp. 264 ff.

14. The exact meaning of the text in Ezekiel is not clear; some modern scholars even doubt that it is to be construed as a direct quotation. Our explanation follows the Rabbinic tradition. Cf. Pirke d-R. Eliezer, end of Chapter Four.

15. Genesis Rabbah XII, 15.

16. See Ezekiel, Chapter 1. This chapter is linked by the Jewish liturgy with Isaiah, Chapter 6 in the prayer, *Kedushah.* See preceding comment on KADOSH, KADOSH, KADOSH.

17. "On Medieval Hebrew Poetry," in *The Jews: Their History, Culture and Religion.*

18. Composed for Simḥat Torah; see Salaman-Brody: *Selected Poems of Yehudah Halevi* (Philadelphia: Jewish Publication Society, 1928), p. 134. The translation is by Nina Salaman.

19. Note that the French ritual omits *V-ha-ḥayyot yeshorayru* on the basis of the Talmudic tradition (Arakhin 10b) that Jews should not "sing" on Rosh Hashanah and Yom Kippur. See *Sefer Tashbetz* (reprint, Jerusalem 5711-1951) p. 19, note 2. The Tosafists (on Arakhin 10b) argue against this omission on the grounds that, though Israel may not "sing," the angels may. Cf. WHY WE DO NOT SAY HALLEL ON ROSH HASHANAH, end of Chapter Four.

20. For extended discussion of Jewish angelology, see *Jewish Encyclopedia,* vol. I, art. "Angelology;" G. F. Moore: *Judaism in the First Centuries of the Christian Era* (Cambridge: Harvard Univ. Press, 1927) vol. II, Index, p. 401; I. Abrahams: *A Companion to the Authorised Daily Prayer Book,* pp. xliv-xlvii.

21. Psalms 104:4.

22. For a fascinating treatment of this aspect of Jewish angelology and demonology, see B. J. Bamberger: *Fallen Angels* (Philadelphia: Jewish Publication Society, 1952).

23. Cf. Rosh Hashanah 26a; Yer. Rosh Hashanah I, 2; Genesis Rabbah 48.

24. See L. Ginzberg: *Legends of the Jews* (Philadelphia: Jewish Publication Society) Index Volume prepared by Boaz Cohen, 1938, p. 85.

25. For the derivation and meaning of *Kataygor*, see M. Jastrow: *Dictionary of the Talmud*, p. 1347.

26. See THE SHOFAR IN JEWISH FOLKLORE AND SUPERSTITION, Chapter Six.

27. See I. Abrahams: *Aspects of Judaism*, p. 20.

28. Betzah 15b-16a.

28a. Translated by Maurice Samuel.

29. Berakhot 17a.

30. *Ḥibbur Ha-Teshuvah*, ed. Schreiber (New York, 1950) p. 265.

31. See RULES FOR THE SHOFAR AND THE TEKIOT, Chapter Six.

32. Two excellent surveys of the *piyyutim* for Rosh Hashanah have been published by Meyer Waxman in *Hadoar*, vol. XXX, issue of Sept. 8, 1950, on Kallir's *piyyutim* for the first day, and vol. XXXIV, issue of Sept. 24, 1954, on Simeon ben Isaac ben Abun's *piyyutim* for the second day.

33. Cf. Berliner: *op. cit.*, I, pp. 69-70 (Hebrew ed., p. 65).

34. See Chapter Two, THE PIYYUTIM. Since the Sephardim do not recite *Kerovot* on Rosh Hashanah, they do not include *Mi-sod ḥakhamim*.

35. For a fuller discussion of the *Reshut* form and its relationship to the *Kerovah*, see Chapter Two, THE PIYYUTIM and the appendix, THE STRUCTURE OF THE KEROVAH.

36. Cf. Chapter Two, THE PIYYUTIM.

37. The Talmudic legend (Rosh Hashanah 17b) pictures God himself as a *Sheliaḥ Tzibbur* demonstrating to Moses the proper method of petitioning Divine forgiveness for the sins of Israel.

38. The *May-ayn Zikhronot* are first mentioned in Soferim XIX, 6 (ed. Higger, pp. 328-29) as having gained acceptance "only with great difficulty" and, at that, only on Rosh Hashanah and Yom Kippur proper but not on the intervening days (as is our present custom). Wolf Jawitz tried unsuccessfully to show that they must have existed in Mishnaic times; see his *Mekor Ha-Berakhot*, p. 27. The medieval decisors (e.g., the *Rosh*, end of Chapter 1 of *Berakhot*) ascribed the *May-ayn Zikhronot* to the Babylonian Geonim; but it is clear that the Geonim were by no means unanimously in favor of admitting them into the liturgy (cf. *Shibolay Ha-Leket*, par. 286). Indeed the earliest reference to *Zokhraynu*, et al., in the Geonic literature, viz., the fascinating *Pirkoi ben Baboi*, constitutes a vehement protest against their insertion in the benedictions of the *Amidah!* (cf. L. Ginzberg: *Ginze Schechter*, II, pp. 512 ff., 553). Nevertheless, *Seder Rav Amram* includes them in substantially the form we now use. Saadiah includes them as a widespread custom. Maimonides includes them as optional, recording that "the majority of the people" recite them. The sources are not at all crystal clear as to the attitudes of the various Geonim on this subject and

copyists' errors in the manuscripts further becloud the picture; but Ginzberg conjectures that, as a general rule, the Geonim of Sura favored the insertion of *Zokhraynu,* et al., while the Geonim of Pumbeditha opposed the practice (*ibid.,* pp. 512-13). Ben Baboi reflects the Pumbeditha tradition; Amram, that of Sura.

An ingenious but implausible suggestion as to the origin and structure of the *May-ayn Zikhronot* was proposed by Israel Davidson. He felt that they must have been older than the period of the Geonim who debate their legitimacy. His conjecture is that the *May-ayn Zikhronot* are the remnants of an older Palestinian *piyyut* (specifically of the *Shivata* type), which also included *U-v'khayn tayn paḥdekha* and *Atah beḥartanu!* See his *Thesaurus,* II, p. 215.

39. Probably this petition originally began *Zekhor raḥamekha* (as in Saadiah's *Siddur*). See comment on the latter prayer in the Musaf service.

40. This explanation is quoted in the *Sefer Ha-Pardes* of Rashi in the name of Saadiah Gaon (ed. Ehrenreich, p. 230).

41. Cf. MALKHUYOT - ZIKHRONOT - SHOFAROT, in Chapter Seven and RULES FOR THE SHOFAR AND THE TEKIOT, in Chapter Six.

42. Such petitions are proscribed in the Talmud (Berakhot 34a) in the first three and last three benedictions of the *Amidah.* An attempt to include similar petitions in the first three benedictions of the Sabbath *Amidah* had failed to gain a foothold (see *Tur Oraḥ Ḥayyim,* section 268; Tosafot on Berakhot 34a). It is on these grounds that the *Pirkoi ben Baboi,* for example, argues against the *May-ayn Zikhronot* (see Ginzberg: *op. cit.,* pp. 508, 553).

43. The observations of Menaḥem Meiri, of thirteenth century Provençe, are most instructive. In his time the controversy over *Zokhraynu l-ḥayyim,* et al. was still alive. Meiri personally favors the new prayers for a variety of reasons: first, though they are petitions, they are not private but collective, and they ask simply for life itself rather than material goods. Second, he fancies the notion of introducing variety — "The nature of man is stirred by any innovation, whether in change of time or in the order of words." Third, "because man is shaken by the mention of death more than by any other matter," Meiri favors prayers which plead for "life." See *Ḥibbur Ha-Teshuvah,* pp. 260, 262-3. For discussion of the "Book of Life" concept, see B-SAYFER ḤAYYIM, at the end of Chapter Four.

44. For a discussion of Kallir, see Chapter Two, THE PIYYUTIM. Davidson lists *Atah hu Elohaynu* as the fourth section (designated *Atah Kadosh*) of Kallir's *Kerovah, At ḥil yom pekudah.*

45. In Nazi extermination camps Jews would often have to write out copies of the Siddur and Maḥzor from memory. Some of these manuscripts (e.g., from Auschwitz) have been preserved.

46. Ruth Rabbah IV, 3 (on Ruth 3:13). Cf. Ecclesiastes Rabbah on Ecclesiastes 1:13 and Song of Songs Rabbah on Song of Songs 1:1. All of these passages are discussed as precursors of *Piyyut* by J. Schirmann in *JQR,* XLIV, 2 (October, 1953) pp. 131-32.

47. Davidson (*Thesaurus,* I, p. 404) opines that the printed editions introduced here the two *melekh evyon* verses from Kallir's *Kerovah, At ḥil yom pekudah.*

In the collection of the *piyyutim* of R. Simeon ben Isaac published by A. M. Haberman in 1938, the complete poem, *Melekh elyon, amitz ha-menusa,* contains *melekh evyon* stanzas that are different from those in question.

48. See Elbogen, *op. cit.*, p. 329.

49. See Berliner, *Randbemerkungen,* I, p. 49 (in the Hebrew edition, p. 48).

49a. *The Small Sanctuary,* p. 246.

50. According to Davidson, *L-El oraykh din* constitutes part nine of Kallir's *Kerovah, At ḥil yom pekudah.* Some communities follow the unusual practice of reciting *L-El oraykh din* in Shaḥarit on the *first* day of Rosh Hashanah and in Musaf (before *U-netaneh tokef)* on the *second* day. This custom is based on the controversy in the Talmud (Avodah Zarah 3b) as to whether God judges mankind on Rosh Hashanah during the "first three hours of the day" (corresponding to Shaḥarit) or during the "second three hours of the day" (corresponding to Musaf). The shifting of the prayer accommodates both views!

51. Cf. KADOSH, KADOSH, KADOSH, earlier in Chapter Four. On weekdays, at the conclusion of the morning service, there is a third *Kedushah,* known as *Kedushah d-Sidra.* On Sabbaths and Festivals, this latter *Kedushah* comes at the beginning of Minḥah; on Yom Kippur, it is transferred to the beginning of Ne'ilah.

The history of the *Kedushah,* in its varying forms, is a highly complex one. For full discussion of the many problems involved, see Elbogen: *op. cit.*, Index, p. 589, for the pertinent passages; Ginzberg: *Geonica,* I, pp. 130-34.

52. The original wording of the third benediction in Palestine was a single sentence which included the "Thrice-Holy." This was later supplemented by the *Kedushah* of the *Amidah* made up of Biblical verses connected by poetic passages – in itself a prototype of *Piyyut!* The third benediction became the focal point for many of the early Palestinian *piyyutim.* Cf. Chapter Two, THE PIYYUTIM and the appendix, THE STRUCTURE OF THE KEROVAH.

53. Cf. comment on KADOSH ATAH, the following prayer.

54. Some old texts (e.g., Maimonides, in his *Seder Tefillot Kol Ha-Shanah*) read *V-az tzadikim.* One manuscript fragment (published by Elbogen) reads simply *Tayn paḥdekha.* In *Seder Rav Amram* all three parts begin *U-v'khayn.*

55. Rav Amram includes them for both Rosh Hashanah and Yom Kippur. Maimonides treats them as a variant custom whose recitation is optional. Jawitz, Brody, Elbogen and Spiegel are among the modern scholars who have detected in the *U-v'khayn* group of prayers a reminiscence of the *Malkhuyot* attributed to Rabbi Yoḥanan ben Nuri by the Mishnah (Rosh Hashanah 4:5). It was he who had argued unsuccessfully that *Malkhuyot,* the prayer for the Kingship of God, be included in this third benediction, *Kedushat Ha-Shem.* The view of Rabbi Akiba, that *Malkhuyot* be associated with the fourth benediction, *Kedushat Ha-Yom,* prevailed. Yoḥanan's usage was Galilean; Akiba's, Judean (Yer. Rosh Hashanah IV, 6). It is noteworthy that Saadiah makes no reference to the *U-v'khayn* prayers; he probably considered them to be the rejected *Malkhuyot* of Rabbi Yoḥanan!

Landshuth saw in the *U-v'khayn* triad an abbreviated version of the three-fold

Malkhuyot-Zikhronot-Shofarot which originally were part of Shaḥarit but now come only in the Musaf service. Actually they parallel only the first of these and thus provide a *Malkhuyot*-type prayer in each *Amidah* of Rosh Hashanah. Davidson (*Thesaurus*, II, p. 215) links the *U-v'khayn* group with the *May-ayn Zikhronot* and *Atah beḥartanu* as parts of an ancient *Shivata* (a seven-part *Kerovah*). See note 38 above and cf. also *Maḥzor Yannai*, p. xxxiii, note 60.

56. *Kuzari*, II, 44.

57. Berakhot 12b, where Rav is also credited with introducing the phrase *ha-Melekh ha-mishpat* into the daily *Amidah* for the Ten Days of Penitence. For Rav's role in the creation of the Rosh Hashanah liturgy, see Chapter One, THE SIDDUR AND THE MAḤZOR.

58. The reading *ha-El ha-kadosh* remains unchanged in all the Palestinian texts. The same is true of the Romanian rite. Saadiah's *Siddur* retains the Palestinian usage but credits also the custom of substituting *ha-Melekh*. For Musaf, the Palestinian Talmud (Rosh Hashanah IV, 6) reads . . . *adir ha-melukhah ha-El ha-kadosh.*

59. Cf. Ginzberg: *Geonica*, I, p. 131.

60. Cf. VA-TODI'AYNU and THE KIDDUSH, in Chapter Three and MELOKH AL KOL HA-OLAM, in Chapter Four. Some of the Geonim continued to recommend the inclusion of *mo'adim l-simḥah*, etc. The Sephardic text retains the festival designation, *yom-tov*; but, as Ginzberg points out, this is "a peculiarity of the Spanish liturgy" and was not in the original *Seder Rav Amram* (see *Geonica*, I, p. 140). On various readings in *Va-titen lanu*, see *Otzar Ha-Tefillot*, I. p. 915; Baer: *Seder Avodat Yisrael*, p. 347.

61. Rosh Hashanah 10a.

62. Cf. EMET VE-EMUNAH, in Chapter Three.

63. The phrase *Ya'aleh v-yavo* is first mentioned in Soferim XIX, 7 (ed. Higger, XIX, 5, p. 327) but the core of the prayer is alluded to in the earlier Talmudic literature (Tos. Berakhot 3:10; Berakhot 49a; Shabbat 24a). Rav Amram, quoting Paltoi Gaon, says that the inclusion of *Ya'aleh v-yavo* in Shaḥarit depends on local custom since, in any event, the precentor recites it as part of the *Zikhronot* of Musaf (ed. Frumkin, II, p. 294). Saadiah includes a somewhat abbreviated version of *Ya'aleh v-yavo* in the *Zikhronot* prayer of his Musaf for Rosh Hashanah (he omits *Ya'aleh v-yavo* from his Shaḥarit service). "Originally *Ya-aleh v-yavo* in Palestine formed a part of every *Amidah* for Festival days, Musaf not excluded. The Babylonians dropped it but retained it, as Paltoi Gaon some sixty years before Saadiah attests, for the Musaf of Rosh Hashanah" (Elbogen in *Saadia Anniversary Volume: Texts and Studies II,* pp. 257-58; (cf. also *Gottesdienst*, pp. 57, 133-35). The Sephardim recite it in both Shaḥarit and Musaf of Rosh Hashanah; in the latter, it forms part of the *Zikhronot.*

63a. Ginzberg, discussing the history of *Ya'alah v-yavo* (in *Ha-Tzofeh May-Eretz Hagar*, vol. III, pp. 181-84 and vol. IV. pp. 97-98) argues against the theory that this prayer originated as part of the *Zikhronot* prayer of Rosh Hashanah, despite the fact that not only modern scholars, like Elbogen, but even some of the early codifiers inclined to this view. He challenges Elbogen's interpretation to this effect of the responsum of Paltoi Gaon (found in *Sefer Ha-Pardes,* end of *Hilkhot Rosh Hashanah*). See also Ginzberg: *A Commentary on the Palestinian Talmud* (New York: Jewish Theological Seminary, 1941) vol. III, p. 436. The historical development of *Ya'aleh v-yavo* is also discussed in detail by Tzvi Karl: *Meḥkarim B-Toldot Ha-Tefillah* (Tel Aviv: N. Twersky, 1950) pp. 96-98, 127-28. Cf. also Atah Zokhayr in The Musaf Service, Chapter Seven.

64. The Sephardic prayerbook actually separates the two halves into distinct paragraphs. The older rites include at this point the unique prayer for the Festivals *(V-hasi'aynu)* but the Ashkenazic authorities deleted it on the grounds that Rosh Hashanah is not a *Yom-tov* but *Yom ha-din.*

65. The struggle is dramatized in the pro-Palestinian Saadiah Gaon's denunciation of those who were substituting such phrases as *mishpat zidkekha,* "Thy righteous judgment," for the older *mo'aday kodshekha,* "Thy sacred festivals." In Rashi's time objections were still being raised to such tampering with the old Palestinian text but the new customs were already well established. Cf. The Kiddush and Va-todi'aynu, in Chapter Three.

66. Meiri explains this usage as a fulfillment of the Rabbinic dictum, "proclaim my Kingship upon you *continually* on Rosh Hashanah" *(Tamid hamlikhuni alaykhem b-Rosh Hashanah).* Schreiber (*op. cit.,* p. 264) failed to discover this statement in the extant Rabbinic literature though a similar phrase occurs in Rosh Hashanah 16a. A parallel passage is also to be found in Sifre, *B-ha'alotekha,* par. 77, ed. Horovitz, p. 71 (especially the last two lines of this page).

67. Menaḥem Meiri, *Ḥibbur Ha-Teshuvah,* ed. Schreiber, p. 263. However, Meiri is heartily in favor of interpolations wherever permitted. See note 43, above.

68. For the concept of the "Book of Life" see the same author's *Festival Studies* (Philadelphia, 1906), pp. 19-24; and Berliner: *Randbemerkungen,* II pp. 15-16 (Hebrew ed., pp. 93-94).

69. On the other hand, as the *Shulḥan Arukh* points out, it is not to be construed as a confessional, for confession of sins is forbidden on Rosh Hashanah.

70. Taanit 25b.

71. *Some Aspects of Rabbinic Theology,* pp. 51, 54.

72. Cf. G. F. Moore: *Judaism,* vol. II, pp. 201 ff. for a complete discussion of the Rabbinic concept of "The Father in Heaven" with special reference to liturgical usage.

73. Cf. *Tur Oraḥ Ḥayyim,* section 602 (Quoted by Zunz: *Ritus,* pp. 118-20).

74. *Levush,* section 584.

75. For general background, see Louis Finkelstein: "The Origin of the Hallel" in *HUCA,* vol. XXIII (part II, 1951), pp. 319-37.

76. Rosh Hashanah 32b, Arakhin 10b.

77. Megillah 10b, Sanhedrin 39b.

78. Pesaḥim 117a. This explanation is given by Shemtob Gaguine in *Keter Shem Tob,* vol. VI (London: S. Dzialowski, 1955) p. 118.

CHAPTER FIVE: THE READING OF THE TORAH

1. The whole question of the origin of the Synagogue has not been finally resolved. The most recent study is by Julian Morgenstern in *Studi Orientalistici in onori di Giorgio Levi Della Vida* (Rome, 1956) pp. 192-201.

2. The elaborate, dramatic ritual for removing the scrolls from the Ark is strictly an innovation without foundation in Rabbinic or Geonic literature. It is first mentioned in the thirteenth century *Sefer Ha-Maḥkim,* and became part of the French and German rites. See Berliner: *Ketavim Nivḥarim,* pp. 104-05. The ceremony remains unique to the Ashkenazic rite.

3. White is also used on Hoshana Rabbah, the seventh day of Sukkot. Jewish mystics associated this day with Rosh Hashanah and Yom Kippur through the teaching that the heavenly verdict written and sealed on the Solemn Days is not issued until Hoshana Rabbah. White is also a familiar color for the prayer for rain *(Geshem)* on Shemini Atzeret and the prayer for dew *(Tal)* on the first day of Pesaḥ. Other traditional colors are red for Shabbat and purple for the Three Festivals. On Tishah B-Av, the national day of mourning, Sephardim use black for the *Parokhet* and Torah vestments.

4. The popular association of the *Kittel* with the burial shroud arises from the fact that the dead are clothed in the *Kittel* precisely because (as Louis Ginzberg pointed out) this garment was the national, festive "dress-suit" of the Jew in ancient times!

5. Yer. Rosh Hashanah I,3.

6. The Talmudic sources (e.g., Rosh Hashanah 17b) fail to inform us exactly how the *Shelosh Esray Middot* are derived from the text of Exodus 34:6, 7. There are a number of divergent views. See the commentaries on this passage, especially that of S. D. Luzzatto and the recent commentary of M. D. Cassuto. The last word of the *Shelosh Esray Middot,* viz., *v-nakay,* is not the natural end of the thought in the Exodus passage. The placing of the period after the word *v-nakay,* truncating the original verse and in fact reversing its meaning, represents a *midrash* intended to emphasize the Divine quality of forgiveness. Cf. Evelyn Garfiel: *The Service of the Heart* (New York: National Academy for Adult Jewish Studies of the United Synagogue, 1958) pp. 209-10.

7. The Sephardic parallel begins, *U-v'khayn, ribbono shel olam.* This is preceded by a special meditation for Rosh Hashanah, beginning *Yehi ratzon.*

8. Their use for *Shalosh Regalim* was introduced by the influential Kabbalistic prayerbook *Sha'aray Zion* of Nathan Hanover, printed 1662 in Prague.

9. For the liturgical potentialities of modern Hebrew poetry see Chapter Two, THE PIYYUTIM.

10. Cf. Soferim XIV, 9 (Higger ed., XIV, 5, p. 258). For discussion, see Elbogen, *op. cit.,* p. 199.

11. See Ginzberg: *A Commentary on the Palestinian Talmud,* vol. III, p. 21.

12. For the technical structure of the cantillation, see P. Minkovski in *Sefer Ha-Mo'adim,* vol. I, p. 98.

13. Rosh Hashanah 16a.

14. Rosh Hashanah 10b-11a.

14a. Adapted from *Selected Essays on Rosh Hashanah,* ed. I. Lipschutz (New York, 1954) pp. 33 ff.

15. In Pirke d-R. Eliezer 30, the demand of Sarah constituted the ninth in a series of "ten trials" to which Abraham was subjected. The last was the *Akaydah.*

16. The Rabbis (through the euphemisms of the Midrash) express surprise at Abraham's submission in the face of injustice. See Genesis Rabbah 54:2.

17. In Moslem tradition the last month of the year is associated with the Binding of Isaac upon the altar and is considered propitious for making the sacred pilgrimage.

18. According to the Midrash, Abraham was put to the supreme test of the *Akaydah* only after Satan had questioned Abraham's piety and integrity. See Sanhedrin 89a; Genesis Rabbah 55:4.

19. "Akedat Yitzhak — The Binding of Isaac" in *Judaism,* vol. VI, no. 1 (Winter, 1957).

20. It seems ironic that one whose life was destined for such tragic dimensions as the *Akaydah* should be given the joyous name of *Yitzḥak.* The paradox was explained — in the best tradition of the Midrash — by the Alexandrian philosopher, Philo, in his *On Abraham.* "The 'laughter' here understood is not the laughter which amusement arouses in the body." It is *eupathy* of the mind. This joy the sage is said to sacrifice as part of his duty to God, thus showing in a parable that rejoicing is most closely associated with God alone, mankind being subject to grief. God, however, "fitly rewards by returning the gift (of joy) insofar as the recipient's capacity allows" (cited by David Baumgardt: "Man's Morals and God's Will" in *Commentary,* March, 1950).

21. Bava Metzia 87a. This legend is the basis of a *piyyut* by Eleazar Kallir beginning *Aym asher b-tzedek,* found only rarely in modern editions of the Maḥzor.

22. Genesis Rabbah 53:19.

23. Bava Kamma 92a.

24. Some modern scholars suspect that the original Torah readings for Rosh Hashanah (like that of Yom Kippur morning even now) were passages like this, dealing with the ritual worship of the Sanctuary. Later, under the influence of the *Zikhronot* (Remembrance) theme, the story of *Akaydat Yitzḥak* came to replace them.

25. *Studies in Judaism,* Second Series, p. 16.

26. See Yalkut Shimoni, section 968, on verse cited. Cf. Bava Kamma 93a.

27. Rosh Hashanah 10b.

27a. *Op cit.,* p. 111.

28. Certain phrases from Hannah's prayer of thanksgiving seem to find an echo in the second part of the prayer *U-netaneh tokef,* e.g., "It is the Lord who causeth death and giveth life . . . The Lord maketh poor and maketh rich; He bringeth low, He also lifteth up."

29. Berakhot 29a. The Midrash states that Hannah's prayer parallels the

"Eighteen Benedictions," the old Palestinian *Amidah* (see Yalkut Shimoni, section 80, quoting Midrash Yelamdenu).

30. The stature of Hannah in later Jewish tradition is considerable. The Talmud (Berakhot 31b) derives several important principles of prayer from the moving petition of Hannah. She may well be also the model for the martyred Hannah of Maccabean times (see end of Midrash Lamentations, interpreting Jeremiah 15:9).

31. The *Akaydah* is also associated by tradition with Yom Kippur. Legend has it that the Binding of Isaac took place on the Day of Atonement; the ashes of the sacrificial ram formed the foundations of the inner altar on which expiatory offerings were brought on Yom Kippur, etc. See Ginzberg: *Legends of the Jews*, vol. I, p. 283; cf. the Notes on this passage.

32. E.g., Taanit 4a; cf. Rashi *ad loc.*

33. *Ḥibbur Ha-Teshuvah*, ed. Schreiber, p. 269.

34. Cf. Jacob Agus: *Guideposts in Modern Judaism* (New York: Bloch, 1954) p. 38, where this interpretation is attributed to Joseph Baer Soloveitchik.

35. "Man's Morals and God's Will" in *Commentary*, March, 1950. An examination of the various levels of meaning in the *Akaydah* may be found in Ernst Simon's essay, *Torat Ḥayyim*, in *Conservative Judaism*, Spring, 1958. The argument that the *Akaydah* was an expiation by Abraham – and, to a lesser degree, by Isaac – for the guilt of casting out Ishmael has been discussed in connection with The Pentateuch Reading for the First Day.

36. "May-Aggadot Ha-Akaydah," in *Alexander Marx Jubilee Volume*, Hebrew volume (New York: Jewish Theological Seminary, 1950) pp. 471 ff.

37. Rosh Hashanah 16a.

38. For discussion of the *Zekhut Avot* concept, see Schechter: *Some Aspects of Rabbinic Theology*, pp. 170-98; Moore: *Judaism*, Vol. I, pp. 537 ff; and Max Kadushin: *The Theology of Seder Eliahu* (New York: Bloch, 1932) pp. 182 ff., pp. 191 ff. Cf. the comment on Zokhraynu B-zikaron Tov, in Chapter Seven.

39. *Op. cit.*, p. 109.

40. Rosh Hashanah 10b (bottom).

41. The similarity between Mother Rachel and Mother Hannah (of the first day's *Haftarah*) is striking and elicited much comment in Rabbinic literature. Even the word *Ramah* evokes associations: the home of Hannah and later of Samuel, her son, was also a town of that name.

41a. Cf. Pesikta Rabbati, ed. Friedmann, ch. 40, fol. 167b. This passage, in discussing the order of worship on Rosh Hashanah, indicates that, immediately following the recitation of the Shema and the *Amidah*, "we listen to the Torah Reading, then to (the message of) the sage."

42. See S. J. Agnon: *Yamim Noraim* (Jerusalem: Schocken, 3rd ed., 1946) pp. 89-90.

43. *Lo A-D-U Rosh* is the Talmudic formula, in which *A* (= *alef*) represents the first day of the week; *D* (= *dalet*), the fourth; and *U*, i.e., *V* (= *vav*), the sixth. This arrangement prevents various conflicts with Shabbat and Festival preparations.

43a. Agnon: *op. cit.*, p. 194.

44. Quoted from Buber: *Tales of the Hasidim, The Early Masters,* p. 133. It is an interesting coincidence that the first mention in Jewish sources of a pulpit may be the "pulpit of wood" upon which Ezra the Scribe stood while expounding the Torah to the Judeans on the first day of Tishre (Nehemiah 8:4). Cf. THE READING OF THE TORAH, beginning of Chapter Five.

CHAPTER SIX: THE SOUNDING OF THE SHOFAR

1. Just what sound the *teruah* is meant to convey and how it was to be made is the subject of considerable debate in the post-Biblical literature. For a thorough historical analysis of the subject, see Sol B. Finesinger's monograph, "The Shofar," in *HUCA*, vols. VIII-IX (1931-32) pp. 193-228. If the term *yom teruah* is obscure, its parallel *zikhron teruah* is infinitely more so. Finesinger *(ibid.)* presents a fascinating though radical reconstruction of the development of *yom teruah* and *zikhron teruah*. Traditionally, *zikhron teruah* is understood in the sense of "ye shall sound the alarm with the trumpets and ye shall be remembered before the Lord your God" (Numbers 10:9).

2. Rosh Hashanah 3:2 and 34a. It is instructive to note here that the Karaites, whose name for Rosh Hashanah is the Biblical *Yom Teruah*, vigorously opposed the Talmudic interpretation. Some of their authorities maintained that *teruah* implied simply the sounds raised in prayer. Others, while agreeing that sounds should be blown on an instrument, contended that *any* instrument sufficed. Especially did they protest the "audacity" of the Rabbis in formulating a benediction to the effect that God has commanded Jews "to hear the sound of the Shofar." See Goldberg: *Karaite Liturgy*, Chapter 14.

3. An excellent anthology of this type is the section devoted to the Shofar (Book I, Chapters 30-47) in Agnon: *Yamim Noraim*; English translation, *Days of Awe* (New York: Schocken Books, 1948). The Shofar has even been treated from the standpoint of the psychoanalyst! See Theodor Reik: *Das Ritual* (1928) Imago-Buecher xi, the section entitled "Das Schofar," pp. 201-330.

4. The word *shofar* is probably related to the Assyro-Babylonian *shuparu,* meaning "horned sheep." See Gaster: *op. cit.*, p. 304.

5. Peter Gradenwitz: *The Music of Israel* (New York: W. W. Norton, 1949) pp. 29-30.

6. Studies made by Julian Morgenstern indicate that originally the Hebrew new year's day was on the tenth of the seventh month, the day of the autumnal equinox. Later the date of the beginning of the new year was transferred to the first of the seventh month and the tenth was celebrated as *Yom Ha-Kippurim.* It is noteworthy that the Shofar is mentioned in Leviticus 25:9 in connection with the tenth, the original new year's day; its later use on the first of the month (a usage not specifically mentioned in the Torah) indicates the shifting of the Shofar-sounding ritual from the former date to the latter. See Morgenstern: "The Three Calendars of Ancient Israel," *HUCA*, vol. I, pp. 13-78; the

additional notes to this article in *HUCA*, vol. III, pp. 77-107; "the Gates of Righteousness," *HUCA*, vol. VI, especially pp. 18-19, 32, 35, 37. These studies are cited in Finesinger, *op. cit., passim.*

7. Rosh Hashanah 3:3, 4.

8. Cf. Rosh Hashanah 27a. On their new year's day, the ancient Babylonians ceremoniously reinstalled their god Marduk in his temple; but their religion never envisioned the universal God-idea embodied in Rosh Hashanah. See Gaster: *op. cit.*, pp. 113 ff.

9. *Ibid.*, pp. 195-213.

10. The Mishnah (Tamid 3:8) records that the daily *tekiot,* sounded at the opening of the Temple gates and at the offering of the daily sacrifices, could be heard as far away as Jericho.

11. Ezekiel 33:3 ff., Amos 3:6, Joel 2:1, Zephaniah 1:14-16.

12. E.g., Absalom's abortive reign in Hebron, II Samuel 15:10; Solomon's coronation in Jerusalem, I Kings 13:4; Jehu's reign over the kingdom of Israel, II Kings 9:13. Cf. Psalms 98:6, Numbers 23:21.

13. See Soferim (ed. Higger, XVIII, 11, pp. 322-23). Mueller's edition on this passage (p. 262, note 3) refers to Rosh Hashanah 30b where Psalm 81 is mentioned as the Rosh Hashanah psalm.

14. Rosh Hashanah 27b. This analogy was characteristically ridiculed by the Karaites. Even when the latter came to accept the implication of blowing an instrument for the word *teruah,* they rejected the Shofar as the exclusive instrument. Earlier they had interpreted *teruah* in a general sense of mood – either jubilation, according to some, or, according to others, alarm and penitence as a prelude to The Day of Atonement. See Goldberg: *Karaite Liturgy,* p. 118. For the opinions of Philo and of the Karaites on the meaning of *Yom Teruah,* see B. Revel in *JQR*, vol. III, pp. 386-87, and note 114 on p. 386.

15. Taanit 1:6.

16. Moed Katan 16a.

17. Niddah 35a and Rashi's comment on the passage.

18. Rosh Hashanah 26a. The Mishnah discusses the proper type of Shofar in Rosh Hashanah 3:2, 3, 5, 6.

19. Rosh Hashanah 16a. The Mishnah, however, is silent on the association of the Shofar with the *Akaydat Yitzḥak.* Rabbi Abbahu, a Palestinian Amora who flourished about the year 300, is the first to mention this association. He was well-known for his polemics against the Christians. It is reasonable to assume, as David Aronson suggests, that "when the Christian missionaries came with their claims that a man's good deeds are not sufficient for salvation, but that he needs the merit of the crucified, the Jewish teachers countered with the 'Merit of the Fathers' and especially with the *Akaydah* story." See *Conservative Judaism* (Spring, 1958) p. 41. The liturgy of Rosh Hashanah makes frequent reference, of course, to the Binding of Isaac and that story constitutes the Scriptural portion for the second day of the New Year.

20. Rosh Hashanah 3:3, 4.

21. *Ibid.,* 4:9. This practice is upheld in the Talmud, Rosh Hashanah 33b-

34a.

22. *Ibid.* The compromise is attributed to Rabbi Abbahu of Caesarea, who figures prominently in discussions of Shofar law and lore (see note 19 above). *Teruah* is taken as "a sound of wailing"; *shevarim* as "a sound of moaning." For a critical examination of *teruah,* see Finesinger, *op. cit.,* pp. 205 ff.

23. This explanation is given by Ibn Yarḥi, *Ha-Manhig, Hilkhot Rosh Hashanah,* 19. Cf. Sukkah 5:5 and 55a. For a critical discussion of whether the Shofar was actually sounded at the time of the New Moon, see Finesinger: *op. cit.,* p. 222.

24. Megillah 2:5 states that "the entire day is permitted . . . for the sounding of the Shofar;" nevertheless – as Rashi comments on this passage in Megillah 20b – the principle that "the zealous perform their religious duty as early as possible" (Pesaḥim 4a; cf. Rosh Hashanah 32b) should be followed.

25. Yer. Rosh Hashanah IV, 8, fol. 59c-59d; cf. Rosh Hashanah 32b.

26. "The Time of Blowing the Shofar on New Year," *HUCA,* vol. IV (1927) pp. 299-301.

27. Obviously this triad of prayers must originally have been recited in Shaḥarit since the *tekiot* were sounded originally in that earlier service, and it is an established principle that "we sound the Shofar according to the order of the special benedictions" (i.e., *Malkhuyot,* et al.) See MALKHUYOT - ZIKHRONOT - SHOFAROT, in THE MUSAF SERVICE, Chapter Seven.

28. See KADDISH TITKABAL – SUPPLEMENTARY TEKIOT, in THE MUSAF SERVICE, Chapter Seven.

29. See THE SHOFAR IN JEWISH FOLKLORE AND SUPERSTITION, in Chapter Six.

30. This accounts for the curious letters *shin* and *bet* found in many old Maḥzorim; they spell *shayv,* "sit." All other explanations are fanciful and superfluous.

31. Some scholars trace this custom to the primitive practice of denying to the populace the sight of sacred objects (cf. Numbers 4:15). See Peter Gradenwitz: *The Music of Israel,* p. 30.

32. Taanit 16b.

33. See Pesaḥim 7b; *Rosh* on Pesaḥim, Ch. 1 and Rosh Hashanah, Ch. 4; *Otzar Ha-Geonim,* Rosh Hashanah, 102-03. It is impossible to reconstruct the original text of the benediction in *Seder Rav Amram*; see Ginzberg: *Geonica,* I, p. 141. Ibn Yarḥi argues in favor of Hai Gaon's reading *lishmo'a,* etc., over *litko'a,* etc. (found in the *She'eltot* of R. Aḥai Gaon) or *al tekiat shofar* (the reading given by Rabbenu Tam) which was the prevalent French practice at that time (see *Ha-Manhig, Hilkhot Rosh Hashanah,* 9).

34. The Rabbinic ruling (Rosh Hashanah 3:7, cf. 4:7) that it is sufficient "to hear" the Shofar may be simply a matter of convenience, but Finesinger ventures a more critical opinion: "The superstitions of the folk with regard to the efficacy of the sound of the shofar may have caused the Rabbis to try to discourage its actual use as much as possible. One way of tempering the crude folk belief would be to say that all that is necessary is to listen to the sound of the shofar." See *op. cit.,* p. 221.

35. *Ibid.*, pp. 195-96.

36. See Rosh Hashanah 4:1; 59b and 29b. Cf. Leviticus Rabbah 29.

37. There were rare exceptions. A learned Bet-Din is theoretically permitted, but Rabbi Isaac Alfasi of medieval Morocco is reported (by Abudarham) to have been the last to exercise the privilege. Meiri curiously reports a tradition based on the Yerushalmi that – according to the Torah – the Shofar is to be sounded only at the Sanctuary where the sacrificial cult was based (see Numbers 10:10). This was also the view of Philo and some Karaites. Their views are refuted by Ibn Ezra (on Numbers 29:1). Josephus nowhere mentions the *Tekiat Shofar*. See Albeck: *Mishnah, Seder Moed* (Jerusalem – Tel Aviv, 1952) p. 490.

38. *Op. cit.*, pp. 203-207.

39. Pirke d-R. Eliezer 46.

40. Rosh Hashanah 33b. Genesis Rabbah 58:5 attributes the demise of Sarah to the shock brought on by the report of Isaac's death. Other passages in the Midrash (Pirke d-R. Eliezer 32, Leviticus Rabbah 20:2, Ecclesiastes Zuta 9:7) associate the sounds of the Shofar on Rosh Hashanah with the sounds of woe emitted by Sarah at the moment of her demise (cf. L. Ginzberg in *Ha-Tzofeh May-Eretz Hagar*, III, pp. 186-88). Abudarham follows these midrashic traditions when he explains that the name *Yom Teruah* is to be interpreted "Day of Wailing," referring to the wailing of Sarah over the presumed sacrifice of Isaac. Thus the Shofar also recalls the anguish of Sarah, a further instance of *Zekhut Avot*. See *Abudarham Ha-Shalem*, p. 269.

41. Suggested by Steinschneider. See H. Malter: *Saadiah Gaon, His Life and Works* (Philadelphia: Jewish Publication Society, 1921) p. 335, cf. p. 315.

41a. *Abudarham Ha-Shalem*, pp. 269 f.

42. Saadiah is the first of the commentators to re-emphasize this significance of the Shofar sounds first pointed out by the Prophets. See Ginzberg: *Ginze Schechter*, II, p. 479. Ginzberg notes there the curious fact that nowhere in the Talmud or Midrash are the *tekiot* interpreted as a call to *teshuvah*! The earliest occurrence after the Bible is in the writings of the Karaite, Daniel Al Kumisi, who was an older contemporary of Saadiah. Since it is inconceivable that Saadiah (who attacked Al Kumisi's writings) would have quoted a Karaite tradition, Ginzberg assumes that both men utilized an ancient *midrash* unknown to us.

42a. *Code, Hilkhot Teshuvah* III, 4.

43. Rosh Hashanah 16b. Cf. *Maḥzor Vitry*, p. 372. Rabbenu Nissim comments here that Satan is only a figure of speech for the "evil inclination" (cf. Bava Batra 16a) but the Satanic personality was too intriguing for the folk imagination to accept rationalistic substitutes. See further THE SHOFAR IN JEWISH FOLKLORE AND SUPERSTITION.

44. Rosh Hashanah 16a.

45. Cf. Rosh Hashanah 34a. Similar thoughts were expressed in an earlier age by Rabbi Jonathan Eibeschuetz in his sermonic work, *Ya'arot Devash*.

46. S. R. Hirsch: *Chorew*, Chapter 32.

47. *Op. cit.*, p. 113.

48. Rosh Hashanah 26a. On the same grounds Maharil forbade the use of a Shofar completely covered with gold. The law, however, permits the Shofar to be gilded so long as the tone is not altered. The Mishnah (Rosh Hashanah 3:3) specificially states that the mouthpiece of the Shofar used in the Temple on Rosh Hashanah was covered with gold.

49. Isaiah 58:1. This verse is part of the *Haftarah* for Yom Kippur morning.

50. *Jewish Homiletics* (London: M. L. Cailingold, 1937), pp. 27-31.

51. It is interesting to note that a prayerbook issued by the Chief Rabbinate of Israel to armed forces of the new State in 1949 advised that the Shofar was not to be sounded if military security were endangered thereby.

52. It is interesting to note that the wall was finally completed on the 25th of Elul, just a few days before Rosh Hashanah (Nehemiah 6:15).

53. Shabbat 35b.

54. Rosh Hashanah 26a.

55. Tanna d-be Eliahu Zuta 22, ed. Friedmann, p. 38.

56. Rosh Hashanah 3:7.

57. Leviticus Rabbah 29:3, ed. Margulies, p. 674.

58. Rosh Hashanah 3:7.

59. Pirke d-R. Eliezer 31. Levinthal's homily is found in his *A New World Is Born* (New York and London: Funk and Wagnalls, 1943) pp. 29-30.

60. In this connection, it is interesting to note that the figure of a Shofar was carved on Jewish tombstones in ancient times, possibly as a symbol of the resurrection.

61. Rosh Hashanah 3:3. Kuk's homily is quoted from *Sefer Ha-Mo'adim,* vol. I, pp. 74-75.

61a. *Ibid.*, p. 69.

62. *Maḥzor Vitry* prescribes a *tekiah gedolah*; others sound *tekiah, shevarim, teruah, tekiah.*

63. *Orḥot Ḥayyim,* part I (Firenze, 1750) p. 108a (cited by Finesinger, *op. cit.*, p. 205, note 28). Finesinger, in keeping with his theory that the Shofar sounding originated on Yom Kippur, sees in the post-Yom Kippur sounding an unconscious vestige of the ancient practice which had been suppressed by the priestly legislators (*ibid.*, p. 210). For other explanations by the Rabbinic commentators, see E. Munk: *Die Welt der Gebete,* vol. II (Frankfurt am Main: Hermon Verlag, 1936) p. 289.

64. *A Commentary on the Palestinian Talmud,* vol. III, pp. 21-22. See also S. Schueck: *Siddur Rashban,* p. 36b.

65. Sifre Numbers, section 77.

66. Theodor H. Gaster: *op. cit.*, p. 112. See also Peter Gradenwitz: *The Music of Israel,* pp. 29-31.

67. Rosh Hashanah 16b. This imagery was employed by the writers of *Piyyut*; a familiar instance is the fifth verse of the Yom Kippur *seliḥah, Omnam kayn,* beginning "*Has kataygor* . . . Silence the Prosecutor." Discussing the two series of Shofar blasts, that sounded during the *Amidah* of Musaf and that blown before it, Finesinger summarizes: "It appears that one is considered an

integral part of the ritual, the other merely a means of confusing Satan. Thus we find two notions about the shofar, one primitive and the other advanced, struggling, perhaps in the mind of one man" (*op. cit.*, p. 219).

68. The number seven has an old history of association with the Shofar. The power of seven Shofars, blown seven times, on the seventh day of the siege of Jericho levels the walls of the city (Joshua 6:20).

69. Zohar, Exodus, 196.

70. Moed Katan 27a.

CHAPTER SEVEN: THE MUSAF SERVICE

1. The Mishnah (Rosh Hashanah 4:9) cites the special enactment of Rabban Gamaliel of Yavneh permitting the Reader to fulfill the obligation of the individual to recite the Musaf. In Geonic times opinions differed as to how much of this complex, unfamiliar Musaf the individual had to recite (see note 6 below). Among the Yemenites, the silent recitation of the Musaf *Amidah* by the congregant is waived entirely in favor of the Reader's chanting on behalf of all. The reason for this practice was the unfamiliarity of the majority with the long, complex prayers (see the rubric before the Rosh Hashanah Musaf in *Tikhlal*); but N. Wieder explains that the institution of this practice by Maimonides is to be attributed to quite different motives, viz., to eliminate the talking and disturbances during services which lowered the esteem of the Jews in the eyes of their Mohammedan neighbors. See his *Islamic Influences on the Jewish Worship* (Oxford: Phaidon Press – East and West Library, 1947) Chapter 3. The western practice calls for a silent recitation of the entire Musaf *Amidah* by the individual followed by the Cantor's repetition *viva voce* (cf. Elbogen: *op. cit.*, p. 144).

2. Avodah Zarah 4b.

3. Quoted from his novel, *The Buried Candelabrum.*

4. It is an old tradition to have a new precentor for the Musaf as it is not permitted for one person to stand in prayer for more than three hours at a time. See Rabbenu Nissim on Rosh Hashanah 4:7.

5. The same melody is also used for the Kaddish that introduces the first *Seliḥot* service in the Ashkenazic ritual.

6. This unusual length of the Rosh Hashanah prayers is noted in Tosefta Berakhot 1:6 and Rosh Hashanah 34b, 35a. See also Yalkut on Isaiah 25:15. The Babylonian Geonim, Sherira and Hai, rule that in the silent recitation the worshipper need not go beyond the seven statutory benedictions of the Rosh Hashanah *Amidah,* leaving the *Malkhuyot,* et al. for the Cantor's repetition alone (see Ginzberg: *Geonica,* II, p. 44).

7. Adapted from Max Arzt: *A Modern Interpretation of the Rosh Hashanah Musaph Service,* p. 16.

8. The Mishnah (Rosh Hashanah 4:5) gives the names of all the benedictions for the *Amidah* of Rosh Hashanah. Some of these names go back to Temple days (see Tamid 5:1).

9. Adapted from M. S. Geshuri in *Sefer Ha-Mo'adim,* vol. I, p. 101.

10. Leviticus Rabbah 29:1; Yalkut Shimoni on *Pinḥas,* section 782 (cited by Heidenheim). There are allusions to this same Aggadah in other Rosh Hashanah prayers, especially in the *Zikhronot* section, e.g., *zikaron l-yom rishon.*

11. Pesaḥim 54a.

12. For the history of the *May-ayn* ("facsimile") *Zikhronot,* see ZOKHRAYNU L-ḤAYYIM, in THE ARVIT SERVICE, Chapter Three.

13. *Tur Oraḥ Ḥayyim,* section 582.

14. For discussion of the *Zekhut Avot* concept, see Notes on Chapter Five, THE READING OF THE TORAH, note 38, and the commentary on the *Zikhronot* section of Musaf, in Chapter Seven.

15. *Proceedings of the Rabbinical Assembly of America* (New York, 1949) pp. 401f.

16. Rosh Hashanah 32b.

17. *Ḥemdat Shelomo,* quoted in B. Yeushson: *Fun Unser Alt'n Oitzer* (reprint ed., New York: Shengold, 1956) chapter on Rosh Hashanah, p. 9.

18. See Davidson: *Thesaurus,* vol. I, p. 323.

19. The Avignon rite preserved this *piyyut* in its entirety.

20. Israel Zangwill, the distinguished translator of *piyyutim,* severely criticized the *payyetanim* for excessively depreciating man in his relationship to the Almighty.

20a. Adapted from Buber: *Tales of the Hasidim, The Later Masters,* pp. 249f.

21. *Basic Judaism* (New York: Harcourt, Brace, 1947) pp. 59-60.

22. On the second day of Rosh Hashanah this is the first *piyyut* recited in the somewhat abbreviated Musaf. Technically it is one link, known as *Silluk,* in the cycle of the *Kerovah.* Cf. the appendix, THE STRUCTURE OF THE KEROVAH. *U-netaneh tokef* exhibits several characteristics of the *Silluk*: it is lengthy, unrhymed, and narrative in style and it is introduced by the required formula, "*U-v'khayn l-kha ta'aleh kedushah* . . . May our sanctification of Thy name ascend unto Thee." We do not know to which *Kerovah*-cycle it originally belonged.

23. True to Sephardic usage, however, the borrowed poem is printed outside the framework of the ritual as an optional prayer.

24. Zunz thought the poem was composed by Meshullam ben Kalonymos the Elder (perhaps in southern Italy) and was popularized by the Amnon legend. A *payyetan* of that name had composed a *Silluk* for this point in the service beginning, *Mi yetaneh.* Berliner points out that our prayer appeared first in the Greek and Italian rites and from there spread to the Ashkenazim. He agrees that it originated in Southern Italy. See *Randbemerkungen,* II, p. 14 or *Ketavim Nivḥarim,* I, p. 92. But see note 27 for the latest evidence pointing to an early Palestinian origin.

25. *Thesaurus,* vol. II, p. 200. Cf. note 27 below.

26. Yer. Taanit II, Bekhorot 9:7; some of the Biblical allusions are Jeremiah 33:13, 29:23; Ezekiel 34:12; Job. 37:7 (cited by Heidenheim).

27. Suggested to the author by Leon J. Liebreich, who has also brought to the

author's attention an interesting passage in Eric Werner's *The Sacred Bridge* (London: Dennis Dobson, New York: Columbia Univ. Press, 1959). Werner states that Menaḥem Zulay made available to him a manuscript of *U-netaneh tokef* (with a number of variant readings) from the Cairo Genizah and added: "There is no doubt whatsoever that the *Unethane toqef* originated in Palestine during the Byzantine rule."

28. Spiegel notes that the long series of clipped phrases beginning with *mi* ("who") is characteristic of the style of *Haykhalot Rabbati*, one of the earliest mystical books.

29. Concerning the obscure opening phrase, *kamah ya'avrun v-khamah yibaray'un,* Berliner offered an ingenious suggestion. Some manuscripts read instead of *ya'avrun,* "shall pass away," a verb of similar appearance but from the root *ubar,* "embryo." The phrase would then be rendered, "How many will be *still-born* and how many will be created?" No parallel with "who shall live and who shall die" is intended. See *Randbemerkungen,* II, p. 63 or *Ketavim Nivḥarim,* I, p. 130.

30. Yer. Taanit II, 1, fol. 65b. See also Genesis Rabbah 44:5, ed. Theodor, p. 434.

31. Cited by Hertz: *Prayer Book,* pp. 138, 840.

32. *Ibid.,* p. 840.

33. Avot 3:19. Cf. Schechter: *Some Aspects of Rabbinic Theology,* p. 285, for discussion of the Rabbinic doctrine of freedom of the will.

34. Niddah 16b.

35. *Code, Hilkhot Teshuvah* V, 1 ff.

36. Avodah Zarah 3b. Leviticus Rabbah 29:8, ed. Margulies, p. 675.

37. Genesis Rabbah 12:15.

38. *Die Religion der Vernunft,* p. 260; cited in *Jamim Noraim, Arbeitsplan und Stoffsammlung,* ed. B. S. Jacobson (Berlin, ca. 1935).

39. M. Zulay: *Piyyute Yannai,* pp. 328, 336-38. Yoḥanan Ha-Kohen is mentioned as the author in the Hamburg manuscript (see *ibid.,* p. 328). For Yannai and his poetry, see Chapter Two, THE PIYYUTIM.

40. Yer. Rosh Hashanah I, 3.

41. Chapter 36, especially vv. 1-5, 8, 16 and 17. This parallel was first noted by Perles in *Orientalische Literatur Zeitung* (1902) p. 493 (cited in Davidson: *Thesaurus,* vol. II, p. 182).

42. See Schechter: *Some Aspects of Rabbinic Theology,* pp. 114-15.

43. *Essays in Science and Philosophy,* quoted by Joshua L. Liebman in *The American Jewish Adventure* (National Jewish Welfare Board pamphlet, New York, 1948).

44. Berakhot 38b.

45. *Studies in Judaism,* Second Series, p. 19.

46. Rapaport and Sachs were the first to note this; see Berliner: *Randbemerkungen,* II, p. 64 (Hebrew ed., p. 130).

47. In this alphabetical scheme, the Hebrew language would not ordinarily permit the letter *vav* to be represented. For this reason, some manuscripts read

vav in place of *alef* in the word *v-yomru,* in the sixth clause (cf. Psalm 139:20 for a similar spelling). Most printed editions include two clauses beginning with the letter *za'yin,* but this repetition probably derives from a misreading of the manuscripts. A confusion of the letters, *bet* and *nun* (which closely resemble one another in Hebrew manuscripts) resulted in the adding of a clause beginning *v-yizBeḥu* to the original clause beginning *v-yizNeḥu.* The correct text is restored in the new edition of the Maḥzor edited by Rabbi Ben Zion Bokser.

48. Translated by the author. The Hebrew original may be found in the recent edition of *Keter Malkhut,* ed. J. A. Zeidman (Jerusalem: Mosad Ha-Rav Kuk, 5710) p. 18.

49. Rosh Hashanah 4:5 and 32a. Rabbi Yoḥanan ben Nuri reported the Galilean practice of inserting *Malkhuyot* in the third benediction, *Kedushat Ha-Shem (ibid.).* His view may have given rise to the three-fold *U-v'khayn* prayers which are included in the *third* benediction and roughly parallel *Malkhuyot.* See Elbogen, *op. cit.,* pp. 141-42; 536, note 3.

50. The antiquity of *Atah beḥartanu* is indicated by the initial word; *atah* is a characteristic beginning of many of the earliest Hebrew prayers (e.g., *Atah gibor, Atah kadosh, Atah ḥonayn, Atak kidashta, Atah hivdalta*). See Berliner: *Randbemerkungen,* II, p. 60 (Hebrew ed., pp. 127-28). Similarly, the *Zikhronot* and *Shofarot* prayers of the Rosh Hashanah Musaf begin *Atah zokhayr* and *Atah niglayta,* respectively. Since *Atah beḥartanu* begins the benediction to which the *Malkhuyot* prayer is attached, the result is that all three parts of this famous prayer-group begin, in a sense, with the word *atah. Atah beḥartanu* is mentioned in the Talmud in Yoma 87b and Betzah 17a. The Palestinian rite reads *Atah baḥarta.*

51. For further discussion of *Atah beḥartanu* and the concept of the "Chosen People," see Berliner: *Ketavim Nivḥarim,* I, pp. 106-09. Cf. Schechter: *Some Aspects of Rabbinic Theology,* Chapter IV.

52. The phrase found in the version for the Three Festivals referring to pilgrimages to Jerusalem is absent, however, from the version for the High Holy Days since they were not occasions for such pilgrimages.

53. The thought is already expressed in the Bible (e.g., Ezekiel 39:23, Ezra 9:7).

54. Yoma 9b.

55. But Ginzberg demonstrates that *U-mi'penay ḥata'aynu* reflects merely Rav's opinion in Yer. Berakhot IV, 6 (in conflict with the view of Samuel) that it is necessary to "make some innovation" in the Musaf prayer to distinguish it from the *Amidah* of the other services. There is no foundation for attributing the authorship to Rav. Originally — as the Genizah texts of the old Palestinian rite clearly demonstrate — all the *Amidot* were virtually the same. The Palestinians adopted Rav's view but added only a brief prosaic phrase; the Babylonians, on the other hand, developed a more elaborate *piyyut*-like text. See Ginzberg: *A Commentary on the Palestinian Talmud,* vol. III, pp. 434-35.

56. Ed. Frumkin, II, pp. 299-300.

57. Soferim XIX, 7 (in Higger ed., XIX, 5, p. 327).

58. For the Palestinian parallel, see Elbogen: *op. cit.*, pp. 134-35 (Hebrew ed., p. 97). Cf. Davidson: *Thesaurus*, vol. II, p. 198; Jawitz: *Mekor Ha-Berakhot*, p. 25.

59. The earliest reference in the Mishnah, Rosh Hashanah 4:5, clearly implies that *Malkhuyot*, et al. formed part of each Rosh Hashanah *Amidah*; but, after the sounding of the Shofar was transferred from Shaḥarit to Musaf, the accompanying prayers were likewise so limited. There remains in the other services, however, a trace of *Malkhuyot* in the form of the three *U-v'khayn* prayers. See Elbogen: *op. cit.*, p. 142.

60. See Elbogen: *op. cit.*, p. 278. Davidson ascribes it to an ancient (i.e., Palestinian) *payyetan*. In the Italian rite, *He'yay im pifiyot* is found before the *Viddui* (confession of sins) in each *Amidah* of the Day of Atonement. For the use of *He'yay im pifiyot* as a prayer for the individual worshipper, see Elbogen: *Monatsschrift*, LV, p. 442 (called to the author's attention by Leon J. Liebreich).

61. See Ginzberg: *Geonica*, I, p. 141. The Maḥzor Romania, which is closely related to the old Palestinian rite, includes *Oḥilah la-El* even in the daily prayers! There is considerable evidence that the Sephardic rite originally included it for individual recitation. In the order of prayers outlined by Maimonides in his *Code, Oḥilah la-El* is even provided with a concluding *berakhah*, viz., *Barukh . . . lamedayni ḥukekha*. The same is found in *Seder Rav Amram*, ed. Frumkin, II, p. 303.

62. See Berliner: *Randbemerkungen*, II, p. 65 (Hebrew ed., I, p. 131). The simple unrhymed language in Biblical style is typical of Yose's writing; in addition, it is followed in the German rite by a poem generally attributed to Yose, the lengthy *Ahalelah Elohai*. Saadiah praises this *piyyut* as the worthiest of the many preludes to *Malkhuyot* and quotes it verbatim in his famous *Siddur*. Elbogen (*op. cit.*, p. 550) conjectures that Yose's poems to *Malkhuyot*, et al. were not preludes at all but actually alternates to the Talmudic prologues such as *Alaynu*; it is significant that they include the Biblical verses, just like the Talmudic prayers. Elbogen inclines to the view that the insertion of *piyyutim* within the *Amidah* began with these sections and that originally the *piyyutim* were thought of as substitutes for, rather than introductions to, the *Malkhuyot*, et al. See *Saadia Anniversary Volume: Texts and Studies II*, p. 260.

62a. This similarity suggests the possibility that the poet-*ḥazzan* may have originally made his entry into the service at this point in the middle of the *Amidah* rather than at the beginning, where the old tradition opposed poetic interpolations.

63. Yer. Rosh Hashanah I, 5; Yer. Avodah Zarah I, 2; Leviticus Rabbah 29; Tanḥuma on *Ha'azinu*. Actually only the introductory section to *Zikhronot* is specified as *Tekiata d-bay Rav* or *Tekiata d-Rav* but the term undoubtedly applies to *Malkhuyot* and *Shofarot* as well.

64. Talmudic authorities derive the need for the three collections from the Torah text itself: Rabbi Nathan from Numbers 10:9-10 (see Sifre, *ad loc.*); Rabbi Eliezer from Leviticus 23:24 (Rosh Hashanah 32a). There is also a disagreement

over the proper order of the three sections (cf. Rosh Hashanah 26b, 34b). This problem is discussed in the comment on THE MALKHUYOT VERSES. Cf. also note 76 below.

65. Rosh Hashanah 16a.

66. *Ikkarim* I,4.

67. *Religion der Vernunft,* pp. 467-70, quoted in B. S. Jacobson: *Jamim noraim,* pp. 81-83.

68. See Bertinoro on Rosh Hashanah 3:5.

69. The *Tur* correctly calls it a *Reshut* to *Malkhuyot.*

70. Elbogen (*op. cit.*, pp. 80-81) dates the transfer to daily recital at about 1300. But the *Roke'aḥ* by Eleazar of Worms (died 1238) already lists *Alaynu* as a daily prayer (in section 324). So does the even earlier *Maḥzor Vitry* (p. 75) with the indication to recite it quietly, evidently because of its controversial beginning. In the ritual of the English Jews before the expulsion in 1290 we find a long version also with a marked polemical allusion (see *JQR*, vol. IV, pp. 56-57). In the Palestinian ritual as preserved in the Genizah fragments, *Alaynu* also seems to be given at the beginning of the daily service (cited by Mann in *HUCA*, vol. IV, pp. 302-03, note 132).

71. *Kol-Bo,* 16.

72. *Some Aspects of Rabbinic Theology,* Chapters V-VII.

73. Adapted from Mordecai M. Kaplan: "What Is Our Human Destiny?" in *Judaism* (July, 1953) p. 197.

74. Not all the authorities indicate complete prostration: Moses Isserles and the *Magen Avraham,* for example, rule that bowing is sufficient. On Yom Kippur, prostration is a feature of the *Avodah* service. The Spanish-Portuguese Jews omit the practice except for the *Avodah* service.

75. Quoted from *Franz Rosenzweig, His Life and Thought,* p. 328.

76. Most of these verses are cited in their present form in the Talmud (Rosh Hashanah 32b). There is disagreement, however, over some of the selections. The Rabbis themselves note the paucity of suitable passages, especially from the Torah. Indeed, only the first of the three verses from the Torah is a clear illustration of the *malkhut* concept. The use of *Shema Yisrael* as a fourth verse from the Torah was necessitated by the lack of a better alternative; indeed, Rabbi Judah rejects it — along with several other suggested verses — because they do not specifically mention *malkhut.*

All of the *Ketuvim* passages are from the book of Psalms. All the Prophetic verses are taken from the Latter Prophets, presumably because they express the consolation *(neḥamah)* which the triumph of God's Kingship will bring to Israel.

The order of the ten verses differs from the more familiar pattern in which the Prophets *(Nevi'im)* precede the Writings *(Ketuvim),* as in the order of the Biblical books themselves. This precedence of the Writings over the Prophets in our verses is ordained by the Talmud itself (Rosh Hashanah 32a); nevertheless, the Tosafists express surprise and can find no explanation more adequate than to point out that the books of Psalms, Proverbs and Job predate the

Prophets, according to tradition. Actually all the verses quoted from the Writings are taken from the Psalms, and thus are attributed to royal Davidic authorship.

In point of fact, the order followed here, viz., Torah, Writings and Prophets, follows the pattern of the ancient Rabbinic homilies. After the text from the Pentateuch is cited, a proem is introduced consisting preferably of a verse from the *Ketuvim,* and the homily is regularly concluded with words of consolation, as a rule, from the Prophets. See Strack: *Introduction to the Talmud and Midrash,* pp. 204-05. Suggested to the author by Leon J. Liebreich.

An old Rabbinic tradition (in Soferim XVIII:4, ed. Higger, p. 315) holds that, with rare exceptions, "Words of Holiness (i.e., the 'Holy Writings,' *Kitvay ha-Kodesh*) take precedence over words of Tradition (*Kabbalah,* i.e., the Prophets)." The Rabbinic term for the third section of Scripture, *Kitvay ha-Kodesh* (cf. Hagiographa, "sacred writings") itself reflects the victorious struggle to gain canonical status for these miscellaneous writings; the criterion for admittance was the inspiration by *Ru'aḥ ha-Kodesh,* "the Holy Spirit."

The more familiar order – i.e., *Torah, Nevi'im, Ketuvim* – is indicated by the Tosefta (Rosh Hashanah 4:6), by the *Maḥzor Vitry* (ed. Horowitz, p. 369) and by *Ha-Manhig.* The latter also states that, "in any case, the law follows the opinion of Rabbi Yoḥanan ben Nuri, that if one said only one verse each from *Torah, Nevi'im* and *Ketuvim,* he has fulfilled his obligation" *(Hilkhot Rosh Hashanah,* 23). Saul Lieberman, however, questions whether the passage in the Tosefta is to be interpreted as indicating an order different from that prescribed by the Talmud (see his *Tosefet Rishonim, ad loc.,* where he cites medieval authorities to this effect).

77. Rosh Hashanah 32b. Cf. THE SHEMA, in Chapter Three.

78. *Seminary Addresses,* p. 26.

79. See Rabbi Akiba's assertion in Rosh Hashanah 4:5. Cf. RULES FOR THE SHOFAR AND THE TEKIOT, in Chapter Six.

80. *Ha-Manhig, Hilkhot Rosh Hashanah,* 20.

81. Our version mentions only the *tekiah* sound. Some manuscripts (mentioned by Heidenheim) substitute a reference to the *teruah* sound after the *Malkhuyot* and *Shofarot* sections.

82. Rosh Hashanah 10b, 11a, 27a. Rabbenu Nissim notes that in Barcelona and its environs the twenty-fifth of Elul was actually celebrated as "The Day of Creation." The Vilna Gaon suggests that this observance may have been the origin of the custom of reciting *Seliḥot* prior to Rosh Hashanah. See Munk, *op. cit.,* p. 189.

83. Leviticus Rabbah 29:1. UPAD MAY-AZ, in Chapter Seven.

84. *The Sabbath* (New York: Farrar, Strauss, and Young, 1951) p. 95. Cf. Gaster: *op. cit.,* p.109.

85. Leviticus Rabbah 29:10.

86. Rabbi Nathan saw in this verse Biblical authority for the recitation of *Malkhuyot, Zikhronot* and *Shofarot* (Sifre, on Numbers 10:10).

87. The old Palestinian practice was to include *Ya'aleh v-yavo* in all

festival Musaf services. Even after this practice was restricted by Babylonian Jewry for other festivals, it was retained for the Musaf of Rosh Hashanah; thus Saadiah's *Siddur* includes *Ya'aleh v-yavo* in the *Zikhronot*, as Sephardim continue to do. See YA'ALEH V-YAVO, in THE SHAḤARIT SERVICE, Chapter Four, and especially the Notes *ad loc.*, for a fuller discussion of the history of this prayer.

88. The appeal to *Brit Avot* forms the refrain for one of the most beloved poems of Yom Kippur evening, *Ki hinay ka-ḥomer.* Another oft-repeated *Seliḥah* begins, "*Zekhor lanu brit avot* . . . Remember unto us the covenant of the patriarchs."

89. Suggested by Lewis N. Dembitz: *Jewish Services in Synagogue and Home,* p. 272.

90. Cf. PENTATEUCH READING FOR THE SECOND DAY, in Chapter Five. David Aronson has suggested that the comparatively late emphasis on the *Akaydah* as part of the *Zekhut Avot* concept may have been a Jewish reaction to the Christian doctrine of "vicarious atonement." See *Conservative Judaism* (Spring, 1958) p. 41.

91. The Mishnah prescribes the recitation of *Zikhronot* verses (as well as *Shofarot* verses and sounding of the ram's horn) for all public fast days. The benediction given there (Taanit 2:4) ends, "*zokhayr ha-nishkaḥot* . . . He remembers things forgotten." The Maḥzor here uses the words, "*zokhayr ha-brit* . . . He remembers the Covenant." For a discussion of the *Zikhronot* and *Shofarot* prayers on public fast days, see Karl: *Meḥkarim B-Toldot Ha-Tefillah,* pp. 88 ff.

92. *Op. cit.*, pp. 108-09.

93. The description of the upheavals in the world of nature occasioned by the Revelation is based on ancient traditions already reflected in several Psalms and noted in the Rabbinic literature (Zevaḥim 116a, Pirke d-R. Eliezer 41).

94. A total of *eleven* Biblical passages is cited here instead of the usual ten. The difference is accounted for by the addition of the 150th Psalm to the conventional three verses from the Writings. The mystical tradition connects the ten verses of *Malkhuyot, Zikhronot* and *Shofarot* with the ten-fold repetition of the verb *hallel,* "praise", found in the 150th Psalm (exclusive of the opening and closing *Halleluyah*). Another explanation for the choice of ten verses is "corresponding to the Ten Commandments" which were given amid the blasts of the Shofar (*Tosafot Yom Tov* on Rosh Hashanah 4:6).

95. It should be noted that the word *shofar* is not explicitly mentioned in this verse (although *ḥatzotzerot,* which are equated by tradition with *shofar,* are). Therefore some authorities (e.g., Naḥmanides and Ibn Giyyat) substitute other verses, a practice frowned on by Asher ben Yeḥiel who reports it.

96. Taanit 2:4. This briefer benediction is preserved in the *Maḥzor Roma* for Rosh Hashanah as well. Cf. note 91.

97. It should be noted that the opening passages are simply a repetition of the tenth benediction of the daily *Amidah.*

98. Sifre Numbers 77.

99. See Gaguine: *Keter Shem Tob,* vol. VI, pp. 68-69.

100. It occurs in *Seder Rav Amram,* where it is included (though only the first half) in all the services of Rosh Hashanah. Abudarham has the verses from *alef* through *kaf.* The German rite has only a few verses from the beginning and end of the alphabet. The complete alphabet is found only in the Musaf of the Roman rite and in some Spanish prayerbooks. See Zunz: *Ritus,* p. 141.

101. *Mateh Levi.*

102. Tanḥuma, *Tazria* 4, *Emor* 11. Ibn Yarḥi relates them to the one hundred sighs presumably uttered by the mother of Sisera, as narrated in Judges 5:28; he reports it as a Babylonian practice (*Ha-Manhig, Hilkhot Rosh Hashanah,* 21). For a discussion of the variant customs see Israel Friedmann: *Sefer Likutay Ha-Mahariḥ* (Marmarossziget, 1903), vol. III, p. 180.

103. Ed. Frumkin, II, p. 307. *Shibolay Ha-Leket* (302), quoting the *Sefer Ha-Ma'or,* cites this same prescription in the name of Saadiah, but our text of Saadiah's *Siddur* makes no mention of this. *Teruah* is used because of the verse, *alah Elohim bi-teruah, Adonai b-kol shofar* (Psalms 47:6).

104. Rosh Hashanah 30a.

CHAPTER EIGHT: THE MINḤAH SERVICE

1. Berakhot 26b.

2. This verse from Isaiah 55:6 is held up by the Sages as a Biblical allusion to the Ten Days of Penitence, the High Holy Day season (Rosh Hashanah 18a).

3. *Op. cit.,* p. 115.

4. See note 54 on Chapter Four, THE SHAḤARIT SERVICE, for variant readings.

5. Buber: *Tales of the Hasidim, The Early Masters,* p. 289.

5a. The logical explanation for this practice is probably that the final verse (*. . . ḥanaynu va-anaynu . . .*) is also part of the daily *Taḥanun* prayer, which is recited silently.

6. See Kaufmann Kohler's article *Alaynu* in *The Jewish Encyclopedia,* vol. I, p. 337. Louis Finkelstein contends that *Malkhuyot* — to which *Alaynu* is the prologue — entered the Rosh Hashanah service during the lifetime of Rabbi Akiba, himself a martyr to the Kingship of God. Cf. Schechter: *Some Aspects of Rabbinic Theology,* pp. 71-72.

7. For possibly earlier use of *Alaynu* as a daily prayer, see note 70 on Chapter Seven, THE MUSAF SERVICE.

8. Translated by Marie Syrkin in *The Jewish Frontier* (September, 1940).

9. For critical discussion of *Tashlikh,* see Jacob Z. Lauterbach: *Rabbinic Essays* (Cincinnati: Hebrew Union College Press, 1951) pp. 299-433; Theodor H. Gaster: *op. cit.,* pp. 122-23.

10. The name is found in Yer. Rosh Hashanah I, fol. 57a. The Babylonian Talmud (Rosh Hashanah 18a) refers to this period as the "ten days between Rosh Hashanah and Yom Ha-Kippurim."

11. *Siḥot R. Naḥman,* 214.

BIBLIOGRAPHY

All of the sources used in the preparation of this work are listed in the Notes and Acknowledgments. However, it was felt that, in addition, a brief bibliography of the major books available in English on Jewish liturgy and on the High Holy Days might be helpful to the reader interested in further study:

Israel Abrahams: *A Companion to the Authorised Daily Prayer Book,* edited and translated by Rev. S. Singer, published by Eyre and Spottiswoode Ltd., London, 1922 (rev. ed.). A historical commentary on the entire prayerbook. The prayers for Rosh Hashanah and Yom Kippur are treated briefly on pages cxcvi - cciii.

Samuel J. Agnon: *Days of Awe,* published by Schocken Books, New York, 1948. A compendium of traditions, legends and commentaries concerning the High Holy Days.

Solomon B. Freehof: *The Small Sanctuary,* published by the Union of American Hebrew Congregations, Cincinnati, 1942. A popular study of the ideas of the prayerbook with emphasis on the Reform liturgy. Chapter Thirteen treats the High Holy Day service.

Evelyn Garfiel: *The Service of the Heart,* published by The National Academy for Adult Jewish Studies of the United Synagogue of America, New York, 1958. A popular exposition of the prayerbook explaining its development and its central ideas. A study guide, prepared by Seymour Siegel, is also available from the same publisher.

Theodor H. Gaster: *Festivals of the Jewish Year,* published by William Sloane Associates, New York, 1953. An anthropological approach to the holidays showing their development and the meanings of their symbols. Chapters Seven and Eight deal with the High Holy Days.

Simon Greenberg: *The Jewish Prayer Book: Its Ideals and Values,* published by the National Academy for Adult Jewish Studies of the United Synagogue of America, New York, 1957. A brief but valuable guide through the main prayers of the Sabbath service with a commentary on their religious significance.

Joseph Herman Hertz: *The Authorised Daily Prayer Book,* rev. ed. with Commentary and Notes, published by Bloch Publishing Co., New York, 1952. A popular commentary on the entire prayerbook. The prayers of Rosh Hashanah and Yom Kippur are treated on pages 838-937.

A. Z. Idelsohn: *Jewish Liturgy and Its Development,* published by Henry Holt & Co. New York, 1932. A standard work on the history of the prayerbook. Chapter Five discusses *Piyyut.* Chapter Seven contains a complete bibliography of the main works and sources on liturgy. Chapter Sixteen deals with the services for the High Holy Days.

Louis Jacobs: *A Guide to Rosh Ha-Shanah,* published by Jewish Chronicle Publications, London, 1959. A brief, popular introduction to the main ideas and rituals of the New Year.

Elie Munk: *The World of Prayer,* published by Philipp Feldheim, New York, 1954. A religious interpretation of the daily services done in the spirit of Samson Raphael Hirsch, the nineteenth century German Orthodox thinker.

Abraham Rosenfeld: *The Authorised Selichot for the Whole Year,* published by I. Labworth and Co., London, 1957 (2nd ed.). A complete collection of the penitential prayers.

Hayyim Schauss: *The Jewish Festivals,* published by the Union of American Hebrew Congregations, Cincinnati, 1938. A study of the popular beliefs and practices associated with each holiday. Traces the development of each holiday from Biblical to modern times. The High Holy Days are extensively treated in Chapters Thirteen - Seventeen.

In addition to the above works, the reader is referred to *The Jewish Encyclopedia* articles on *Piyyut, Seliḥah, Shofar* and other prayers, poems and rituals treated in the Commentary.